Endorsements

Dr. Bill Williams was five years ahead of everyone else at the turn of the turn of the century when it came to marketing your practice on the internet. It is exactly that progressive vision combined with his compassion for the dental profession and the people we serve that makes it imperative to hear his message. He's has put together the best of the best marketing information to get you on track to experience your best practice ever. Once you learn this information, I know that you'll be following his lead!

—CHRIS KAMMER, DDS
Past-President American Academy of Cosmetic Dentistry
Past-President American Academy for Oral Systemic Health
Madison, Wisconsin

"A new dental paradigm? You bet. The good news—your customers still appreciate value. The bad news—what they value has changed, and it's up to you to figure that out! But don't worry. Bill Williams spells it all out in this book. Every dentist who wants a thriving dental practice has to own this book."

—MARTHA HANLON
President, Wide Awake Marketing

"Dr Bill Williams has put together a comprehensive and easy to follow roadmap for success. His willingness to share the good as well as failure increases the value for all dentists. In my opinion this book is a must read! It's wonderful to have someone so willing to share their years of experience. Job well done, Bill!"

—DR. BRUCE B. BAIRD
Founder of "The Productive Dentist Academy" and
"Comprehensive Finance" Granbury, Texas

"Dr. Bill Williams has knocked the ball out of the park. He has been blessed because of what he gives back. This book of his experiences and dreams will help every health practice, not just dentists. It is a must read! It's all here! Step by step the Why's and the How To's of the incredible dental practice. Bill Williams shares the true complexity behind the excellence of the Million Dollar Practice. The magic of what is possible with this wisdom will take you to the top of the mountain. Go for it and enjoy a wonderful life and the joy of helping others."

—RONALD C. McCONNELL DDS, MSD
Founder, Quest Management Program Richardson, Texas

"Dr. Williams has been a very good friend for almost 30 years! There is a saying that goes something like this; "If you want to be successful, do what successful people do.." Dr. Williams has studied from the most important thought leaders in dentistry and he has taken that knowledge and used it to create a practice that is in the top 1/2 of 1% in the country. I am so thrilled that he wrote this book because he defines precisely what you need to do to develop a successful practice. This book is coming at exactly the right time for the Dental Profession. If you want to achieve your full potential read this book and follow Dr. Williams' counsel."

—GARY TAKACS
Founder, Takacs Learning Center
Scottsdale, AZ Takacslearningcenter.com

"If you're interested in growing your dental practice in any economy, then this is the book for you. Speaking directly from the trenches of dentistry, Bill shares his insights on opening a start-up practice to building a multi-million dollar dental empire. The magic of this book is that he spells out exactly how he did it and how you can too. He has graciously provided the blueprint for success! Most 'how-to' dental books will put you to sleep, but this book will inspire you to think outside the box and help you understand the psychology behind selling and marketing (which is often the last thing we in dentistry take time to learn).

Most importantly, this book will cause a shift in your thinking and make you realize that without the best marketing and mindset, even the best dentist will struggle. After reading this book, as Bill says, you will have "a future of choice, not a future of chance." Why not learn decades' worth of knowledge in a few short days? Get this book! Change your life!"

—DR. EJAZ TAHIR
Orthodontist, Berwyn and Oak Lawn, IL Coolbraces.com

"Thanks for giving me the chance to read your book. It is a well written, nothing but 'meat' study of where every practice should be when we think about marketing. The best thing I saw was that it was logical and very easy to read and apply. I would recommend this to every doctor I know. This book needs to part of every doctor's library. There was not one chapter that I would not endorse."

—MICHAEL ABERNATHY DDS
Founder, Summit Practice Solutions and McKinney Dental
McKinney, Texas

"Dr. Bill Williams has once again demonstrated how to 'CatchFire' in your Practice. This must read will show all practitioners how to go about marketing their 'babies' with less time and effort as he has shown others for decades.

—Dr. Chandler George, D.C.
President, CatchFireCoaching.com   Trophy Club, TX

"I have known Dr. Bill Williams since 1975. Bill graduated from the Medical College of Georgia the same year I began my dental career at the MCG School of Dentistry. Our paths crossed many times over the years. I have always admired Bill's constant search for clinical and managerial excellence. Bill has the rare combination of drive, determination, clinical excellence, managerial skill, futuristic thinking, and an insatiable desire to be the best he can be in everything he does. This book is truly a gift for those dentists seeking a highly successful dental practice. As Omer Reed said, 'If it has already been done, it is probably possible.' Bill has done it, and you can too. By following the key concepts in his book, you will be able to unlock the doors to marketing success which will lead to a dental practice you never dreamed possible."

—J. Brad Bynum, DMD, FAGD, FDOCS
Valdosta, GA

"This book is a must read for today's successful dentist. Bill has synthesized 30 years of experience and practice. He has stolen ideas from the best minds in dentistry. He put those ideas into action and created two of the most lucrative practices dentistry has ever seen. However, the most remarkable thing about Bill is that he is willing and able to share in every detail how he is achieved that success. This book is a harvest of ideas synthesized and implemented by a stellar mind with a great philosophy. His singular mission in this book is to help you achieve the practice you really want."

—Joe M Ellis, DDS PLLC
Houston, Texas www.4Smiling.com

"Dr. Williams, Is The Real Deal. If you want to turbo charge your marketing strategy follow his advice. Whether or not you want to be in the top 1% of the nation's dentists or just be better than where you are, he's been there and done that. I have known him for almost 30 years and have watched his journeys of success unfold into the book you have in your hand. So no matter where you are in your practice career, you can find concise and helpful guidance from this master clinician and marketer."

—Dr. Nicholas J Meyer, DDS, DND, MICCMO, FICOI
Past President, International Academy of Biological Dentistry & Medicine
Scottsdale, Arizona

"I have known Bill for the past 15 years and he is a man of integrity, passion and wisdom beyond his years. He is a man of God, who walks the walk, and is there for his fellow man always. He is a Master in the field of Dentistry who has been able to use his profession to minister, teach and help his colleagues not only become better Dentists, but better people. This book is much more than a book about marketing tactics. It will inspire you to reevaluate your life and purpose, how you can blend work, play, family and worship, and how you can make sure your priorities are in order."

—DINA JACKSON GIESLER, DDS, MAGD
CEO, Atlanta Smiles and Wellness
Founder, Atlanta Smiles Foundation

"Dr. Bill understands the importance of marketing in today's new economy! His keen knowledge and experience with what works and what doesn't work will provide any professional with a blueprint for increasing profits and streamlining efficiency. He's the real deal."

—SCOTT F. PETERSON, DDS
Family & Implant Dentistry Hurst Texas

"Bill has hit the nail on the head again! The successful minority of practices in the future will be those willing to adapt in a climate of increasing corporate practice, insurance and competitive constraints. Effective marketing solutions and strategy will allow fee-for-service practices prosper in the new economy."

—BRADY FRANK, DDS
Founder and CEO, OsteoReady Practical Implant Solutions
Ashland, Oregon

"Healthcare and dentistry are at a crossroads today. It's "differentiate or die." While clinical competence and hi-tech will always play an important part of the delivery of dental care, it's the business of dentistry, including a heavy emphasis on marketing, that will make or break the practices of the future. Unfortunately, there is no time to teach these survival topics in dental school. Competing as a commodity based on low price (as insurance and healthcare regulations would like), will unfortunately be the demise of many private practitioners.

But there is good news! Chaos creates opportunity! Dr. Bill William's Marketing The Million Dollar Practice is the ultimate reference guide for dental practitioners for the New Economy. Written as a story board beginning with his own graduation from dental school in the mid 70's, Bill takes the reader through a novel-like approach with lessons learned... both from trial and error and more importantly, from the many mentors and coaches with whom he associated (there's a tip... hire a coach!).

Having spent a great deal of time with Bill Williams, I know him to be a very humble man, a servant, putting his faith and family first. He walks the talk. At the twilight of his practice career, he is very much in demand as a speaker, coach and mentor, as well as a leader of mission trips, setting up dental clinics in Kenya, Tanzania, Haiti and Honduras. His awards and accomplishments are many; he is a lifelong student of his passion.

While he talks about the Million Dollar Practice, the fact is that Dr. Williams recently sold his Five Million Dollar practice. He is what I call, a "decathlon dentist." He does it all. Virtually every clinical procedure as well as being a student of business operations and marketing. As Bill aptly puts it, "if it's been done, it's probably possible."

If you are a dentist, or a member of a dental team and want the exquisite treatise on what it will take to re-position yourself for success in the coming years, Marketing The Million Dollar Practice is the book for you."

—DAVID PHELPS, **DDS**
Founder, The Dentist Freedom Blueprint Rockwall, Texas

"I recently read your book, Marketing the Million Dollar Practice. Congratulations! From cover to cover it is filled with pearls of dental marketing wisdom. I have already begun to incorporate your ideas into my practice. If anyone is looking for the guru of dental marketing it is Dr. Bill Williams! Thanks for all the help and support."
—RAYMOND SHERIDAN, **DDS** *Grove City, OH*

"Ask yourself one question—Do you want to know how to grow a multi-million dollar business? If the Answer is no then you need to go to the self-help section instead. On the other hand if you want to see how one man with a plan grew his business to over 5 million plus—and even better will share with you exactly how he did it and how you can do the same (or at least apply it) to your business no matter what you offer —Then You Are In The Right Place.

My name is Mike Crow (founder of Coach Blueprint) and I work with people in every type of industry and when Bill shares with others how he has grown and continues to grow his business others listen and then want more—You will fill the same way about this information—Simple secrets that can be applied to any business to help move you to the next level even quicker, more effectively and with more profit. Get this information now and consume it—mark it up and review it regularly—you will benefit in ways you didn't even expect."

—MIKE CROW *Founder, Coach Blueprint Dallas, Texas*

"Dr. Bill Williams, a proven mega successful dentist, has done a brilliant job of producing a very valuable book in a much needed area, that of marketing the dental practice. This is not a book about gimmicks or tricks to produce a large practice, but about excellence in dentistry and exceptional service to the public, which results in sustainable hyper-growth. The powerful ideas written about in this book have not only been produced from the authors own strategic thinking, but from contributions from other brilliant minds as well. These are not just great ideas in theory, but have been well proven in the daily trenches of a dynamic dental practice. This powerful book is a must read for any success seeking dentist, dental practice manager or dental management consultant for that matter. It is that good!"

—S. KENT LAUSON, DDS, MS
Orthodontist, Aurora, Colorado, and author of
"Straight Talk About Crooked Teeth" The New Orthodontics

"Never afraid of success or the efforts and steps required to reach it, Dr. Bill Williams has set a new bar for excellence with his new book 'Marketing the Million Dollar Practice.'

They say it's better to copy genius than invent mediocrity. Dr. Bill Williams makes it so easy to copy his genius and model his success— and to avoid the mistakes made trying to go it alone. His genius comes from a very well thought out yet fearless charge forward to see what works, and what doesn't—and then packaging it in an easily understandable manner for literally anyone to follow!

In the 25+ years I've known and worked with Bill, I am constantly inspired by his work ethic, integrity, insight, confidence and humility. Plus it doesn't hurt that he is just one of the smartest and most accomplished dental health professionals we have in our profession! Thankfully, in addition to his passion to achieve, he has a passion to teach and to lift and to inspire others to be what and where he is—and more.

Now he takes it a step further and blesses us with this "best of the best" marketing book about the "million dollar practice" (never mind that it should be read "multi-million dollar practice.") While the dollar figures and specific goals may vary, what doesn't vary is his commitment to excellence and in challenging people to move beyond their boundaries and limitations, to think outside the box, and to achieve and be more than they think they can. He is the perfect example of "if it's been done, it's probably possible!"

A consummate student and example to us all, I give a big two thumbs up to Bill, his marketing book, and his Solstice Dental Advisors practice and personal coaching efforts. Thank you Bill."

—LEE OSTLER, DDS
President, American Academy of Oral and Systemic Health
The Center For Dental Health Richland, WA

"We were dental school classmates. The recession hit and initially we were still busy, I watched my income go down, overhead go up, new patients dwindle and something I had never experienced in 30 years of practice—I routinely found holes in my schedule. Despite the recession, Bill's practice was still producing and growing when others around us were bemoaning their plight and even closing their doors. It dawned on me that the difference in his practice was having systems in place, scripting for every situation, internal and external marketing, and constant communication with staff and patients as well as hands-on, consistent management. These things were lacking in my practice, yet utilized in Bill's practice. It's what he teaches others to do in his coaching program, Solstice Dental Advisors.

It has taken me a long time to realize and was difficult to admit, but Bill was right all along. The best service, best dentistry, or best personality won't assure success unless you are letting your patients and the community know about them in a positive professional way. Referrals won't occur unless you ask for them. People won't know what you do unless you tell them. Practice success doesn't mean only financial rewards. Dentistry is a service profession but think of the service you could render with a financially successful and sound practice. Real success means being able to donate your time, energy, skill and yes money to those in need or for the good of you community. I see Bill living that out. Just maybe you and I need to listen. His new book Marketing the Million Dollar Practice is a great place to start to learn from a master."

—LARRY L. TILLEY, DMD, FAGD, MICCMO, DABCP
President, American Academy of Craniofacial Pain Calhoun, GA

Foreword by Dr. Omer K. Reed

marketing the

MILLION DOLLAR

practice

27 Steps to Follow to Grow 1/2 Million a Year

Dr. Bill Williams, DMD, MAGD, MICCMO

Author: **Dr. Bill Williams, DMD, MAGD, MICCMO**

Published By:

SEGR Publishing LLC
2150 W. Northwest Hwy
Ste 114-1168
Grapevine, Texas 76051
(972) 600-2310
Email: info@SEGRpublishing.com

Cover Design By:
Andrea Ferguson, 320 Designs
www.320designs.com

Page Layout and Design By:
Lynn M. Snyder
Nosy Rosy Designs
nosyrosydesigns@gmail.com

ISBN-10: 1619200228
ISBN-13: 978-1-61920-022-7

Printed in the United States

*A*cknowledgements

PARTNERING WITH THE FOLLOWING "bluechip" professionals allowed me to assimilate and put into practice what this book teaches. I wish to acknowledge each one of them as a meaningful contributor to this book, my practice and my life.

My wife Sheila has been there since day one as my only chairside assistant to CFO of a five million dollar group practice, Angie, my loyal office manager and excellent treatment coordinator, Justin and Tyler, my sons who have been involved in marketing and teaching, Amy, Mistie, and Marti, my current chairside dental assistants who represent a score of other fine dental professionals whom I have had the privilege of sitting knee to knee with over patients, Jennifer, Brooke, Derrelle, our family of McDonalds who represent our able business assistants over the many years over which we have honed our management systems, Andrea who was my personal assistant and communications coordinator, Caren, Jennifer, Lena, Amy, Kayla and Beth who are my Suwanee Dental Hygienists who have pioneered with me our unique NST and Laser Periodontal Therapy.

Dr. Bill Gelfond, my first associate ever who represents ALL of my invaluable 16 associate dentists over the years, my primary mentors, Dr. Omer Reed, Dr. Ron McConnell, Jay Conrad Levinson, Brian Blomgren, Mike Crow, Armand Morin, and Dr. Justin Jones, my classmate at MCG, Dr. Larry Tilley, who along with Dr. Dennis Simmons and Dr. Dale Madsen, partnered with me in the TMJ Framework, my original fellow Solstice Research Group members, Dr. Lee Ostler, Dr. Joe Ellis Dr. John Willoughby, Dr. Steve Cobble, Dr. Geoff Pratt, Dr. Nick Meyer, Dr. Tommy Oppenheim and Dr. Tony Roeder, and last but not least, my able friend and publisher of this book Bob Bare, with his excellent editor Heidi Clingen.

Dedication

THIS BOOK IS DEDICATED TO MY FAMILY for their many sacrifices: my loving wife, Sheila Harrison Williams, my two fine sons, William Justin and Tyler Harrison Williams, who allowed me to stretch my wings and become who I am. And to my parents, Dr. Bill & Anne Williams, who shared their love and dreams with me for 62 years, bringing me up in the way of the Lord.

Table of Contents

Endorsements................................ i - vii

Acknowledgements............................... xi

Dedication xii

Table of Contents .... xiv-xv

Forward by Omer K. Reed, DDS 17

Introduction.................................... 21

Chapter 1 The Way It Is 29

Chapter 2 Mid-life Crisis 39

Chapter 3 WebCentric Marketing 49

Chapter 4: It All Starts With... Your Image........... 55

Chapter 5: The New Resident Letter................ 61

Chapter 6: The Brochure for Your Practice........... 67

Chapter 7: Message-On-Hold Systems 75

Chapter 8: New Resident Follow-up Postcards:
           Make It A Campaign 81

Chapter 9: Using the *Yellow Pages* to Your Benefit,
           Now That They Are Almost Dead........ 85

Chapter 10: Local Links: The Winners Circle.......... 97

Chapter 11: Marketing Your Practice Through the Health
           History Part I :Psychographics 107

Chapter 12: Marketing Your Practice Through the Health
           History Part II: New Patient Intake Form . 113

Chapter 13: The New Patient Experience............ 127

Chapter 14: Direct Email........................ 141

Chapter 15: Affinity Groups 153

Chapter 16: Neighborhood Directories. 161

Chapter 17: Autoresponders 165

Chapter 18: PowerCore: Networking Teams. 171

Chapter 19: Word-of-Mouth Advertising 177

Chapter 20: Word-of-Mouth Patient Referrals 183

Chapter 22: A Sign of the Times 189

Chapter 21: Developing the E-Based Practice. 195

Chapter 23: Impressions: The Name Game 201

Chapter 24: Coffee News 211

Chapter 25 Time in a Bottle 215

Chapter 26: The Experience Economy 221

Chapter 27: Daycare Dynamite and the Tooth Fairy. . . . 229

Chapter 28: The Prayer of Jabez 233

Chapter 29: Sugar Hill Mission Project and the

        Deserving Diva Makeovers 245

Chapter 30: High Tech—Soft Touch Perception 253

Chapter 31: Dental Missions Fallout 261

Chapter 32: The 12 Differentors 273

Chapter 33: The Seven Mountain Marketing Strategy . . 281

Chapter 34: Conclusion But Not The End 295

Epilogue 305

Resources 307

Bonuses. 309

About The Author. 311

Forward

"WOW!... AN AMAZING COMPILATION of tried and true methods for marketing your dental practice to achieve the now obtainable "Million Dollar Practice." Bill Williams has done an outstanding job of sharing his expertise gained through his own efforts and that of his mentors over the last 30+ years in building his own dental practices.

CONTEXTUAL CONGRUITY

Back in 1988, Dr. Williams set a goal to be a presenter at our Napili VIII Million Dollar Round Table: The Anatomy of the Accelerated Practice. Of course the criterion to be invited to speak was that the practice had to produce over one million dollars. By the next year he had achieved that goal and Marci and I invited him and his wife Sheila to our home in Phoenix, Arizona. There he was our guest instructor, one of three dentists who gave their 'Stepping Stones To Success' presentation. Dr. Ron McConnell, himself a previous Napili VIII speaker and the founder of the Quest Management Program, attended and called it 'World Class.' Little did I know what was to evolve from that session! As the founder of Napili and Pentegra, of which Bill was an active member and participant, I'm pleased and proud to say that many of my tenets and philosophies of practice, taught in Napili-Pentegra, are still influencing the next generation of dental professionals.

HOW IT CAME TO BE

At that particular Napili VIII was birthed the original Solstice Dental Study Club, or Solstice Group, as they became known. No less than eight of those members became internationally known clinicians, authors and presenters. Meeting as a true mastermind, they were my hand-picked group of geographically diverse, future-focused, forward-thinking dentists who began to meet twice yearly on or about the summer and winter solstice, hence the origin of their name. With Dr. Joe Ellis of Houston, Texas, as point man, they organized, strategized and implemented their way as a collective mind to successively higher levels of practice achievement. This book is a result of ten years of deliberations within that group. Dr. Williams applied their deliberations to his new start-from-scratch practice in 1997 and the rest is, as they say, history.

WHY IT IS IMPORTANT?

Because of the mastermind effect, unearthed for us through the business classic, Think And Grow Rich by Napoleon Hill, his is a new classic, a "must read" for ALL dentists in practice, including new practitioners. It is an annual checklist for all established dental practices. Adding to your marketing mix on a regular basis is the only way to keep up and preferably stay ahead of your competition. I know they will be reading this book and implementing much of what Bill has suggested. You will find it easy to read with step by step how-to's and resources for every phase of marketing, both internal and external. You'll be surprised at the level of completeness you'll achieve in your life if you truly implement his success formula, focusing faithfully on family, work, self and spiritual balance. You see, as you travel the road and vicariously live through what Bill has done, you'll find yourself on a different plain by the end of the journey. I know, in fact, I guarantee, that you'll not be the same person you were when you started reading this book. As Bill says, "Change happens at the speed of life!"

WHO THIS IS FOR?

The past is behind us and the future belongs to those who embrace new concepts and technology. What worked in the 70's and 80's will still work but so much better when combined with the power of what was learned in the 90's and 2,000's. Many of the new graduates (2,000 and on) have never been exposed to the golden nuggets, the proven gems of the great dental and business masterminds of the last 30 years of the 20th century. This book will tie a lot of loose ends together for those who have been searching for that missing link. Connecting into the taproot of why we do what we do and what matters most in life is correlated with the nuances of the psychology of sales, WebCentric marketing action planning, and our fast flow into the mobile, digital, video-driven, social media age of marketing. Think of it as Sinatra meets Elvis, meets Bono, meets Pink: a medley of classical hits, modern marketing tactics and wisdom of the ages from dental sages.

WHEN THE PARADIGM SHIFTS, EVERYONE STARTS AT THE BEGINNING

That is why Marketing The Million Dollar Practice is a critical "must read" approach for the successful process of planning and executing the concept of marketing a practice that focuses and satisfies today's high tech dental patient. The author is now sharing his journey, through the decades, complete with the paradigm shift he traversed, and unifying the many methods and strategies that work in this modern-day marketing environment. His concepts via experience in his own practice and sitting at the feet of 'The Masters' build upon one another to arrive at a very concrete and successful conclusion that can and has been replicated. Again, this is a new classic for all dentists that want to be on the cutting edge of soft touch—high tech marketing and management resulting in a million dollar plus practice.

MARKETING HAS COME A LONG WAY. THE PARADIGM HAS SHIFTED!

—OMER K. REED, DDS
Phoenix, Arizona

Introduction

THE AMAZING SHRINKING DENTAL PRACTICE

ALL ACROSS THE COUNTRY dental practices are contracting, shrinking at an alarming rate. New patients joining the practice are down and the back door seems wide open as discount programs and PPO's drain the profitability of the average dentist's fee for service practice.

New dentists are coming out of dental school without a quality practice to join. As more older dentists defer their retirement plans due to the poor results of their stock market and real estate portfolios, the future for younger graduates is cloudy, murky, and down right scary.

THE WORLD OF DENTISTRY IS CHANGING

The days of a new graduate opening his or her new practice right out of dental school and automatically succeeding have vanished. Used to be it was the norm for a practice in our area to set up from scratch. The dental equipment companies fought among one another for recent graduates to place in the expanding suburbs of our metro areas. Dentists followed the housing and population booms of the 1970's, 1980's and 1990's. Banks forked out money to anyone with a DDS or DMD and waited to rake in the deposits from their rapidly burgeoning practices.

> The days of a new graduate opening his or her new practice right out of dental school and automatically succeeding have vanished.

Equipment costs were reasonable back then. I only spent

$54,000 to fully equip two Pelton Crane Executive units and build out the entire space for my 1200 square foot first practice in a leased space at the Hidden Hills Shopping Center in Decatur, Georgia. The year was 1975, men out-numbered women in dental school classes ten to one, extractions cost patients $10, and a crown could be had for $150 with a $30 lab fee for the dentist.

THE NEW DENTAL PARADIGM

What you must do today to succeed in dentistry didn't exist thirty, twenty or even ten years ago. There were no dental practice "PC" computers three decades ago; there were no lasers in dentistry just over twenty years ago, and within the last decade has come Google, Facebook, Groupon and Pinterest. It's enough to make you Yelp!

We are faced with escalating technological achievements, miraculous advances in our scientific understanding of human genetics and the disease process. Plus, we have a heightened ability to help our patients because we now more fully understand the oral-systemic connection, how oral inflammation influences the vascular, endocrine and nervous systems of the human body. Microchips and nano particles create opportunities for digital everything and improved smaller versions of anything. Analog is dead; hail king digital, plug and play, and the Cloud.

With such technological explosion comes opportunity. "When a paradigm shift happens," says futurist Joel Barker, "everyone starts back at zero." The old ways no longer offer security and may even not have viability in the new paradigm. The new way of doing things offers those who adopt them "leap frog" capability. The new opportunity is to charge to the front of the line, to rearrange the chairs on the deck. The dentist who embraces change, understands it and makes the most of it is the big winner in the new economy, in the new dental paradigm in which we practice.

WIN-LOSE-WIN

My story in dentistry in a like a lot of others, filled with peaks and valleys, wins and losses. But my peaks have been Mt. McKinley and my valleys Death Valley: very high and very low. I remember cruising past Dr. Bob Levoy's $100,000 practice and saying that wasn't too difficult. I remember Rick Mercer saying in our consult with him in Eugene, Oregon that he had never seen such a large savings and retirement plan as I had amassed in such a short time as a dentist back in 1986, in my first ten years of dentistry. Yes those were the halcyon days of the 1970's and 1980's.

Somewhere in the 1990's I lost my fire. The flame flickered and almost went out and my gut said sell, move on, get out of dentistry. The area where we practiced had turned rough, killings on the corner and burglars breaking into our building drove me away. I sold the practice in 1993 only to have to take it back in two years. My extra-dental business ventures all flopped and our once huge investment portfolio was a shadow of it's former self. Those were gut-wrenching, Death Valley days.

So, in 1996, I sold the $1.8 million dollar practice once again and this time included the building with it. It was an 8000-square-foot, magnificent facility with 12 operatories and lease space for a primary care physician's practice. All for $900,000. I paid off all my debts with that and basically started over. I was right back to square "two." I felt just like a new graduate. I had to start over, make a new beginning. I needed to open my own new practice. But this time something was different. My heart said it was right and the focus was on a future of infinite potential.

I say square "two" because while I was starting over, there was one big advantage... a ton of experience and knowledge from running my own practice for 23 years. The short, sweet version of my success story, The Last Win, was that I found, through much prayer and good blessings from the Lord, the ideal location for growth and practice development for our next dental adventure. My wife and I chose Suwanee, Georgia, a suburb on the northeast outskirts of Atlanta, my home town, and applied a series of marketing and management principles to a new scratch practice start up.

The new practice, named Suwanee Dental Care, grew from zero to $600,000 in our first year (working three days a week from August to October... then four days a week for the next nine months). On average, production increased $500,000 a year for the next ten years in Suwanee. We expanded our dental facility space from 1,200 to 3,000 to 9,000 square feet and increased our staff from three to 24 over that decade. Profits grew and what was early on a seven figure gross became a seven figure net.

Now, I'm enjoying the scenery, often from the rail of a cruise ship in the Mediterranean or the inner passage of Alaska. I'm working three days a week, producing on average $12,000-$14,000 a day myself while my team of three dentists and four hygienists produce $15,000 to $20,000 additional each and every day of the week. I have now employed three "Million Dollar Dentists" and am enjoying teaching and mentoring other dentists.

THE OPPORTUNITY TO INSPIRE THE NEXT GENERATION

I am inspired to see my dental colleagues align their systems to create those "perfect dental storms." I'm having fun at the office working with patients, working with staff, working with other dentists. And, I'm here to show you, too, that it's possible and that you, too, can build a similar high-impact dental team, that you, too, can generate the kind of new patient flow and a high personal income which will allow you to set your course for a future of choice, not a future of chance.

I'm here to show you how we did it. I want to show you the step-by-step actions we took to become among the top 1% of dental practices in the country. It's a system and a formula with visible frameworks to follow. I've begun to put it all down on paper in books, documented it in Power Point presentations, captured many of the technologies and systems on video and will deliver them in classes at live seminars and online with webinars. But, I'm getting ahead of myself.

The reason you will want to get through this book, *Marketing The Million Dollar Practice,* is that you need to know what it takes to reach the seven-figure plateau. In this very book, we show you how we break through where most dental practices stop growing. We cover the strong marketing focus you need to succeed. We give you the dentist's perspective on the psychology of sales, the very tactics needed to propel you on to multiple millions of practice growth. Read on, if propelling your practice to much higher levels is your goal.

THIS MAY NOT BE WHAT YOU WANT

1. Maybe you don't want a "Big Practice" like ours with a couple of associates working for you producing every day while you you're there or not. Maybe you don't want to have a relatively large staff to manage, even though they can be taught to be twice as productive per person than the average dental staff. But if you do want to have these things, this book can help you take your practice to the next level.

It could be that you need staff management and executive leadership skills to stabilize your volatile practice situation. Perhaps you want to be more efficient in your procedures. It is possible to learn how to produce twice the dentistry in half the time. We can show you that top quality can happen at the speed of laser light. Leadership skills are a part of the Solstice team teaching, and we find that it is one of the key ingredients many dentists want and need. The sky is the limit when there is excellence in leadership.

Marketing, which this book focuses on exclusively, is not the whole answer to being highly productive. There are more things to learn. There are systems, strategies, and a vision of a grand future for dentists that I want to share with you. You will use a resource guide and an implementation list to plot your next strategy in the evolution of your practice. Let me tweak your curiosity and say that there is a nice surprise waiting for you once you have finished this book. I hope you'll soon take advantage of it!

THE BLUEPRINT

2. Marketing *The Million Dollar Practice* is laid out as a template or a framework for you to follow. I've designed the flow of this book to follow the chronological steps I went through to grow my own brand new, start-up, dental practice first to one million dollars, then two, then three, and beyond. I'm showing you every major marketing strategy and chess move I made. I cover for you every internal and external marketing action item we used and the implementation plan that was set up to run each. I show you the three most important action items to do first.

Next, I focus your attention on the top ten marketing steps you must make this year, in this economy. There are forty, detailed marketing plays that will give you the lead over your dental competitors. Finally, I share the psychology of sales behind each one of them. It's a treasure trove of ideas. This has never before been put together in one book for dentists, or any business for that matter!

3. Finally, at the end of this book is a "What's Next?" section. You should see this book—a simple book on marketing and sales psychology—as only the tip of the iceberg for creating the practice of your dreams, in which you work three days a week, have a five million dollar practice, or a seven figure income. Perhaps your dream is taking six or seven weeks of vacation a year, or perhaps it's the ability to travel on missions like we do for two to three weeks a year. What's next is up to what you want. What's next is your future of choice. You can choose the end and how it will look.

Enjoy the journey. The journey IS the thing. Take this journey with your friends, your peers, and you will see that it is the real deal!

·

CHAPTER 1

The Way It Is

*D*ENTISTRY IS IN AN UPHEAVAL. To be successful in our current economic climate, dentists need to be intelligent marketers. The reality is few dentists have the interest or have been well trained in marketing. Unless one has a natural affinity for that kind of subject, it's the exact polar opposite of the personality, style, and training that leads to (1) who applies to dental school, (2) what dental schools create, and (3) what a new graduate wants to be or do. A clinical dentist marketing expert is an oxymoron.

In marketing, it's always been thought that to make a lot of money, you have to spend a lot of money. New dentists starting out fresh out of school, residency or even as an associate for a few early years never have a lot of money... so they don't market well—if at all. Dentists who barely scrape by don't run extensive marketing campaigns, which are the ones that work best. They take individual shots in the dark, hit or miss—mostly miss. The Madison Avenue approach is the picture most dentists think of when they hear the word marketing: newspaper ads, magazine full-page glossy features, radio, TV and direct mail postcards.

> Dentistry is an upheaval. To be successful in our current economic climate, dentists need to be intelligent marketers. The reality is few dentists have the interest or have been well trained in marketing.

The plethora of dental consultants have been around for decades and they sold us on the one-two punch of putting our practice names on tooth brushes and coffee cups. But they cannot pull us out of this economic morass with those yesteryear strategies, however well they once worked. We've had cute, positive posters on the wall and flowers at the front desk checkout as "thank you" tokens for over twenty years. All this is still done, in the name of internal marketing and keeping patient "good will," but it is not enough.

The dentist of the new millennium, one much younger than I, will know and recognize the value of the Internet to the practice. They will readily interface with Facebook and Twitter, be able to code in HTML and navigate Word Press, perhaps, and rely upon mobile devices to carry out their daily tasks. Yes, times have changed and the new era of marketing in dentistry is upon us.

It was a stoke of luck that I rolled into the Internet age when I was selling my first practice and starting my second. As an early adopter and a leading-edge thinker, I embrace new ideas and analyze them. With the Internet, I found the time-shifting tools at our disposal. I combined them with the psychology of sales into a unique system, the Solstice WebCentric Marketing Action Plan.

CHANGE HAPPENS

What changed for me was how the breadth and depth of my marketing could grow with very little effort and very little expense. I found that I could gain as much visibility and presence in the market with hundreds of dollars using my new-found guerilla marketing ideas as someone paying tens of thousands of dollars to an ad agency or marketing firm. The Internet was hot and getting hotter when I began my practice. I rode that practice website train all the way to the top of the hill and still have a seat in the first class cabin.

We're still focused on our WebCentric game plan and I'm still promoting this technique as the #1 most important marketing tactic a practice must have in place to succeed today.

When I started the second practice in the late 1990's, I had five or six spokes on my wheel, the WebCentric wheel. Now, over a decade later, we still need to feed a big, dynamic, patient-eating machine, and we're doing it, even in what some call a real recession. Your marketing should be able to feed the beast... or it's not doing its job.

Show me idle dentists or empty treatment rooms and I'll show you an executive who has poor planning and management ability. The more busy and profitable a practice, the smoother and well-tuned their practice marketing will be. Practices grow by intention, not by accident. Populations of people support dentists by the natural process of desire and decay taking its daily toll. Yet, it's the story of the haves and the have nots. Some dentists seem to have all the patients they need and some dentists sit around wondering why they don't.

So, in essence, marketing has grown much more involved, more technical, more digital, more focused, and especially for the near future, reliant on more online video. The new era of marketing will blend a hearty mix of online and offline activities. It will involve you, your staff and a group of out-source marketing helpers. They will handle your web design, web hosting, video production, print ad creation, mailing lists, auto responder, social media management, community events and sponsorships, athletic team sponsorships, and more.

THE BAD NEWS

You've seen it before; it's not news to you. The bad news is that dentists are awful at marketing. Generally we were given no real business training, not in dental school and not in college. We were too busy with biochemistry, cell biology, cardiology, genetics, prosthodontics, and dental materials to get a real grounding in cost analysis, marketing formulas, balance sheets, management structures, or key performance indicators.

The other bad news is that the old ways of marketing, even if you did learn them, are now out-dated and in need of a marketing plan overhaul. Gone are the halcyon days of opening a practice with a three-inch high sign on the door and instant success, Now it's digital this and laser that. It's You Tube and Yelp, not CBS and WSB. New era dentists have more tech-savvy skills and value the web and all it offers. Our purpose here, in this book, is to unite the "experienced" with the "high tech" and produce a new superior way to market your dental practice, the WebCentric way.

THE NEW APPROACH

Web Centric Dental Marketing and Design (Web Centric DMD) is a concept that I coined in 1997. The spokes of that version of the marketing wheel have grown from six spokes to nearly sixty spokes now. The practice has grown accordingly. Our practice is approximately ten times larger in 2011 than it was at the end of our first year in 1998 ($600,00 to $1,000,000). The new WebCentric approach has worked consistently well in each and every year over the last 14 years. We've remained at our average of $5 million as a group even during the recession for the past four years. Our new WebCentric model of marketing and our Solstice 5M System that you can follow has recommendations of the places to go, the people to contact, the emphasis to place and the dollars to spend to reach your practice goals.

Do you want twenty new patients a month for each dentist in your practice? Do you want thirty or forty? How many actual new patients does a practice need to flourish? What is your conversion rate and how do you calculate your ROI?

Return on investment is critical to know in marketing and is important to monitor each and every month. All of these things are part of management's basic statistics knowledge in a stellar dental practice. It all starts with marketing to get those new patients coming through the front door.

What course in dental school covered "the funnel?" What instructors had the private practice model solved well enough that they could teach you the "fool proof" way to always sell your high-end , top-dollar cases. Are you comfortable saying: "That'll be $45,000." Can you remain silent long enough to let the patient speak just after that mind-blowing number? Are you an expert at sales?

WINNERS AND LOSERS

Who wins in the next ten years and who loses will largely depend on who has the open mind, the curiosity to leave the "dental school box" and who has the interest to go outside for more avenues, more options. If you only rely on traditional "marketing gurus" to coach you, just as they coached sixty or seventy other dental practices, you'll merely end up looking like just one more striped fish in a pond full of stripers!

Today, differentiation is the key to success. In the book, *Differentiate Or Die,* Jack Trout, talks about the secret to ultimate marketing success. The book, in the early chapters, clearly identifies what are *not* usually key factors in this success:

(Chapter 4)   Quality and Customer Orientation Are Rarely Differentiating Ideas

(Chapter 5)   Creativity Is Not a Differentiating Idea

(Chapter 6)   Price Is Rarely a Differentiating Idea

Later on in this landmark book on marketing, the lines of distinction are drawn and what Trout identifies as success principles are these:

(Chapter 10) Being First is a Differentiating Idea

(Chapter 11) Attribute Ownership is a Way to Differentiate

(Chapter 12) Leadership is a Way to Differentiate

(Chapter 13) Heritage is a Differentiating Idea

(Chapter 14) Market Specialty is a Differentiating Idea

(Chapter 15) Preference is a Differentiating Idea

(Chapter 16) How a Product is Made Can Be a Differentiating Idea

(Chapter 17) Being the Latest Can Be a Differentiating Idea

(Chapter 18) Hotness is a Way to Differentiate

In the new era of dentistry, that time called The Digital Age, The Nano Particle age, and The Time-Shift Age, you can quickly and easily seize the day and become relevant to your patients and to your team once you embrace these new technologies. The winners of tomorrow will utilize mobile devices, keep their data "in the Cloud" and communicate with their community on a regular basis in a real and transparent way. The power of "push technology" will give way to pull the technology that the younger generation prefers. Your marketing messages will be forever lost as time-shifting clears out the waste bins of junky advertising and only the clever, strong and relevant survive.

The losers will be those who are stuck in the 1990's. They are those who refuse to see the train coming towards them at one hundred miles per hour. Overhead costs will rise, yet new patient numbers will drop. Dismay turns to discouragement and depression. It's not a dog's life that's being described; it's a dentist's life, one who forgot to differentiate or die.

Okay, so you don't want to be one of the dental statistics they talk about. You choose immortality over mere mortality. You want be a dental god to your staff and your patients!

How you say? By doing what's been done! In this book, *Marketing The Million Dollar Practice,* we'll open the door and show you the steps to take to become a true legend in your own space—a real hometown, dental hero.

Later on, in the next chapter, I'm going to tell you the whole story, my woe-to-win scenario and how all that happened, both the good and the bad. I had it made after a hard-fought battle to succeed and basically threw it away with the help of some dumb choices I made along the way. I'll share some of that with you because I don't want any dentist to make the same mistakes I did. The climb back to the top can be long and painful.

PREPARE TO WIN

To put together this revolutionary Solstice 5M system I had the best mentors money could buy, took the best courses I could find, and committed to the result I visualized and wanted. I had a goal in mind; I set it in stone, and worked hard to achieve it, no matter the cost or effort required. Along the way I had a splendid journey, met wonderful friends, and traveled the world. It's been said that "where you are next year will depend on the people you've met and the books you've read." I believe it and have the stories to convince you, too!

I exposed my mind to the best dental and business thinkers of our times, read their books, joined their coaching programs, and took their seminars. It all started with *Guerrilla Marketing Attack,* a book by J. Conrad Levinson. I took a hundred ideas from his seminal book on low-cost marketing tactics and created a game plan. Then, I learned for a year under Charles Martin DDS in his Dallas Mastermind. I took the five-year Georgia AGD Mastertrack program from Dr. James Curtis and Dr. Carol Wooden. I spent one year with Dr. Tony Feck of Sunrise Dental Solutions and four years of weekly one-on-one coaching from Brian Blomgren of Action Coaching, an international firm founded by Australian billionaire, Brad Sugars. Earlier in my dental career I spent a couple of years with my number-one guru/teacher Omer Reed DDS in Phoenix, Arizona.

Major, year-long stints with Dr. Carl Misch, the AAID Maxi Course, Dr. Hilt Tatum and Dr. Ed Mills led the way to comfort doing big implant cases. Five years in the USDI, the last four as their Senior TMJ Instructor, gave me my strong background in orthodontics. I cofounded TMJ Framework and Framework Seminars teaching in that 16-day mini-residency for nearly nine years in the 1980's and 1990's.

But beyond the obvious dental and business courses, the most significant move I made was in following the recent crop of business superstars, those who grew up in and made their millions on the Internet, in the digital, nano particle, time-shifted winners of how it is done now. I followed Armand Morin, Brendon Burchard, Ed Kennedy, Loral Langemeier, and Mike Crow, all multi-multimillionaires in their businesses. I figured out how their work relates to dentistry and applied it. I applied the brilliance of multiple multimillionaires to dentistry so that we can all benefit. What you will see in the following pages will elevate you and inspire you, I hope, to go forth with an open mind and to seek the value that other professionals, often outside our dental sphere, have to offer to you and your dental practice.

I've boiled it down, focused what is relevant to dentistry for you and now it's in a framework you can easily see and understand. And better than that, you don't have to spend all the time and all the money putting this all-together like I did. It's right here for you in synopsis form. The cliff notes are good and you are free to use them to grow and enjoy.

The New Paradigm Blue Print: The Basis of our Solstice 5M Strategy is:

1. Become the Authority—It's Combining Image and Knowledge

2. The New Patient Experience with 93% Case Acceptance
3. Web Centric Marketing Action Plan is the "Secret Sauce"
4. Decathlon Dentistry: Separates the Men and Women from the Boys and Girls
5. Solstice Systems List: Systems Run the Practice
6. Team Gold: People Run the Systems
7. Efficiency Gold: Producing Twice the Dentistry in Half the Time
8. Loyalty Reward Systems: For Patients, Team and the Doctor
9. Strategic Planning for Success
10. Gold Key List: Your Guaranteed Way to Succeed

So this framework/blueprint/formula is the total package that helped us create our $5.8 million dollar practice. I call it Solstice 5M. And, I want to help you do the same thing, grow your practice a bit, at least to a million dollars, perhaps two, three or four! You choose; I help. I'm focused primarily in this book, *Marketing the Million Dollar Practice,* on just the WebCentric Marketing Action Plan and some of the systems that surround it. As you go forward in this book you'll be exposed to the New Patient Experience, the Loyal Patient Rewards System, elements of the Solstice Strategic Planning model and the use of Expert Status and Authority as it relates to the Psychology of Sales.

Reading this book will place you light years ahead of your competition, yet won't answer your entire set of questions. Make a list of those questions and let me know how I can help you get answers. Send me a note when you've finished this book.

CHAPTER 2

Mid-life Crisis

*C*LIMBING THE LADDER OF SUCCESS is an
exhilarating ride but, the higher one gets, the
closer to the top and the further one gets away from
the ground, the greater their potential fall. In the
early 1990s my wife and I began to feel the effects of over
twenty years of burning the proverbial candle at both ends.
My practice peaked at $1.8 million and we were having a
hard time finding a buyer/partner. Staffing was becoming a
difficult issue as the neighborhood where my practice was
located became more dangerous. Dentistry wasn't as fun as it
had once been.

Also, TMJ Framework, the seminar group that I had
founded seven years earlier began to dissolve. I wanted
to step down as its leader and began looking for M.S.I's,
multiple sources of income, to supplement my dental
income. So, I diverted my attention away from dentistry a
bit and focused on direct marketing. I started new business
ventures in places like Costa Rica, Colombia, Greece, and
Indonesia as well as nationally. By the early 1990's I was
ready for a change yet there was no real income being
created by any of these new options. I looked at the future
of staying where I was and doing what I was doing and I did
not like what I saw. I wanted a way out. An alternative game
plan became an option and a way out. I took the leap.

During this time, world events led to the leveling of
the Berlin Wall. Before the Iron Curtain fell, I had been
to Moscow. It was 1986 and the leaders of the Academy
of General Dentistry went as a dental delegation to study
the systems in Denmark, Sweden and the U.S.S.R. Later, I
was to go there twice more, first in 1993 and then again in

1994 with the World Business Network, seeking to gain a foothold in the period of Glasnost and Perestroika. WBN attempted to start American businesses in Russia, the Ukraine and Kazakhstan in the building, lottery and oil industries. We were hunting bear and we had a full load of buckshot in our barrels.

TRANSITIONS

> I now believe that I went through a stage of clinical depression without ever realizing it... what else do you call playing computer solitaire for five or six hours, day after day, while listening to the same songs from Vince Gill and Reba McIntire over and over?

I passed through the decade of the 90s in a funk. This for many reasons was the lowest point of my life, my Death Valley moment, looking back. I now believe that I went through a stage of clinical depression without ever realizing it... what else do you call playing computer solitaire for five or six hours, day after day, while listening to the same songs from Vince Gill and Reba McIntire over and over?

I can count four reasons for my depression. First, my Framework Seminars company broke up soon after we lost a key employee to an unexpected and tragic circumstance. Two, the sale of the practice fell through after two years and I had to take it back and run it by myself. The third death knell struck, also entirely by surprise: my MLM up-line stole my entire down-line in Bogota, Columbia, the one that I had built via the Internet and two trips into South America.

The last big reason for being depressed and hitting rock bottom followed the loss of my down-line. All of my heavy investments in Russia and Indonesia went belly up and burst in flames. That streak of bad luck eventually did in my once-promising retirement plans. At age 46, I was destined to work for a long time to come. I was in a place I did not want to be and the future looked bleak.

Now, more info on the failure of the sale of the practice is important to share with you. Selling our big practice was always my concern. The bigger it got, the more our financial advisers at Cain-Watters and Associates contended that there would be fewer and fewer buyers in the market for it. They were correct. I had three associates come and go who had initially planned on buying in. Finally it was a dentist from one of my TMJ classes who came along and was interested enough to purchase the practice. So, I sold the practice, my 20-year-old baby, to a dentist who had earlier completed my TMJ Framework program. I knew him and figured he was a pretty safe bet. But I was wrong.

Believe me, the details were like Days Of Our Lives, but for real. Because he suffered a series of severe personal setbacks that affected the practice as well as his personal life, I ended up just where I had started three years prior.

I had made the mistake of financing it myself even though it was through a local broker. I had been the associate dentist for two and one half years. I got the practice back and I was solo in an 8,000-square-foot building with twelve operatories. This is the point at which I started playing solitaire and listening to depressing country music for hours on end when I got home from the office. I felt like the weight of the world was on my shoulders… and it was.

TURNAROUND

I hired a Russian dentist to work for me but that went nowhere in terms of his buying into the practice. He did, however, offer some help. He told me about a friend of his who had just returned to Atlanta from his dental implant residency at Loma Linda. This new dentist, Dr. Bernee Dunson, liked our practice and it was he who eventually did buy the practice as well as the 8,000-square-foot building. Bernee was an excellent dentist and we would work well together for a year. It was blessing from God, a total turnaround of fortune for us. We were delivered from the depths of our depression. Just like that, in a matter of months, we were freed to seek our ultimate destiny, if we could just figure out what that was! But, oh, how that year passed so quickly. I was soon in need of finding a new source of income… and quick. It was April and we were only six months from having to leave the Stone Mountain practice.

FINDING SUWANEE

How do you identify the perfect practice location? After selling our Stone Mountain practice, we wanted to make doubly sure that our next location held the key to our preferred future. We learned a lot from our earlier choices about what to do and what not to do as far as choosing a practice location. Sheila, my wife, and I relied on lots of hard work and lots of prayer. Over a six months period, we drove through every major crossroad in Northeast Atlanta looking for the perfect dental office location. We wanted to build a nice, small, boutique practice of approximately 3,000 square feet.

Number one, we wanted to be at or right off a major crossroad. Number two, we wanted to be on a major highway, preferably one that had direct access to the Interstate system. Number three, I wanted to be located in a metro Atlanta town or community that was growing and that had land values which were increasing. I was looking for maximum local traffic, ease of recognition of location, and the perception by potential patients of this community being an excellent place to raise a family, to work and to play.

We rode the county roads from Cumming to Covington and from Gainesville to Doraville. We searched the neighborhoods for signs of community deterioration and impending problems with the schools and local businesses. In Cumming we liked a building at the intersection of Georgia Highway 20 and Georgia 400. To the far northeast we investigated and liked Hamilton Mill Road and I-85. And in Suwanee there was a nice green patch of woods at the corner of Peachtree Industrial Boulevard and Suwanee Dam Road. We passed on the Hamilton Mill area because it was located in the Hog Mountain area. I did not want a practice called Hog Mountain Dental. Then, there was Shake Rag in Fulton County. I did not want to be Shake Rag Dental Group either. You see, I had a formula already in mind and I was sticking to my strategic plan. The complete picture of WebCentric was not yet a focus but in just a few months, the idea was to be born.

The year was 1997, it was early April and I had six months left to work as an associate at my former practice during what was termed "the transition period." I had a one-year contract. We had been looking diligently for six months for a place to locate a new start-up dental practice. While driving down Suwanee Dam Road one day, I stopped and attempted to turn around but backed my Ivy Green Jeep Grand Cherokee into a ditch on a dirt road. As I tried to get out, the wheel slipped deeper into the ditch and we were stuck, the wheel spinning in thin air. It looked like we were trapped in the middle of nowhere. But, not a minute went by before a truck stopped; the driver got out and offered to pull us out with a heavy chain. He freed us and we were on our way within mere minutes of being helpless in Suwanee. He was our saving angel sent from heaven and it was the first sign that Suwanee was to be our destiny.

The second confirmation for us came one week later. An Atlanta Dental Supply Practice Location Specialist named Dean Cox, whom I had known for 25 years and who was the one who helped me find my first location in Decatur, passed on to us information about a recently abandoned dental space. He said that he heard we may be looking for place to locate a new practice. There was an older 1200-square-foot office recently vacated by a dentist and was now up for lease in Suwanee. We were interested and had booked an appointment in our new office for our first patient in Suwanee, all within six weeks of falling in that ditch.

NO *YELLOW PAGES*, NO PATIENTS, NO PROBLEM

Yes I felt like I had been zapped. Lightning had struck twice in Suwanee and we were in our own space and ready to work. But no one knew we were there. The leasing agent had really laid one on me with this two star industrial office space. I was glad to have anything at this point, so I was not complaining. I just knew we had to make the best of it and plan for the future. This place was old and it was hidden. I mean it was down the hill… literally a full 10 feet below street level. It was down in a hole and there was no curb appeal. Zero, *nada*, nothing about it appealed to passersby. We opened our new practice in Suwanee with zero visibility to automobile traffic. There was no foot traffic, either.

On top of that, I leased that old dental space in May, two months after the *Yellow Pages* deadline for the 1998 phone book. What was I to do? In Stone Mountain we routinely received one hundred or more new patients a month in our two-man group practice. There, we relied on the *Yellow Pages* almost exclusively as our marketing activity. Sure we had good word-of-mouth referrals and were known as a progressive, high quality practice, but we did not stand out from the crowd in a whole lot of ways down in Stone Mountain. We sort of blended in and were pretty much a standard dental practice with some extra TMJ, ortho and implant dentistry training.

For a couple of years I had been into CompuServe, AOL, Prodigy and before them various BBSs (Bulletin Board Services). E-mail as a business tool was in its infancy and I had learned to scour the Internet collecting names and E-mail addresses as I built my international direct marketing businesses. I chose to reach out to the people of Costa Rica, Colombia, and Greece. What I needed was contact with new people to build my downlines. I needed the World Wide Web. That was the beginning of my experiences on the Internet and from it I developed a plan that would propel me into the 21st century and ultimately change my entire life. As you read this, you should know that it's that quest to find people in another country who had e-mail that ultimately led me to you today. Let me explain...

So, being an early adopter, and having missed the Yellow Page deadline, I chose to focus all my marketing expertise on the use of E-mail and on some website fundamentals that I had recently learned. I became my own webmaster and began putting up copy and working with HTML programming of my own site. I uploaded photographs and added links to local area businesses. I went out into the community to visit all of my personal and business connections, giving them my new web address and my e-mail address. Sending them to the Suwanee Dental Care online brochure web site, giving them a dynamic, ever-present, ever-ready, easily accessible Yellow-Page-on-steroids web site, all twelve pages of it, was the goal. Yes there were some things to learn, and, yes, we'll talk about that later in more detail. The bottom line is we got started. It was ready, aim, fire. We hit the ground running with a web site and a plan. 1997 was ground zero for the 5 million dollar practice that started in a hole.

PASSING THE $1 MILLION MARK

I'm down in the hole and I have no patients. I have no *Yellow Pages*. I do have a plan and know how that plan should work. It's called the Web Centric strategy and I envisioned all of our marketing efforts funneling every one of our prospects to a webpage to make a case for excellence in dentistry, Suwanee Dental Care style excellence. The promotion of our brand was a calculated one: the comprehensive dentist, the dentist who can perform all of the dental services a patient might need. This is the Decathlon Dentist that we are describing to our audience, to whomever is viewing our web site across Atlanta, throughout Georgia or the Southeast.

Because we had previously been very successful in our dental practice, I knew I could do it again. While it had taken us thirteen years with two dentists to achieve our first million-dollar practice production year back in Stone Mountain, I did it on my own in just two years in our Suwanee location. In 1997, I was one dentist starting over, but now I'm starting over with a new mindset related to marketing. I was still using the same dental skills and knowledge that led me to success in Stone Mountain. The only difference was that I had no patients in Suwanee but I did have the Internet. I had a voice and I chose to use it to reach out to people in the area and state my case for excellence, Suwanee Dental Care excellence.

The good thing about starting over and starting out with a fresh slate is that you don't often make the same mistakes twice. In Suwanee we were slim; we worked in 1200 square feet with three operatories. We were small, just three employees. By networking locally and by marketing earnestly, we succeeded. Getting the word out in a number of unique ways allowed us, in our first year in Suwanee, grow to $600,000. In the second year, we passed $1.1 million. Somewhere in the night our marketing kicked in and we continued to grow at a record pace. We passed what to most dentists and most dental consultants was a rare milestone, a near-to-impossible feat, the $2 million dollar mark for a one doctor dental practice. We kept working and kept marketing and never looked back. The year was 1998. It was time to expand and the building I had planned on moving into was nearly ready to break ground.

3,000 SQUARE FEET OF HEAVEN

When I first decided to move to Suwanee, after our angel had rescued us on that deserted highway and after having been miraculously placed in an abandoned, small and fully operable dental office space, I was already planning my next practice. It would be a unique, small, efficient, and profitable boutique practice. So with great anticipation, we went to bid on a piece of land for sale on the core Suwanee Dam Road and Peachtree Industrial Boulevard. That was 1997 just a few months after setting up shop in "the hole."

Well, the developer didn't sell it to us after all the discussions. He did, however, build a new brick box office complex in which we were to be the anchor tenant. We planned the ideal amount of area for one hard-working, visionary dentist, 3000 square feet of interior space. It was a place to be proud of one day soon we hoped. But, because it took over two years for the process to go from concept to lease we were busting at the seams of the older 1,200-square-foot office: so much for not owning the project and the building.

We occupied 3000 square feet on the top floor of a two-story office of a 10,000-square-foot building. Wonderful wooded views from all five of our operatories gave the practice a unique outdoor flavor. The décor inside was based on my love of American Indian and western art and was the basis for our choosing to bring some of the Southwestern desert motif of Santa Fe into Suwanee.

THE ASSOCIATE

I told everyone when I moved to Suwanee that I would build a small boutique practice. I would do this and work two or three days a week while dabbling in the stock market or international trade for my main source of income. But by 2001 the millennium bug had come and gone, my direct marketing world sales empire dreams had been thwarted and I saw that my last best option for any real solid income was to continue to be known as a world-class dentist and to stay chained to my dental chair with those golden handcuffs for years to come. I was too knowledgeable to waste my experience and my 401(k) was not yet complete enough to not make one last grab at the brass ring.

So, once again the practice was put on the growth plan using our WebCentric formula and we ratcheted it into a higher gear. I took off the shackles and let her run. No longer was boutique in my vocabulary. Now my buzz words were empire and domination, associates and expansion. I was just about to turn 50 and my newly acquired debt motivated me to work just that much harder and that much smarter. We were gearing up for an even bigger run. Little did I know just how big. I went to the Internet and found my first Suwanee associate in 2001. She started just a few days before I went to Africa. God sent me my second angel just in time for our first dental mission to Kenya.

CHAPTER 3

WebCentric Marketing

ISING LIKE A PHOENIX out of the ashes after I had crashed and burned, starting a new practice, I discovered the power of the World Wide Web, the Internet. I saw connections and relationships that I had never before seen in my previous 23 years of practice. In 1997, I created a web portal for the practice and focused all of our marketing towards the site. Online, offline, feet on the ground, article in print, hot dogs and pony rides for kids—it all became part of the plan! WebCentric Marketing was born and our web-centered marketing action plan was developed to

> Rising like a phoenix out of the ashes after I had crashed and burned, starting a new practice, I discovered the power of the World Wide Web, the Internet.

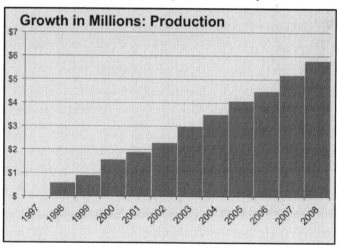

Growth in Millions: Production

propel our new start-up practice over the first hurdle.

Your practice website is the hub of all your marketing. Every new patient flows through your website. They select your practice, in large part, because of what experience they have on your web site, just as much as they stay in your practice by what experience they have in your office. WebCentric Marketing is about finding and attracting more business to your practice. If you apply the laws of attraction to your community with your practice as the hub, you will be successful. There are natural laws in effect, formulas that work and results that occur when the equation is fully implemented.

THE SOLUTION

What I'm going to teach you in this book, *Marketing The Million Dollar Practice,* is exactly what I did to grow from zero to $5.8 million dollars in just ten years. I'm going to take the wrapping off of the present and show you the inside-the-box story. You see, it's not just the vehicle of the marketing that you need to know—it's the psychology behind it. To be uber-successful, you will want to go beyond cursory tactics. You need strategic focus on the reasons people buy—the psychology of sales in your marketing message. It may look to outsiders like you're aiming at the public with a shot gun approach, but in actuality you are laser-focused with a platoon of rifles at your disposal. With WebCentric marketing you select your targets and take aim with precision.

THE BIGGEST OBSTACLE

The biggest obstacle to overcome is getting known. Visibility is required. A new dentist must make a statement, must get outside his or her natural comfort zone and become a marketer. As a small business owner, you have to go from riding in the back of the bus (as a well-protected dental student) to the bus driver yourself. There is no hiding out, waiting for someone else to write your ticket, punch your card, or row your boat. It's you or no one!

Does that sound familiar? Is that how it was for you when you just got started in practice? Or is that still the way it is for you? Well, if it is, I've got good news. This chapter will unlock the door for you to change all that. I'll show you some simple steps you can take to overcome the inertia of dental school thinking and put you squarely in the driver's seat, taking charge of your practice growth, and ultimately overall practice success.

As I've mentioned previously, I started my new Suwanee practice thirty miles from the Stone Mountain office that I sold in April in the middle of the year between the telephone company's *"Yellow Pages"* cycle. Southern Bell only printed the *Yellow Pages* of the telephone book once a year and if you missed getting in the book, your marketing was kaput for an entire year for that avenue. I had been online for ten years with AOL, CompuServe, Prodigy, bulletin boards, email and the like.

The World Wide Web had just recently been born in the mid 1990's and I was an early adopter. I was computerized with Alpha Health Care on Amos operating system in 1981, began using the Myotronics K5-AR Kinesiograph, the precursor to the K-7 and the Bioresearch's Biopak, in 1979, and developed businesses in Costa Rica, Greece and Columbia via email and the Internet in 1995. I saw wide open opportunity with the World Wide Web. I saw the hub of the wheel and I saw the spokes leading in to that hub. I envisioned the galaxy of input coming to that hub from all of the various sources ,people, events, and marketing mediums.

I believed that WebCentric Marketing would be the way

to get a fledgling dental practice up and off the ground.

They say you can't start a new practice and grow it to average size ($500,000) in a year—yet we did it! They say you can't continue to grow at that rate year after year after year—yet we did it! They say you can't sustain a $5 million dollar practice through an economy such as we've had over the past three or four years—yet we've done it.

Well, maybe there is some truth to their statements. Perhaps "they can't do it." Maybe they are blind to the potential for dentists today. Could be "they" don't have the belief that they can do it. Perhaps "they" don't have a mentor to look to, pattern after, or follow. Maybe "they" haven't taken the time to turn over that rock to see how someone else did just what is possible.

CREATE A MARKETING MACHINE

But you are not "they!" You are curious; you desire change, growth, and new input. You want to know more about how to marry the key elements of WebCentric and Guerrilla Marketing to the psychology of sales. You believe you can do it and that it's your time. So, just follow along. Study the chapters on specific spokes of the WebCentric

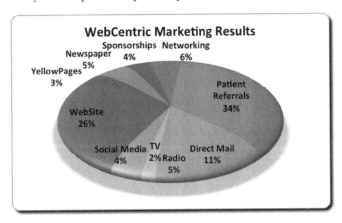

wheel. Get your hub, your website working for you. It's your 24/7 slave. Let it work. You sleep, it works. You drill; it works. You eat; it works. Get the picture? A WebCentric marketing machine is what you need, always on, always working to feed your practice with new business, new patients.

You can see from the growth of the spokes on the wheel that WebCentric marketing is not all about the Internet. Every lead, every new patient, however, you want to filter through your web site as a part of the process. You want them to get to know you through this interactive, in-depth, dynamic online picture of who you are and what you stand for. You want the discovery process to start way before they set foot in your practice. You want to win them over, bond them to your practice before they even meet you in person. An excellent website can do that, if that is your intention, if you apply the psychology of sales to all of your marketing effects.

It looks overwhelming, to say the least, if you look at the 2013 version of our WebCentric marketing framework. Let's step back then and take it one step at a time. I'll show you the top three things you will want to put in place for your own WebCentric Marketing Action Plan (MAP).

TOP THREE REQUIREMENTS

#1 You need a website. You need a website that you can control, add to, modify, update and one that lets patients be interactive with your practice.

#2 You need a team. You need a team to help you design two types of marketing activities—internal marketing (what you do inside your office that helps drive new business to your practice) and external marketing (what you do that is outside your facility that teaches people so that they know more and more about you, your interests, your capability, your passion and your expertise). You want your uniqueness to shine through all of your marketing efforts, both internal and external. Once you dedicate a team to each area, internal and external marketing, you need part three of the plan.

#3 You need a strategy. You need a strategy of how you'll conquer the hill. Succeeding in business, especially a small business like a dental practice, is like capturing a hill in battle. There is territory that must be taken. There are those on the hill who have it now. You want it, so you design a strategy to take it! You have your team, your army. You have your main weapon, your website. What you need to complete the MAP are sequential additions of the spokes to the wheel. These are your tactics that added together and implemented become your strategy.

Over the next thirty chapters of *Marketing The Million Dollar Practice,* we'll cover what steps we added, starting in 1997. I'll identify which steps I feel are most appropriate to implement in your practice this year, in the current state of the economy. I'm excited to share with you my story. I'm even more excited to see your practice grow and prosper by using some of the approaches we've used over the past few years.

CHAPTER 4

It All Starts With...
Your Image

*I*MAGE IS EVERYTHING! More than location, your image in the community dictates your results. Want to be the quickie filling and extraction practice on the corner of Highway 3 and Main Street? Or do you want to be the quality boutique practice in the quiet suburbs? Where do your highest caliber clients live? Where would you like to live? Want a one-hour commute or a three-minute commute? It's all related to the image you project. You will get the type of patients to whom you promote yourself and your practice.

The number one source for referrals is in a glowing personal recommendation. We acknowledge that and will hold that thought for discussion in another chapter. Right now, I will speak about creating an outstanding first impression. Truism: you only get one chance to make a good first impression. So don't blow it. Create it. Make it

> Truism: you only get one chance to make a good first impression. So don't blow it. Create it. Make it happen.

happen. Also, your impressions, and, therefore, your images (that is plural on purpose) must be consistent. You see, you get to create a first impression many times. Imagine your potential new patient's first sight of your office building, the first sound they hear in your practice or even on the telephone (whose voice is it?), that first smell (is it fresh pine or that "dental-office-smell-of-clove oil"), the dental hygienists first touch, the dentists first injection, the thoroughness of that first exam. In our practice, we developed the "New Patient Experience," an introduction to the practice for new clients which is memorable in its uniqueness. This will be the basis of one of my marketing "best practices" and a full chapter unto itself.

HOW PATIENTS FIND YOU

Potential patients (clients) find you through a number of sources. It is your job as CEO of your practice to ensure that each potential interface with the public is a potential "outstanding first impression." Consider their first look into the *Yellow Pages*, that first look at the Internet search results, that dental directory listing on the web, that look at the first page of your web site, what's "above the fold," the first typing of your email address into their computer, the first phone call to your answering machine or answering service. What was that potential client's first thought about you, about your practice? Did your image ooze out of that interaction as you would have preferred? Were you in control of the result or was it totally out of control? Do you even know or measure your results?

Knowing what people think of you and your business means you understand your Business Intelligence Quotient and should be a routine part of your leadership systems.

Marketing a dental practice in the midst of Madison Avenue, MTV, CNN, ESPN, Yahoo, 1-800-DENTIST, Facebook, Twitter, You-Tube and the like takes more than we were initially equipped to conceive in dental school, much less achieve. As dental entrepreneurs, CEO's of our practices, we need to be savvy in many business areas. Smart dental executives know to spend 3-10% of our gross income on marketing, depending on our stage of practice growth and their goals for the practice. More than anything, dentists need their marketing dollars to count, to get results. Having a Marketing Action Plan is that initial step towards success.

Back to creating your image and that perfect first impression. Have you ever called your office and listened? How about that first phone call, the voice, the words, the on-hold silence, music, or message? Did it portray quality? Was caring and concern evident in the message? Does your first impression portray high tech, competence, confidence? In a nutshell, is what your patients hear synonymous with your desired image? Or, would you rather not discuss it!

Do you market to new residents in your community? How do you do that? Do you send information to them or do you just wait for them to find you? Is there an opt-in box on your web sites front page? What if you could stack the deck in your favor so that 95% of all newcomers in your local area want to come to your practice, want you to be their dentist? That should be your goal and you can set up your systems and your practice management to achieve just that goal.

CASE 1

Here is an example of my day today at the dental practice, related to marketing. One pharmaceutical sales and technology fellow came in today, as a new patient with a toothache, large caries in a virgin #31. He had buccal caries surrounding the tooth in addition to caries burrowing occlusally towards the pulp, undermining both buccal and lingual cusps. We digitally imaged the tooth, could not see a pulpal entry, and it hardly looked bombed out due to the diffuse decay. Using our Dexis Digital Radiographic software to enhance the gray scale radiograph, the patient was shown and actually liked the Technicolor green color that the caries glowed in the Dexis color mode. We removed half of the caries to verify that it was undermining the cusps. I then took a photograph with the digital camera and had it printed for the patient's records/insurance company if requested. The brown/red/yellow caries was dramatic… much more intimidating to an insurance adjuster than a black and white radiograph. I would dare him to try and kick that crown off his desk into file 13. Crown prepped, buildup completed, patient happy, case closed.

Anyway, back to why this clinical case was interesting in a marketing sense. I asked him, the pharmaceutical rep, how he found out about our dental practice, as I do each and every patient. We record it, computerize it, and study the demographic results of our marketing efforts and dollars spent. He reported that he found us on the Internet. Bingo! I asked, "How so?" He stated, "In a search engine." Double bingo! "Yahoo to be exact"… everyone's favorite and yours too, I'll bet at one time. Now, there is Google and Bing. It's not a one man game. "Too many URL's," he said, so he narrowed the search down to Georgia, then Gwinnett County, then, most importantly, our area specifically. We came up in the top one or two listing in the search, he said. He looked over our web site, liked what he saw, and now our web site has just today paid a dividend equal to what would be equal to 100% of a whole year's hosting and directory listing fee.

CASE 2

The owner of the PowerHouse Gym came in today as a new patient, through the hygiene department. I had placed an 8" x 10" paid advertisement on the gym announcement board. There are several businesses advertised on this commercially created board. It has our business cards and office brochures in a plastic slot for their clients to take. He stated that he had met me when I came in to check on the board one day. I make it a practice to meet owners and workers in all businesses that I deal with, shop with, visit.

I usually leave a card and tell them to let me know if I can help them in any way.

Oh, and by the way, all he needed, clinically, was four buccal pit restorations. What he wanted was four porcelain veneers to close his anterior spaces once we have whitened his teeth. I am sure that he is open to getting his 16 molars and bicuspids sealed as a preventive measure, based on our wellness conversation in the hygiene room today. Marketing to fitness businesses is logical for cosmetic-minded practices.

After watching Atlanta and John Smoltz demolish the Cubs 7-1 one sunny afternoon, my family and I went to dinner at a local comfort food diner. My wife was bragging about its good southern cooking so we had to try it out. Upon our departure, I saw my card on the checkout cork board above the cash register. Of course the card has my email address and my practice web site address. Seems that people carry our cards around with them and give them out to folks everywhere. I wonder where they got that idea? Could it be that I asked them to take a few with them as they left our office one day? Who knows.

As in the Naked City (you do remember Sergeant Joe Friday on the TV show Dragnet, don't you?!), this town has a million stories. Every patient that comes in our office has some interesting story about how they found us. We believe that there are no coincidences. We believe that people are led to us for a reason. Of course, that is the image that we have created. Our patients, for the most part, arrive knowing that they are in the right place. That is the magic of what we call WebCentric Marketing. Stay tuned for more on that very subject as it's the core of our marketing framework.

When we continue with our next marketing tip in the next chapter, we will discuss the importance of the new resident letter and how it captivates the imagination of potential clients and leads them to your front door by way of your WebCentric Internet site.

TAKE-AWAY POINTS

- First Impressions Count Most
- Create Your Image In Your Community
- Personal Referrals Are #1 Way To Grow
- Reach Out To New Residents First
- Engage Your Marketing Audience and Your Patients

CHAPTER 5

The New Resident Letter

REACH OUT AND TOUCH SOMEONE. Join the Pepsi generation. Buy Loreal, because you're worth it.

The purpose of advertising and sales media is to motivate your prospective clients to do something, to make a choice that is favorable to you, the advertiser. In writing and sending a letter in the mail to new residents in your community, you are attempting to duplicate the same thing Madison Avenue does… gain a patient.

Your goal is to create an outstanding first impression of your dental practice in a new resident's mind. Most people say that 80% of dental appointments are made by women. In our practice, 50% of the appointments are for men. I suppose that means that most men delegate the choosing of a dentist for a family to the woman in the household. Therefore, the letter should appeal to women, no doubt about it. See if you think our example does, later in this chapter. Bottom line is to know your audience. Know who the power brokers are in the relationship. In selecting the family dentist, women rule!

FIRST IMPRESSIONS

Remember, first impressions start with look and feel. Go first class mail, not bulk mail. Mail class reflects your class. You're not second class, so why advertise anything less. Have you ever received a mailer from Mercedes Benz, from Jaguar, from Rolex or Mont Blanc? I guarantee that it was classy and expensive looking.

Stationery is about image. Look sharp, feel the quality. Your potential clients will notice what you say subliminally by the weight of your envelope and stationery, the color, texture, the font of your typeset. Is there a logo that is unique? Is it consistent throughout all of your marketing pieces? Look at your stationery and see if it appeals to other dentists or to patients. Perhaps two styles of stationery are appropriate for your practice, one for other professionals, one for clients. We use just one style because our logo is well known in the community.

Content separates the amateurs from the professionals. Write the perfect welcome letter and attract perfect clients.

> **Remember, you get what you give out. Give class; get class.**

Remember, you get what you give out. Give class; get class. Read our new resident letter at the end of this chapter. Think about how you would feel if you were a new resident to the area. Start with the obvious, no beating around the bush. "We're looking for a few good patients" is our initial line. Sounds bold doesn't it? It is, and we are.

DON'T ASSUME THEY KNOW

That is a D.M.D. (or D.D.S. for those of you who didn't go to MCG, Alabama, Kentucky, Harvard and a few others) tattooed on our buccal mucosa in amalgam isn't it. Dentists are special people, no doubt. We feel that it is an honor for a patient to have a spot in our practice. Likewise, we feel honored to have our patients chose us as their dental practice. We display this mutual desire in our initial letter. We are creating our preferred future before we ever meet our new patients. There are no accidents; we create our results.

Acknowledge that you know they are new to the area, next. Omer Reed calls it "speaking to the obvious." Welcome them. Explain your "unique selling proposition" i.e., why they should choose YOU above all those other dentists who sent them mail, also. This should be number one... your experience, number two... your comprehensive services, number three... your practice emphasis, and number four... your convenient location. These are the top four reasons why people choose a dentist, in my opinion.

I emphasize being a fair value if I mention fees, but never refer to being cheap or low cost. You may want to offer a free or introductory offer to new clients in this letter. I have not found it necessary, but it does increase the number of clients who respond to your letter.

THE LAW OF RECIPROCITY

Remember, you get what you put out... don't send out too clear a message that you accept, promote, or expect discounts, freebies, low profit procedures or you will have a practice full of patients who expect that at each and every appointment.

Practice emphasis is a key: how many of you strive to be the gentle, comfortable, painless, on-time, caring dentist who is good with fearful, phobic, gagging, frightened, terrified patients? That is a good niche to dominate, especially now that sedation dentistry with DOCS training is so reliable and simple. And don't forget to include your talents in ortho, TMJ, implants, endo, perio, pedo, veneers, sleep medicine... whatever. I got two new patients yesterday because my Yellow Page ad said I treat TMJ. Who would think the *Yellow Pages* still matter!

But more people have fear or dental phobia than TMJ. Speaking to the obvious, focus your marketing that you are comfortable treating their fear. You will be blessed with any number of people who have never visited the dentist. On a regular basis… and they become your most loyal dental patients. Not all dentists want to promote or even accept a lot of phobic patients. However, I love this kind of patient because we "turn" them around so frequently. A little TLC, understanding, good listening, plus sedation dentistry and they are your loyal friend for life.

Finally, keep it short, to one page. Tell your new resident to visit your web site by all means. Start the process early and do it often. Provide your telephone number and ask for a call to set up an appointment. Explain that you can only take 25 new families a month. This acts as a magnet. People want to go to an exclusive dentist. Exclusivity leads to attraction. Our practice never turns away new patients, but we are so busy that one of our dentists can't see more than 25 new families a month.

Enclose the following items in your new resident envelope along with the new resident letter: a tooth-shaped refrigerator magnet, two business cards in a presentation folder marked respectively, "His" and "Hers," and your dental practice brochure which contains the crucial details which you alluded to in your letter.

THE LETTER THAT STARTED IT ALL

The following is the new resident letter that we used for our entire first year. We kept it similar for 13 years, mailing it to all of the new residents in our zip code month after month after month. That number was approximately 600-700 families a year. We put it on our web site on the New Patient Welcome page and updated it as the size of the practice and the number of dentists increased.

NEW RESIDENT LETTER

Dear Thomas,

It's a match made in heaven! You're looking for a good, new dentist. We are looking for a few good clients. We would love to have a group of fine Suwanee folks who become patients and friends. After 22 years of practicing family dentistry (including orthodontics, cosmetics, implants and oral surgery) in Stone Mountain, we have opened our office here in Suwanee, I want to invite you to consider us to become your family dentist. Here's why...

If you are like me, your move to Suwanee was based on attaining superior quality of life for your family. Our practice is small, personal, state-of-the-art and innovative. We focus on being comprehensive. That means you will not have to go to three or four doctors for your dentistry. We take our time and work well with those patients who don't find going to the dentist their favorite pastime!

If thoroughness, competency, superior quality and gentleness matter to you, then we are your type of dentist. You won't find mercury fillings, quickie cleanings, or two-hour waits at our office. Since we are a private care dentist, you will not have to wait 6-8 weeks for an appointment which frequently is the case at those large PPO clinics.

Since we are both relatively new to the area, we already have lots in common. If you would be inclined to become part of our family, do check us out and call us for an appointment. At this time, we can accommodate about 25 new families a month. We are serious about the level of care that we provide and we want to truly serve those who appreciate our exceptional level of care, skill and judgment.

You may learn more about us in the enclosed brochure, on the web at www.suwaneedental.com, or by stopping by our office for a tour any day of the week (Monday-Friday). We welcome and encourage your careful inspection and evaluation. We know that choosing the right family dentist is an important step in relocating to a new community.

Sincerely yours,
William B. Williams, DMD, FAGD, MICCMO
WBW/ABC

In the next chapter of *Marketing The Million Dollar Practice,* we'll discuss the Practice Brochure and how it feeds the desire of potential clients to know about you and your practice and how this leads them to your front door by way of your WebCentric, branded, Internet site.

TAKE-AWAY POINTS

- Make an Outstanding First Impression
- Speak to the Obvious
- Focus on Their Wishes
- Explain Who You Are
- Tell Them "Why They Should Join Your Practice"
- Ask For the Call / Appointment
- Add Scarcity

CHAPTER 6

The Brochure for Your Practice

The Prescription for Success

EVERYONE NEEDS A COLOR, customized, interesting practice brochure. Throw away those dull, drab, two-color, policy wonk pieces of trash and start making a good first impression. Be interesting.

Get a seriously good photo of yourself made by a professional photographer. Don't settle for anything second rate. Proper lighting and minimal shadows are the key. Also, smile a friendly smile. One problem I have seen repeatedly in professional photos is that the selections tend to be too arty, that is, they are just too dark, too shadowy, too strange. If the viewer can't see both eyes, the teeth, the hair (a problem when a dark background is chosen) or if the hands cover the face in any way (would you want to go to a dentist who has his hands in his mouth all the time?), then the photo is not ideal for a dental office brochure.

Don't confuse a wonderful portrait for the ideal marketing photo. In this marketing photo, you want to show the whole face, the entire countenance. And, if you wear glasses, please don't put photo-gray or tinted lenses in this photograph. It only hides the face and makes, even if subliminally, the viewer suspicious. Didn't those go out in the 70's with disco, polyester, and stacked heels?

Go for the fresh look, the trustworthy look. You are selling yourself. And a final note on photos, if you are not particularly photogenic, skip this feature if you wish. Put a stock photo of a pretty smile, similar to those smiles we put on our web sites. They draw attention and interest. They work.

SIZE AND SHAPE

What is the best size brochure? I suggest a 6-panel, bi-fold. This gives you plenty of space for lots of information. It fits into a purse or pocket, too. Use bullets, a quote, a map, headlines and text boxes. If it looks interesting, it will get read. Drop the office policy information; that can come later, at the office, after they are in your confines, after being cuddled and coddled by your warm, caring office staff.

In your brochure, you need to do two things: attract the curious and show that you understand what they want. Once you do that you can tell about yourself and your advanced education, your service mix, your hours and days open, your staff, how convenient your location is.

Most of all, identify your web site. Push, pull and steer those potential clients to your well-developed web site. If you've got 'em floss, 'em. Every time you get a chance, identify the site to your clients. Give them a reason why they should log on and earmark, bookmark, save the link for future reference.

> Most of all, identify your web site. Push, pull and steer those potential clients to your well-developed web site. If you've got 'em floss, 'em. Every time you get a chance, identify the site to your clients.

PROMOTIONS

Offer a promotional if you wish. Statistics show this does increase calls to your office. I personally did not offer anything for free or a discount in our practice brochure. It was not the initial image that I wanted to present, as you know from the last chapter. I saved that strategy for *Yellow Page* coupons, direct mail coupons and newspaper ads. That way, I could change the promotional without incurring large costs. Changing the practice brochure is costly if your printer has to use a multicolor plate. One way to add promotions to your brochure is to make a separate page for a promotion that can be updated as needed and placed inside the formal practice brochure.

Coupons have been worthwhile, just not as the mainstay of our marketing efforts. I will discuss promotionals and coupons more in the future from a different perspective, but only after thoroughly discussing the other important methods of practice marketing and growth. It's important to know how they fit into the whole marketing action plan. They are not an entire strategy in and of themselves.

Speaking of promotionals, our first year, we featured a raffle that offered a cruise in the Caribbean. We held a free pony ride for children and a barbecue for adults when we first opened our doors in Suwanee. Twice in our practice, we rented the three-decker riverboat, Scarlet O'Hara, steamed out across Stone Mountain Lake and had a disc jockey, buffet and prizes for all of our practice patients. Once we had a hay ride on the train that encircles Stone Mountain.

Most promotionals are for items, like cleanings, exams, and/or tooth whitening. We will offer them sparingly. I always wanted to give away a free root canal when civic groups would come by for donations to raffles. Never got any takers!

THE "LOOK" OF YOUR BROCHURE

What LOOK should you choose? I like multicolored brochures. The best is four color slick. I like medium weight paper stock with texture, not a board stock, which is heavier. It costs less but is very professional, and is easier and cheaper to mail. One drawback with textured stock, photographs do not look as impressive. I use postcards for that purpose.

WHAT'S IN A NAME?

A large headline should announce your practice name and location. My favorite practice name includes your location: i.e. Stone Mountain Dental Group, Suwanee Dental Care, Dental Care of Stamford, especially if you are located in a metropolitan area.

People look for convenience first. Identify where you are and you win the location game. Be merely "a doctor's name" and you are just one of many. Differentiation is a key to marketing success. Be proud of your name, your degree, use it to your advantage, but consider the lack of differentiation it offers. If you want to still use your name in your practice promotion, consider hyphenated names, such as Suwanee Dental Care—W.B. Williams, D.M.D. I list both in the *Yellow Pages*. On the web, search engines should find both your doctor's name and the name of your practice.

When would a dentist's name be a positive? In an ethnic neighborhood, say the Russian district of Chicago. Dr. Andrekov may do better at attracting clients initially than a Dr. Youngblood. Locals may identify

> Remember, your business is no dress rehearsal. Life happens at the speed of thought and what a person's first impression is determines the eventual outcome for you. Business is business and it is your business to run your business like a business.

with language and culture. The reverse also holds true. When foreign names that are hardly pronounceable are shown on signs outside a clinic, the chance of drop ins from the majority of locals is hardly enhanced. Would it not be better to make the first impression be one of location, caring, concern, education, and quality rather than highlighting the differences in culture, language, and heaven forbid, training in a foreign dental school?

Remember, your business is no dress rehearsal. Life happens at the speed of thought and what a person's first impression is determines the eventual outcome for you. Business is business and it is your business to run your business like a business.

THE BULLET POINTS

What information do you put in your brochure? A few salient points are much better, more likely to be read, than a solid paragraph. Therefore, use brevity, use highlighted statements called to attention by bullets. Most dental brochures are merely paragraphs end on end... boring. Also, forget the clip art if it's cheesy. Develop that nice logo. Make it thematic. Sell the sizzle. Always include a map and send potential patients to your web site. Don't forget to highlight your practice phone number in a big, bold font.

Remember what the experts in marketing say, "The headline is the most important part of the message." Always make your headline be an attention grabber, something the patient will pay attention to. Go for the one thing that will get them to read further.

Bullet your most notable educational accomplishments. Got

> List your special high tech equipment. It is a major draw. Believe this if you believe nothing else I have written.

your FAGD or MAGD? Use it. Write a paragraph about your family, your practice duration, and community involvement. People love to go to the most experienced dentist in town. If you are a new graduate, hide that fact. Make an effort to highlight your up-to-date training instead.

List your special high tech equipment. It is a major draw. Believe this if you believe nothing else I have written. What's new and in-the-news, sells. Its the sizzle that comes with the steak. What is the only positive thing you ever hear about dentistry in the national news? New technology, new breakthroughs, high tech equipment. Why not capitalize on the market that is there, waiting to be tapped?

Bullet your "Why Choose Us," a list of impressive items such as gentle touch, reasonable fees, number of years of experience, comprehensive dentistry, fantastic staff, great with children, orthodontics, implants, or TMJ. Make them value your abilities before they even meet you. I find "Listens to his patients" and "Gentle touch" very meaningful to patients. "Understands your fears" is also excellent, if you do.

Brochures go wherever we need them, so spread them all around your community. They are not just for potential clients, although we send them out mainly to new residents. They go home with current clients when we ask for referrals. They go to other businesses. They are in every operatory in our office. If you can place your practice brochures in other professional offices, i.e. physicians, veterinarians, chiropractors, beauty salons, then you are making your presence become ubiquitous. Or, as we say in Atlanta, Covering Dixie Like the Dew. That is your goal. If someone thinks of needing a dentist, they should think of you first.

BEYOND THE PAPER BROCHURE

Many people think of their web page as an online brochure accessible 24 hours a day, 365 days a year, from any place in the world with an Internet link. We can send brochures by mail. We can send email with our web site connected to it as an attachment. Whatever we can do with a practice brochure, we can do with our web site. In *Marketing The Million Dollar Practice,* you'll find scores of ideas on how to market your practice via the Internet proactively. Preparing the public to receive your message is one function of good public relations and marketing.

As web sites become more complex, interactivity becomes increasingly important. At this juncture, the web site "brochure" becomes more than the online practice snap shot. It becomes the way patients reach you, through email and maps, and promotions, and interest building dental stories, demonstrations, and articles.

Blogs keep people with an interest in your practice connected and always within arms length. You-Tube and other embedded videos on your web site can become your online practice brochures. Become the video-capable dental practice and watch the competition fade in your rear view mirror!

That's it for brochure talk. Your next step is to draw it up, get your printer to make a mockup and proof it. You may want to make it yourself in Microsoft Publisher as I did and give it nearly complete to your printer. They can finalize it and do the graphics as you wish. Or, you can have them do the entire thing from your notes.

Time is all we have, so spend it wisely. Remember, unless you are graphically gifted, technically talented or cosmically crazy, you do not want to be developing your own marketing pieces, web sites or office brochures. Let the professionals do the majority of the work.

I am continually surprised at the number of dentists who want to save $500 to $1000 on their marketing budget by doing it themselves. They will spend 10 to 20 hours or longer, do a poor-to-middling job that looks exactly as amateurish as it can be when they could have worked one day in the dental practice and earned three times the money to purchase professional results. I have been guilty of that one, believe me. I learned early on in the area of manual labor, making web sites, like mowing the grass and digging holes around the yard, is for the birds. Believe it or not, I am proud of the fact that I have never once pushed a lawn mower around in circles since I started my practice of dentistry 1976. If only I had learned that lesson in the marketing game at the beginning of my career.

When we continue with our next marketing tip, we will discuss the MESSAGE ON HOLD system and how it informs current and potential clients about you and your practice and how this leads them to your front door by way of your WebCentric Internet site. Again, consistently moving clients from one information source, through the web site, into the front door.

TAKE-AWAY POINTS

- Select a Top Shelf, Four-Color Brochure
- Have a Professional Portrait Made
- Use a Six-Panel, Bi-Fold Brochure
- Headlines are Critical: Location, Location, Location
- Employ Powerful Bullet Points and a Map
- Always Point to the Web Site and Phone Number

CHAPTER 7

Message-On-Hold Systems

*P*HONES RINGING OFF THE HOOK? Your receptionist too busy checking out patients, doing consults, making appointments? You need a message-on-hold system, you need a Secret Assistant. Ever have this scenario: you first hygienist is talking too loud about bleeding gums to Mrs. Jones in operatory four as the Cavitron whines in hygiene operatory three across the hall? All this is disturbing your slightly phobic dental patient who is trying to relax as she waits for her anesthesia to become profound? Wouldn't it be good to cancel out that noise with a music overhead system of your own choosing? You need a personal sound track for your office, one that you can control in both volume and content.

Yes, patients sometimes must be put on hold; patients sometimes have to wait in a room unattended. What we don't want is for them to have complete silence on the telephone if they are on hold and we don't want them hearing the office chatter between staff or with other patients or dental procedures being performed once they are already in the office. What would be even better than no silence or neutralizing those noises would be the giving of valuable and wanted information to patients who call and have to be placed on hold or to those who are sitting in the reception room or operatories waiting for treatment.

PERSONALIZATION OF THE MESSAGE

To be able to impart information in a normally "down" time for the patient is a smart idea. Personalized message-on-hold and personalized overhead music with value-added content about your office helps in keeping patients happier, occupying their minds, and often saving your staff the necessity of answering routine questions over and over again.

> Turn a negative into a positive. Give patients and prospects personal, accurate, up-to-date information on you and your practice as they wait on the telephone line.

Turn a negative into a positive. Give patients and prospects personal, accurate, up-to-date information on you and your practice as they wait on the telephone line. What can you share: offer insights into cosmetic dentistry, your Loyal Patients Savings and Rewards program, explain how to get to your practice location, list your office hours, describe your insurance policies and financial options, make the patients aware of your extensive experience and advanced training, highlight your special promotions that change each quarter/month, etc.

GUIDING PATIENTS TO YOUR PRACTICE FOCUS

Message-on-hold is pleasant to hear, informative and makes patients ask for specific services when their needs are known. Our system is a looped system of about 20 minutes duration. No one has to hold through an entire cycle so the length assures that they will hear new material most times they call and have to hold.

Written professionally with your guidance, recorded

professionally in both male and female voices and including background music of your choice, message-on-hold is truly your Secret Assistant on those busy dental days. Overhead music with value-added practice advertising typically comes as a package with the message-on-hold and allows a seamless integration from the telephone to the office music environment.

PLEASING TO THE EAR

One of the best features of the music overhead system is that it allows for you to select the genre of music from scores of categories and can be changed during the day with the click of a button. When the mood changes and you want calm jazz instead of rock 'n roll, you can have it within a minute. A patient who is spending all day with you for a full mouth reconstruction doesn't have to listen to country music all day long. They can have total quiet (turn the system off in each room if you have a room control setup), smooth-as-silk, calming music, or fast-paced, lively music.

PUBLIC SERVICE ANNOUNCEMENTS

Automatically, between songs, there will be, at intervals you specify, a PSA, (public service announcement) or advertisement that you write and that the messaging company professionally records with their voice talent. Utilize this marketing vehicle to offer specials, discuss recent CE your doctor has attended, new procedures being offered, results of scientific dental research of interest to patients, or to welcome a new team member to your practice by introducing them to all of your patients for a few months. These messages on the overhead music system can be changed at any time and can be set in a seasonal rotation highlighting Christmas, New Years, Thanksgiving, Memorial Day, and so on.

What should you put on your Message-On-Hold related to your Marketing Action Plan? How about your practice web site information? You should make several references to the web site, giving its domain name (address) as the message rolls. Direct people to the site and tell them that there are specials on it, if you wish. The more you create the traffic flow, the greater its value to your bottom line. Message-On-Hold is essentially a verbal brochure or verbal web site. Its purpose is information transfer more than sales. Basic need-to-know information for new patients is a must.

What's new is also important for all patients. It is a medium that will be used by 100% of your patients some time during the year. Being put on hold can become a blessing for the practice if the marketing is done properly.

MARKETING IS NOT AN EXPENSE: IT'S AN INVESTMENT

Systems like these actually pay for themselves. One way to keep overhead down is to use a message-on-hold system. This saves having to hire additional staff. Once the system is in place, it has a very low cost. The marketing that goes out from overhead and on-hold systems promotes products and services as well as promoting good behaviors that save the practice lost revenue.

Of course, Solstice Dental Advisors is a source for more information on this service. Because we have used the top four companies over the years that offer these types of systems, we have a good idea about the features and benefits of each system. We'll be glad to share with you what we feel are the top of line systems available and the ones we believe will be best for your practice. All you need to do is ask and we will send you information. Call our office if you wish to listen to our message on hold system. You can reach us at 770-614-7301. Identify yourself as a Solstice client or potential client and give our dental practice your email address. Ask my receptionist to put you on hold so that you may listen to our messages. Just hang up once you are finished listening.

TAKE-AWAY POINTS

- Combine Message-On-Hold With Overhead Music System
- Continual Marketing to Patients
- Eliminates Dead Space On Hold
- Customized Scripts
- Customized Music
- Plays Like A Radio Station Only With Only Your Announcements

CHAPTER 8

New Resident Follow-up Postcards: Make it a Campaign

L ET'S SAY THAT YOU HAVE, by now, developed an outstanding new resident letter to introduce your practice. You mailed out a batch to cover the new homeowners in your surrounding zip codes encompassing the previous 6-12 months. You have a standing order with the local mail list company to send you a new resident list via email each month. Your initial mailing was to 500-1000 homes with a recurring initial letter to 50-200 homes, depending on the area you include. That was your rifle shot in the dark. You shot where you thought the prize would be most likely located... in your own zip code!

The question is, what do you do now? Will this strategy alone work for you to gain many more new patients or will it require some additional support mechanism to create the result you really want? Knowledgeable marketing professionals say that direct mail campaigns (such as this new resident letter program) only work well if done consistently and over a period of time to allow for "multiple impressions."

MULTIPLE IMPRESSIONS

Multiple impressions are how all advertising works. That is the rationale behind the WebCentric Marketing Action Plan. It is a fact that you must put your name out there, in front of your intended public early and often if you are to be successful with your advertising. As they say in the dove hunting plantations of Georgia, "You'll bring home more dinner for the kids with a shotgun than a rifle."

Therefore, it is important to do follow-up mailings to your new resident letter. Here, I am talking about a series of post cards. Four reasons for this are:

(1) repeat impressions keep your practice name in mind and you know that dentistry is often an impulse purchase based on need;

(2) this gives your practice the ability to focus on a single issue on the face of that card;

(3) post cards are more readily read—a graphically interesting post card is much more effective than a familiar letter that must be opened; and

(4) postage is much less when sending post cards. It takes my Friday staff person 45-60 minutes per month to complete the creation and mailing of these cards. You could out-source the entire process to a mail house, too.

CALL TO ACTION

Each post card should have a call to action, to ask for a phone call to set an appointment. Highlight your web site and include a cartoon or interesting photo or graphic. You may want to print them yourself from Microsoft Publisher onto Office Depot stock post cards so that you can be flexible and economic in sending as few as 50-200 cards at a time. Another option is to buy bulk and then customize to fit your needs. I have used post cards in bulk that can cost as low as $0.36 including printing and mailing.

The post card is sent one month after the new resident letter. In this first card, detail your laser and air-abrasion drill-less dentistry systems if you have them. A month later, your third contact, send another post card. For instance, we focus on Fresh Breath and your CloSys anti-bactericidal mouth rinse and tooth paste system. The cartoon on the card is irresistible… people just have to read it. It makes a definite, certain, defined impression.

You could emphasize anything in your post cards. It is a way of individualizing and personalizing your message to potential clients. You could continue your monthly mailings, either as post cards, as a newsletter or as an informative letter. Mixing the medium is a positive step to keeping interest high. The cost is minimal compared to the results you will get.

REPETITION AND FOLLOW-UP

I draw the line at three mailings currently because our marketing program is working so well. Right now, we are booked three months solid and are looking at how to overcome this business challenge. I wrote my first edition of this particular marketing advice when I was still in solo practice! I'm still busy at 100% every day I work but I also have three associate dentists now helping me keep the wait for appointments to a minimum. Problems like this, I like. At least I worry in a different way than when there were multiple holes in our schedules, as was the case years ago in my former practice.

So, how do you gauge your results? One way is by the dramatic increase in hits to your web site when you mail out your letters and post cards. Stop the cards and the number of hits goes down. People do go to your web site when it is mentioned in your post

> You can see why this is called WebCentric marketing: everything points to your web site. The web site is your most flexible, most interactive, most detailed piece of marketing material. It also has the highest demographic audience… the most ideal, discriminating, dental customer.

card ads, your message-on-hold, your Yellow Page ad, and your newspaper ads. You can see why this is called WebCentric marketing: everything points to your web site. The web site is your most flexible, most interactive, most detailed piece of marketing material. It also has the highest demographic audience… the most ideal, discriminating, dental customer.

Another point to focus on is to use a tracking phone number when you create your postcard. This will allow you to know what is working in your marketing. And, when you put a promotion on your direct mail piece, make sure the instructions say, "Bring Post Card To Appointment to Receive This Special Promotion."

Although it won't be covered in detail in this chapter, what about the addition of email, audio and video to the campaign mix for your new resident follow-ups? Would that make an even bigger impact on those potential patients and how they feel your practice? The well-organized marketing campaign is the wave of the future for dental practices to thrive in the new economy. Stay tuned for a lot more about this favorable option for growing your practice.

Next on the *Marketing The Million Dollar Practice* agenda is *Yellow Page* Advertising. Love it or hate it, its a fact of life that we need to be there. The good news is that I cut my Yellow Page costs in half by moving to the WebCentric method of marketing during my early years in practice in Suwanee, and now have cut it by three fourths as we replace the large full page ads with tightly placed specific listings.

TAKE-AWAY POINTS

- Mail to Targeted Zip Codes
- Create Multiple Impressions
- Post Cards are Inexpensive
- Include a Call-to-Action
- Cartoons Work
- Promotions Work

CHAPTER 9

Using the *Yellow Pages* to Your Benefit, Now That They Are Almost Dead

*T*HIS WILL BE THE TALE OF TWO CITIES. How it was and how it is. Where I was that worked so well with *Yellow Page* support as our sole support. But let me tell you about where I am now and how we blew open the doors to new patient growth in spite of not having *Yellow Pages* for the first year or two in our new practice location.

IN DAYS OF OLD

In the past, I used *Yellow Page* advertising in one big book to anchor our entire external marketing campaign. That was when we had 13 operatories, 12-16 staff, a $60,000 monthly overhead, over 100 new patients a month, and million dollar plus gross each year. It was spectacular in its results. What did we do that spelled success then and what did we change to move into our boutique practice of three operatories and three staff? And finally what did we do, regarding the *Yellow Pages*, as we grew over the last decade to our current 15 operatory, 22 member staff.

Back in the Stone Mountain office, which I sold in 1996, we placed a half page ad in the BIG BOOK for over 15 years. This approach is still valid and can certainly work well for a dental practice, especially in small towns. We approached the public in a way that showed our differences, not our similarities. We chose our ad size to mark our success as well as to plan our success. Size is always a winner: bigger is better... and more costly. People realize that successful practices do things right and having a large *Yellow Page* ad means to the public that you are successful.

Next we added color. Color makes people pay attention, and it costs more. Funny how that seems to always be the case, if it works, it costs more. If it tastes better, it costs more. If it's more natural, it costs more. If you want to run with the big dogs, you have to do what the big dogs do.

> **Funny how that seems to always be the case, if it works, it costs more. If it tastes better, it costs more. If it's more natural, it costs more. If you want to run with the big dogs, you have to do what the big dogs do.**

What was the most important factor in our *Yellow Page* success? One word spells the tale: LOCATION, location, location. We identified where our practice was in the ad in bold print, big enough for all to see when flipping the pages. We even went as far, as you probably remember from an earlier chapter of *Marketing The Million Dollar Practice,* in naming our practice after our location. We were Stone Mountain Dental Group then. We are now Suwanee Dental Care. If the public knows where they are, and they usually do, then all you have to do to get them interested in your office is to let them know where you are. See the connection?

People love convenience and will most often, unless a dental practice's USP (unique selling proposition) is very strong, choose a dental practice purely based on location and convenience to their work or where they live. It is important to play the name game and be primed for success.

Keep in mind your overall image in designing your *yellow*

page piece. Don't shoot yourself in the foot by advertising a special $10 x-ray, exam and cleaning if you don't want to attract the "takers" of the world. Dentists using the *Yellow Pages* were notorious in the beginning of dental advertising for offering specials to get John Q. Public in the door. Yes, Mr. Public did arrive in droves to the discounting dental practices but with a name change. Upon sign-in at the reception desk he should have scrawled his real name, John Q. Poverty, instead of John Q. Public.

Most of the early takers of the discount offers were looking for that "once-every-five-year, freebie cleaning," not the full-mouth reconstruction that the dentist had hoped for. They were worth little to the practice and cost a lot to get in the door, especially after breaking those first two appointments with the hygienist. Sound familiar?

BUILD ON QUALITY, THEN SPEND ON QUANTITY

So, my advice is to go for quality first, then go for quantity in your advertising. Announce your special education, your high tech equipment, your special attentiveness to fearful patients and of course your gentle touch. These items are meaningful to patients. Features are good but benefits are better, benefits to your patient. In fact, the *Yellow Page* ad is essentially your scaled down practice brochure that we discussed earlier

In your *Yellow Page* ad, include a nice photo of yourself for best results. Other than that, a nice female smile works well. Your goal is to first catch their eye and then get them to read your copy. Copy, photos, maps, headlines, white space... "Oh, that's a lot!" you say." "It's a big ad, it costs so much." Well, if you want a big practice, you must spend money to grow it. Think of it as dental vitamins, right up there with continuing education and updated equipment.

You have to swallow'um whole even if they taste bad and make you sick. Paying for all that "white space" is good medicine, so get used to it!

What is this about white space? The quantity of white space sets your practice apart. It's a way to draw attention to your ad. Since most dentists want to cram so much information into their ad, and the phone company wants to sell a lot of ads, there is often little empty space on a typical yellow page. White space is restful to the eye and brings in the casual searcher for more careful attention to the real message so artfully placed before him. Take a trip, letting your fingers do the walking through the newspaper, the business section especially, and notice the way large, powerful and profitable companies make use of "white space." This speaks volumes.

> Speaking of ad design, guess which way Americans read? They start at the top left and scan down to the bottom and left to right.

Speaking of ad design, guess which way Americans read? They start at the top left and scan down to the bottom and left to right. Instinctively they start at the first graphic and go down and to the right. Anything to the left of the graphic and above it gets less attention.

Writing advertising copy is a science. Make use of the Golden Triangle of ad copy writing and see improved results in all of your ads. Your practice logo should be in the upper left hand corner and your phone number bold in the upper left hand corner. A photo and a map are important ingredients of your ad design. Correct placement of the right information on the page is significant to your success.

I like a map in the *Yellow Page* ad because it speaks volumes in simple graphic language. It should be a simple line drawing with the major roads identified and an arrow pointing to your exact spot. Not too detailed and not hard to decipher.

I like our web site highlighted in bold, even in color. If I could do one thing right now with my *Yellow Page* ad, it would be to magically and instantly move people from my static *Yellow Page* ad to the dynamic, interactive web site about our practice. Putting a discount or offer in your *Yellow Page* ad is one way to get people to your web site. Have the details explained on the web site. An offer is a good way to push people to the web site. It gives people a reason to go there. Promises of gold, diamonds, lottery jackpot numbers, trips to Jamaica, eternal youth... anything to move them off the dime and into your online, interactive, patient-grabbing practice web site!

THE TWELVE WARNING SIGNS OF HEALTH

One of my telephone book ads in our local neighborhood directory has The Twelve Warning Signs of Health (I bullet point listed the twelve signs) and our Philosophy of Healthy Longevity (a sentence) that I paraphrased from my good friend, Dr. Joe Ellis of Houston, Texas. The entire ad was just that and our web site address, name, location and phone number. It was the thinking man's approach. I figured that people interested in becoming patients could read all about the dental stuff on the web.

I wanted to grab the attention of the dental decision maker of the family while she was sipping her Earl Grey tea in the morning, after the kids were off to school. It's pointedly non-dental but wholly health-related. Healthy Longevity is just the thing to make a potential patient, especially a mom, think of us as the caring, off-beat, humorous folks that we are.

If you are guilty, like me, of practicing comprehensive dentistry, performing all phases of the art and science of odontology, then be sure to spell out that fact in your *Yellow Page* ads. It brings in more people than most other reasons I know of combined (except, of course, location). People love to shop in one place.

One of our first dental clients, whom we assisted with the web design and marketing of his practice, created a slogan for his practice called One Location Care. They are on the cusp of high-end, niche marketing with that as their marketing slogan. Our practice in Suwanee has often used "Everything Under One Roof" and Your One-Stop Shop For All Your Family's Dental Needs" as a means of attracting patients, and it does work.

PROMOTE THE TELEPHONE NUMBER

You should have a notable phone number prominently listed on the *Yellow Page* ad. In our area, we draw from four area codes, so we include our 770 ahead of the regular phone number. If you expect people to drive to see you, then announce to them that many of your patients drive from other area codes to your office. That is a measure of social proof.

> Remember, a call to action for a potential patient to pick up the phone and call now is critical to good results in advertising and marketing.

How about the 1-800 numbers? If you are a big referral practice or have a multi-state practice draw, by all means become rarefied in your *Yellow Page* ad and include your 1-800 number for your out-of-town, out-of-state, and out-of-country patients.

When you move to a new location, consider choosing your practice's main number wisely. Go for easy to remember. I went for easy to dial in Stone Mountain, all the numbers either 1,2 or 3. In Suwanee, I choose lots of zeros, 614-7300. You could spell a word with your number, but that is really a bother for most people to key in a word. But, if your last name is four letters long, go for it! There are some words that stick in a person's mind and when you can use a word like "smile" for 770-93-SMILE, "dentist" in 770-DENTIST or "root" with 770-41-ROOT as your phone number, you can't lose. Remember, a call to action for a potential patient to pick up the phone and call now is critical to good results in advertising and marketing.

While you are thinking of all that goes onto a *Yellow Page* ad, consider the essential marketing rules: Speak to the Obvious. Patients want to know what BENEFITS there are for them at your office. They know you do dentistry, but they don't know what kind, how good, how different you are. Spell out in bullets your significant benefits for them. Paragraphs are to be kept small, mainly as quotes. People love to read a quote, because only happy people give quotes! Did you ever see a quote from an unhappy patient in a dentist's ad?

I created an ad once that ran for three or four years with phenomenal success that highlighted our "Let the Patient be in Charge" attitude. It was disarming to them and, in their eyes, differentiated us from all other dentists. It was like a Patients' Bill of Rights and spoke to our ability to listen and our understanding and concern for our patients' feelings. I can tell you that it drove lots of phobics to our practice. We got very good at dealing with their emotional needs and their phobia concerns.

NICHES CREATE RICHES

Now we are quite happy to see those often difficult patients. We have since created a niche for treating phobic patients, utilizing oral conscious sedation, IV sedation and

NuCalm natural sedation. Once turned around, those folks become the most loyal and conscientious of all clients. And, as you know, they have an above average level of pathology compared to non-phobics and they tend to need more extensive dental work to be made whole again.

So, that is what we used to do that brought us over 100 new clients a month for years. Now, since 1997, we have spread our dollars around, don't use the big book alone, have smaller ads, down to quarter page or less, and target market the communities directly around us. People still like the small *Yellow Page* books, I find, so consider them if you can.

If you are getting started in a new location, go bigger and bolder. If you are established, be more modest, but don't hide out in the fine print with most of the other dentists. People still think success is spelled "size of ad." The purpose of your ads today is to PUSH people to your web site as well as iden- tify your location. I give equal emphasis to each need now.

BEYOND THE BIG YELLOW BOOK

In our practice, 95% of my new patients have an email address. This may be high compared to most areas, but you will see that in your region sooner, rather than later, too. You must capitalize on the trends and digital was coming rapidly to the forefront in the late 1990's when I designed the "post-yellow page strategies" of WebCentric Marketing. That system is now sine qua non in the current millennium, ten years later. And as such, following and capitalizing on the digital revolution is a marketing bonanza for those who already own that turf.

Fortunately, with the proliferation of *Yellow Page*-type books, the cost per ad has come down. I find that the companies will bargain on price. Don't ever take the first offer. Get color or an additional geographical area thrown in for your good support of their service. Extras are easier to come by than price breaks. Recently the Southern Bell *Yellow Pages* threw in the yellow book ad for free when I signed up for the digital on-line listing. The world is turning on its head.

How do you gauge your results? Track each and every new patient who comes in the door. Know where they live, where they work, who referred them, whether it's a person, an ad, a mailer, the website, or the *Yellow Pages*. Ask which *Yellow Page* book it was that pointed them to your practice. In our Atlanta metro area, there have been at least five *Yellow Page* books, ranging from the BIG Real *Yellow Pages* by Ma Bell and her sons, several startup "baby" *Yellow Pages* and then regional, county and town *Yellow Pages* put together by various companies and groups.

We even have the neighborhood cook books, calendars, and spiral bound subdivision resident lists with our ads. We divide our dollars up judiciously between all these potential referral sources. As time goes on, we study the ROI of each directory and eliminate the losers. We keep a presence in those that return a positive number. Keeping up with your numbers is a key component of your marketing action plan.

A CHANGE OF HEART

In the past, I would spend $3,000-$4,000 a month on *Yellow Page* ads. And the truth is that I hated every cent I spent on them. Once we moved to our new location and started our new practice, for the first four or five years, our total budget per month was less than that for all of our marketing.

My change of heart on marketing came out of necessity and not having the *Yellow Pages* available. What developed as a result was our new focus on spreading the drops, our advertising budget, around covering more territory, being ubiquitous. Remember, "It Pays to Cover Dixie Like the

Dew. If they think of dentist, they should think of you."

People do go to your web site when it is mentioned in your post card ads, your message-on-hold, your *Yellow Page* ads, your newspaper ads. This is why we call this WebCentric marketing: everything points to your web site. Again, the reason for this is that the web site is your most flexible, most interactive, most detailed piece of marketing material.

> I find that *Yellow Page* advertising is worthwhile when the ad copy is tasteful, high class, and indicative of what and who we are. Combine that with the push to the web site and you have a winning formula.

The web site also has the highest demographic audience... the most ideal, discriminating, dental customer. I find that *Yellow Page* advertising is worthwhile when the ad copy is tasteful, high class, and indicative of what and who we are. Combine that with the push to the web site and you have a winning formula.

As digital overtakes print in some communities, it pays to be aware of the shift in where people go for information. While the death of the *Yellow Pages* has been prematurely announced, their impact is mediated by the growth of Google, Yahoo and Bing search engines. Dental online directories are showing up in increasing numbers with mini-sites which spotlight dental practices. They include maps, procedures, patient reviews and doctor ratings. I'll develop this concept more on these evolving phenomena in a chapter to follow.

Bottom line: transfer all of your thinking from paper to digital as it relates to the *Yellow Pages*. Don't just use the Bell system's pages, use everyone's. In small towns, the real *Yellow Page* book may still give you a good bang for your buck.

Next in *Marketing The Million Dollar Practice* is the importance of having Local Links on your web site. This is a form of partnership advertising, piggyback marketing, or the buddy system. From your web page, you link to other businesses that are also on the web. You receive clients by referral from other businesses because you are recommended by those businesses, 24/7/365, as a link on their site. Co-marketing can be a powerful medium to expand your audience of potential patients.

TAKE-AWAY POINTS

- You Must Be Listed Online and Offline
- Location, Location, Location
- Copy is King
- Headlines Matter Most
- Include Map, Phone Number, Website URL
- Consider Alternative Directories of All Sorts Online and Offline

CHAPTER 10

Local Links:
The Winners Circle

*L*ET'S TALK SPECIFICALLY about one of my favorite subjects, the World Wide Web. I was a young dentist at the tender age of 33, just eight years out of dental school from the Medical College of Georgia when my first associate dentist walked in with a Kaypro mini-computer and spoke about something called CompuServe. I wasn't hooked then, but by the time 1985 came around, I was online, doing the BBS routine, downloading files, and beginning to understand the power of the Ethernet world.

LIFE AS A DENTIST IN THE EARLY DAYS

I saw the commercial birth of the Internet and the beginnings of Prodigy, CompuServe as a GUI interface, AOL and the Mosaic browser, which was the mother to Netscape. If only I had a crystal ball then. Knowing what we now do, if we had invested in this early technology, we wouldn't be doing dentistry on screaming kids or writing articles for fun today, would we!

FUSION MARKETING

"Local Links" is the topic of this chapter, a form of partnership advertising, piggyback marketing, or the buddy system. Recently it has been called Fusion Marketing. It happens on your web page. It happens on your neighbors' web site and it causes increased traffic to your site.

Local Links is a circle of like-minded businesses, friends, or associations, linking each others' web sites together with clickable links. Some call it a "Web Ring." I like the Fusion Marketing model because it encompasses not just web links, but email and direct mail.

On a web site, there are areas which serve to give information to the customer (the data), areas which encourage a customer to act (buy, call, surf to the next page, etc.), and there are those areas which act to support more traffic being generated towards your web site (for instance the local link). From your web page, you can link to other businesses that are also on the web.

You receive clients by referral from other businesses because you are recommended by those businesses, 24 hours a day, 7 days a week, and all 365 days of the year, working for you as a link on their site to your site. This co-marketing strategy is a powerful medium to expand your audience of potential patients. Using the power of relationship, that intangible but momentous force, your base of potential patients can be doubled or tripled by the judicious use of relationship mining.

> This co-marketing strategy is a powerful medium to expand your audience of potential patients. Using the power of relationship, that intangible but momentous force, your base of potential patients can be doubled or tripled by the judicious use of relationship mining.

RELATIONSHIP MINING

"What is "relationship mining ?" It is when you know that there is a purpose in knowing someone, but you just don't know what it is. You just have to go after it and find out. It's a bit like going on a blind date; someone knows you both and is trying to make a match that is good: You just have to see if there will more to it than you currently can see or understand.

One thing I have learned in surfing the web, is to be watchful, mindful of what passes by me on a given day. Opportunities abound and present themselves with uncanny regularity. If your mind is tuned in to marketing, as it should be,, then local links makes perfect sense. Okay, not all of you think that way, so… let's explain what we did in the beginning.

First, I developed my www.SuwaneeDental.com practice web site according to my own value system, according to the image I wanted to portray, and it's my "data" that is displayed. We'll get into web site content later on in this book. The goal is to have properly structured pages being connected so that there is a logical progression from one thought to another.

The patient surfing your site should access the index or table of contents at will on almost every page. Make it easy for a net surfer to come and go throughout the site. If you don't, he will exit. Period. No more visits, no creating a bookmark of your web site, no deposit, no return. Your site must be easy to use.

Second, the priority list of index items needs to be prominently displayed. Today, the most prevalent index items are: Home, About, Services, News, and Contact Us.

LOCAL LINKS PAGE

Finally, there is one page called the "Local Links" page. It is listed in the index on the front or home page and nearly every page after that. The index is the list of words on the left or along the top of the web site, usually, which, when clicked, sends you on to the topic you chose.

On a Local Links page, you can include a logo, a name,

and a contact person's name plus a statement about the person, place, web site or business to which you are linking. Try to build interest so that people will want to go to these sites. Now, this seems to contradict the purpose of your own web site: generating calls to your office. But, in reality, this stimulates business.

You should have the local links situated so that most people go to them after they have tired of looking at your dental information. The Local Links page is at the bottom of my index or nearly so. This is like a vacation, a breather, a break from the reality of pyorrhea, facts about bloody extractions and ugly, pitted and cracked amalgam for the patients.

Who should you include as links… anyone who wishes usually. If they want to be on your page, ask if you can be on theirs. It's a reciprocal, tacit agreement. Of all the links to have, you'll love to link to groups. Personal web pages are nice, but they have a limited audience, therefore a more limited appeal for this purpose. You may want to go "real local" by creating a separate page for individuals who are already patients to "show off" their personal web sites, like a family album. Put in the right context, it will still draw traffic to your web site.

CASE STUDY 1: OURHOMEFIELD.COM

I once had on my local links page a link to a web site called Our Home Field, designed by an entrepreneur/patient who set up the site to list the scores and standings of all of the local sports teams each week, game by game. He had coaches putting up the scores, tabulating the standings in football, soccer, baseball, basketball, all ages, boys and girls. Can you imagine the thousands of viewer hits to that sports scores web page who would view your practice logo, name, and phone number? How many new patients would you get if your site were linked to this fellow's page?

And, of course, there is the all-important "link" to your practice web site. An athlete seeking his updated batting average can, in my case, come directly to our Suwanee Dental Care web site from this Our Home Field site. We are on his first page! Of all the good fortune, that is the best one could hope for. It does help that I am his dentist and that I feed him helpful hints now and then, about the web of course. Who cares about plaque and cavities when you can talk baseball with the kids!

That's just one concept. How much is it worth? Can you think of another way to put yourself in front of that many new faces repetitively, at no real cost to you? Another link I had on my first web site was to my brother's church, Conyers First Methodist. It's a bit different from what most dentists do but I like to have it there… for me, it adds meaning to life. When I was a client of Rick Mercer, back in the 1980's, he said get rid of all the "junk" in your life, but if it "adds meaning to your life, keep it!"

WHO YOU KNOW AND LINK TO MATTERS

On the Local Links web page, were also links to local churches. I have visited and know the pastors at several fine religious institutions near Suwanee. I make it a matter of course to offer to be of assistance to anyone in these pastor's congregations who sincerely needs our help, as a dentist. It's a way of making friends and doing good community service at the same time. Spread the good will and the good fortune and it will be returned ten-fold. That's scriptural and true.

SuwaneeDental.com links to the Atlanta Falcons, the official City of Suwanee web site and the Powerhouse Gym. The Powerhouse Gym created traffic. Suwanee Dental Care advertises on their entry hall message board with an 11" x 14" poster under glass. The message says go to our web site at SuwaneeDental.com and there are brochures in a holder on the message board.

CASE STUDY 2: SUWANEE SPORTS ACADEMY

Recently, I purchased, for $300 a year, a similar message poster space in the Suwanee Sports Academy, a basketball, volleyball, indoor track complex that will handle approximately 250,000 folks during that year. Every single one of them will pass my sign, stop and look at the daily bulletin board info, as they go to and from lockers, courts, bathrooms and dining areas.

Our team periodically goes to the gym and to the sports academy to replenish the brochures and speak to the owners, coaches and whoever is hanging around. They all become patients eventually. Cosmetics, youth, staying in shape, looking good, and "being on top of your game" all have a connecting point in which dentistry. We fill a niche in the marketing of self, just as the sports palaces of America do. Don't forget that significant source of patients.

> We fill a niche in the marketing of self, just as the sports palaces of America do. Don't forget that significant source of patients.

I could go on and on about each link and why I chose it. But, why not tell you how I found them instead. Early on, there was a cool tool called The Informant, from the Ivy League brainchildren at Dartmouth College. With this internet tool, key words are placed and this netbot (robot) searches day and night, day after day, on multiple search engines for your special key words: Suwanee, Buford, Duluth, Sugar Hill and more. Those are the towns in my local drawing area.

KEEP YOUR SITE UPDATED

When a new or updated web site comes online, anywhere on the web, The Informant notifies me in an email. I can also list certain URL's that I am interested in following and The Informant will keep track of them, notifying me if any changes are made. That is great for PR, dropping my online friends a line when their site is updated.

Here is what an online reviewer says about The Informant:

"The Informant is a free service that will save your favorite search engine queries and web sites, check them periodically, and send you email whenever there are new or updated web pages. You can enter up to three sets of keywords. At a periodic interval of 3, 7, 14, 30 or 60 days (which you specify), The Informant uses the AltaVista, Lycos, Excite, and Infoseek search engines (in addition to your local Internet search engines) to find the ten Web pages that are most relevant to your keywords. If a new page appears in the top ten, or if one of the pages from your previous top ten list has been updated, The Informant sends you an e-mail message. You can enter up to five URL's that are of particular interest to you. At a periodic interval of 3, 7, 14, 30 or 60 days (which you specify), The Informant checks these Web pages and sends you e-mails if one or more of them have been updated."

The Informant was purchased by TracerLock.com and now incurs a cost (though very inexpensive at $4/month). It is the most user-friendly tool we have found on the market. It is easy to subscribe to and easy to update your profile.

KEEPING UP-TO-DATE WITH NEWS

Another way to get started is to go into one of the major search engines (Google, Yahoo, or Bing) and type in your hometown name. Search for interesting local businesses, personal web sites, associations, and city and county governmental sites. When you find something interesting, look for a contact person, an email link on the site.

E-mail that contact person a note asking if you can add their link to your Local Links web page. Of course, list your business name and contact info, including web address on all your email in the signature portion of your email. You could also send an attachment via email, which is the home page to your dental web site. Do this to show them your site, so that they will see that it is professional and worthy of being linked to their web site.

The Law of Reciprocity says you can benefit. Perhaps, you will get an offer in return to have them put your logo and link on their web site. You know the drill. Sometimes, its best to just go ahead and ask if they would be so kind as to link to your page also. It is a good symbiotic relationship in a local area and the savvy businessmen and women know this.

> **During our first year after starting our practice in our new location, we had 700 patients since we opened our doors. Approximately 500 came to us through the diligent data mining we did with email.**

During our first year after starting our practice in our new location, we had 700 patients since we opened our doors. Approximately 500 came to us through the diligent data mining we did with email.

Taking your news gathering to another level, you can connect with a web monitoring and news clipping service. These online companies monitor all that is produced on the news and on the Internet every day and you are sent "clippings" of what you are most interested in. Keeping up with what your competition is doing, what your local linked friends are focused on can benefit your practice. It's good business intelligence and good public relations. Some of the major players in that arena are WebRoot, BurrellesLuce and MetroMonitor. For those who want a simple solution, Google has excellent free services that keep you up-to-date on any topic that is online.

NETWORKING PAYS DIVIDENDS

What else about local links is there to know? You just need to know that they work. You need to use them just like any other business- development tool. If you make a contact, figure out if you can help each other. Give first and you will receive in kind much more than you gave. Try to speak to your local businesses and ask if they have a web site. Ask for their cards with email and web addresses.

Local linking is all about networking with your business referral base.Give them a card and ask for them to surf on over, check out your new web site and (I stress this) ask them to tell you what they think. If they do, they will be snagged, hook, line, sinker, rod, reel, and bass boat. Getting constructive criticism directed towards your site builds your audience in this business.

The general public does not frequently search web sites for dentists. But when a need arises for dental care and that person does not have a dentist, the web is the first place they go. It's then a hot topic among the bridge club, ladies workout group or golfing buddies. Everyone always asks for social proof of the top three or four dental practices that they found on the web.

Your site will not get a bad critique if you've done it right. That is unless you treated your web site like a red headed stepchild. Don't get caught exhibiting your third cousin's nephew's free but awfully made-especially-for-you dental web site. Create it in your image, professional and to the point. Dentists know what I mean. There's a plug in here somewhere. Save it for when you need it. If your boat is sinking, use the plug.

In our next chapter in *Marketing The Million Dollar Practice,* we will be making hay with health histories. You heard me right, marketing the dental practice with the dull, drab health history. Just wait until you see what we do with this. Its magic, its outrageous, it sets us apart. I think it even drives off the lower end of the spectrum in come cases. "Low" as in no fun, stiff and stodgy. Until then, look for the logical local links living in your immediate locale to locate onto your web site.

TAKE-AWAY POINTS

- Select Fusion Partners
- Capture Local Links
- Ask For Reciprocity
- Display Fusion Partner Logos and Local Links
- Help Others Succeed and Reap the Rewards

CHAPTER 11

Marketing Your Practice Through the Health History
Part I : Psychographics

WHO SAYS that filling out forms has to be dull? What practice management guru said you must use the standard ADA health history form? Perhaps after reading this chapter, you will never fill out another health history yourself without thinking about the missed opportunity that that doctor just lost. Hopefully, you will update your own New Patient Intake Forms before you lose this valuable opportunity.

In the beginning, when I first started my dental practice in 1976, I received a pre-printed patient information health history pad of forms from the dental supply company that helped set me up. Years went by before I updated it under the guidance of a practice management consultant. It was only 10% different, asked all the same questions but was technically more legal in the financial area.

THE GREAT INFLUENCERS

In the mid 1980's, tutelage by Dr. Omer Reed and Avrom King, both of Phoenix, AZ, led me to understand and recognize the value of psychographics. I knew the value of knowing patients' geographic, chronological, demographic, genealogical and occupational data. If I could also determine with some accuracy their social style, chief motivators, dental IQ, and habit patterns, then I could more adequately predict what approach to take towards examination, consultation and delivery of dental care. And, in that vein, I developed my first psychographic (values clarification) intake form for the dental practice.

IF YOU MUST SPEAK, ASK QUESTIONS

> Central to the success of my New Patient Intake Form is its list of unconventional questions.

Central to the success of my New Patient Intake Form is its list of unconventional questions. I employed multiple choice answers and requested the patient to check all that applied. Information was gathered in the standard way on the Personal/Family Information Area and the Insurance/Financial Area— by fill in the blank. Check boxes worked well for the medical, dental and psychographic history sections. I especially aimed at understanding my patients' attitudes and past behaviors. Questions about previous dental experiences, services, recommendations, plus current concerns and known dental problems highlighted the dental area.

Specifically, I wanted to know past reasons why needed work was not completed. The big three answers were TIME, COST and FEAR. I subdivided fear into fear of shots, noise, and pain. Later, I added "no perceived problem" to the list. Historically, fear and cost were by far #1 and 2 on the list.

SPEAK TO THE OBVIOUS

To understand a patient's future behavior and therefore their chance of success in your office, it would be good to know their past behavior. We attempted, in the mid 80's to elicit data on frequency of dental visits and the "why" of the routine visits. We strove to learn the motivations for dental care, such as going to the dentist

(1) twice a year,

(2) once a year,

(3) emergency only.

This initially helped us to understand some of our patients' motivations, but, we were more accurately tuned-in when we asked questions on why they were there in the present.

Their answers included that they (1) Want a complete exam and they know needs are present, (2) want a comprehensive exam and consultation, (3) have pain and need immediate assistance, or (4) "I'm in great shape, I just want my teeth cleaned as soon as possible."

This was effective and significantly different from the standard dental office New Patient Intake Form. It showed us as being a different kind of dental place, too, a goal I was interested in achieving with our new patients. When combined with our complete dental examination with the dentist, which we called the New Patient Experience, our intake exam revolutionized our practice.

The New Patient Experience was so successful, and continues to be over 25 years later, that it deserves to be the focus of an entire chapter. It is one of the crown jewels in our extremely successful marketing effort.

I used our psychographic intake form from 1986 to 1993. In 1993 I sold my million dollar practice. The purchaser eventually went to a dental guru for advice and promptly changed our intake forms and discontinued the new patient experience as we knew it. I was working my way out of the practice as an associate for three, then two and supposedly one day a week over three years following the sale.

So, I gave up control and did not insist that the old, successful ways be continued. I was easing out of the 18-

wheeler practice that I had created over 18 years as the new owner took over the reins. As you may surmise, year three never materialized into a one-day-work week for me there. It was clearly evident that my production was critical and was absolutely required to keep profitability intact.

The new owner had not marketed well and had not planned for my eventual drop in production as my days working were reduced. He had not planned well as there was no new associate dentist waiting in the wings, being groomed to step in as I stepped down. Eventually, the three D's, debt, drugs, and divorce emotionally, spiritually and financially bankrupted the doctor who had bought my once shining castle on the hill. By default, I got the practice back. There is a good lesson here for those who think financing a sale yourself is a wise move. It may be easy but not always wise.

First thing I did upon regaining control of my practice was to reinstitute the psychographic New Patient Intake Form and the New Patient Experience. We turned the foundering ship around and steamed into Port Profitability within three months. First impressions make an astounding difference. We learned much from this unfortunate transition.

Fortunately, I found another excellent dentist/buyer and was out of the practice again within a year this time. The reasons this second transition was successful, in

> First thing I did upon regaining control of my practice was to reinstitute the psychographic New Patient Intake Form and the New Patient Experience. We turned the foundering ship around and steamed into Port Profitability within three months. First impressions make an astounding difference. We learned much from this unfortunate transition.

my opinion are:
   (1) the purchaser borrowed the purchase price from a bank through the AGD SBA program,
   (2) I only agreed to stay one year, and
   (3) he kept using the psychographic New Patient Intake Form and the New Patient Experience.

The new owner of my practice became a master at the same techniques that had made us successful.

NEW BEGINNINGS CAN BE A SHOT IN THE ARM

Now for the hot, new material....the WebCentric Marketing addition to the New Patient Intake Form! My move to a boutique practice in Suwanee followed my 23 years of building the Stone Mountain 18-wheeler practice.

My goal was to stay small, keep the overhead reasonable, enjoy dentistry and get a rapid start. So, it was at this time that I introduced marketing to the New Patient Intake Form. That was the shot in the arm that I had developed during my planning stage between selling the former practice and starting the new one. I was planning my move, developing a marketing plan, growing my knowledge and interest in the World Wide Web. The year was 1997.

If you have read between the lines in this book so far, you will have realized that I am defining the spokes on the wheel. The wheel is called the WebCentric Marketing Action Plan. The spokes are the independent structural components or campaigns and the hub is the practice's Internet web site. Understanding the whole will help you focus on the utility of the new WebCentric patient intake forms.

Gathering and feeding this patient data into your practice management systems so that it can be analyzed and used to help you make decisions requires work. We have come up with a novel way to achieve this and keep up with the software updates. I hope you will search on the Internet the term "psychographics" and see what is possible by understanding its power.

In part two of this chapter, we will be making more hay with health histories. After more than twenty years using this format, we changed it, so let's dig into the details about how we use our current WebCentric Patient Intake Form.

TAKE-AWAY POINTS

- Look For Opportunities Everywhere
- Dare to Be Different
- Capture Demographic and Psychographic Information
- Seek to Find Out Why People Make Choices They Do

CHAPTER 12

Marketing Your Practice Through the Health History

Part II:
New Patient Intake Form

FLEXIBILITY

A KEY QUESTION that gets little attention in most practices is, "How do you ensure compatibility between your dental practice management software and your new dental patient intake forms that the patients fill out?" Another question more commonly asked is, "How do you get this information in time to create a smooth flow of the patient into the practice on their first appointment?"

Our practice uses the Practice Works Dental Management Software for our administrative, practice management and chairside charting systems. Our digital SLR and intraoral cameras are linked to Practice Works with Zoom and Kodak imaging software. A bridge to Dexis digital radiography allows us to manipulate images and send them via email. Linking to the Internet with a T-1 line connects us online for browsing, email and file transfer. It makes good sense to use your New Patient Intake Form to gather information for your practice management system and a lot of other areas, too.

One excellent feature of the Practice Works software is the patient data entry. Once in, it is everywhere we need it to be. All current dental management software systems have this feature. But, one problem all dental software systems created for the masses is that they are not readily customizable to the individual practice. The data entry page, for instance, is the same for all dental practices. Your administrative team needs to gather the patient information in its correct "order" and then input it into the computer in that same sequence on the patient information screen. What you need is the flexibility to update and change your New Patient Intake Forms.

DO IT YOURSELF WORKS FINE

I had this in mind when designing our Suwanee Dental Care New Patient Intake Form on Microsoft Publisher. With it, you have the ability to update, cut and paste, anytime you need a change. You can print 1.000 or 100 or 10 forms right now on the laser printer. There is no waiting for the local printer to send a proof, go through the printing process and the time involved, particularly if there is color involved. Cost savings can be a major benefit when small numbers of copies are needed. Your administrative team will love you for your foresight on this flexibility issue.

How often does your office manager ask if she can change the practice forms? There may be times in your practice when you need to meet that need based on when changes in your practice management system screen format make it necessary, when HIPPA rules change, when OSHA interferes with your systems, or when the FCC, DEA, ADA, IRS, or a hundred other alphabet soup governmental/regulatory agencies intrude and require us to manage information in a specified manner. This is our #1 recommendation for those who wish to take control of this process. Build flexibility into your forms. Use Microsoft Publisher.

MEDICAL HISTORY

For example, serious medical information surfaced that patients who had taken Fen-Phen may have developed heart valve damage and may have been in need of antibiotic premedication. We just added a check box to our intake form and were back in business within ten minutes with our New Patient Intake Forms and our Medical History Patient Update Forms… What did you do?

As software updates occur, practice focus changes, and scientific and medical discoveries come to light, we need the ability to reflect these changes on our patient forms. As the news of bisphosphonate induced osteonecrosis spread across the dental, medical and legal landscape, dentists had to add questions to their health histories about osteoporosis and cancer drug treatment with a long list of drug names representing the bisphosphonate categories. They had to update their informed consent forms for extractions, periodontal surgery and dental implants. Again, planning for flexibility allows you to anticipate change and not be stymied by it.

History tends to repeat itself. A change must occur and a person's attitude or feelings must shift or he or she is apt to do the same thing when faced with a similar decision. To overcome negative actions and the consequences of those untoward actions, the New Patient Intake Form has questions designed to find out why patients do what they do and act as they do. Questions like, "Why did you leave your last dentist?"; "What kept you from completing your needed dentistry in the past?"; and "What do you want to accomplish on your first visit with us today?" are all good open-ended questions that begin a conversation if the patient begins by filling in the blank or checks the appropriate box.

MARKETING DATA

The obvious question is how to use the New Patient Intake Forms to gather marketing information.

There are three pages to our primary New Patient Intake Form: page one is personal and insurance information, page two is medical and dental history, page three is marketing and motivational information.

We gather the personal and insurance data on our form's first page to please our team. That is a concession to our front office staff who wanted it on the front page for easy input into the computer screen. I have a personal feeling that "speaking to the obvious"—the dental health history—is perhaps a better way to introduce the patient to our considerable uniqueness, but, in this case, my pragmatic staff won the battle over the order of pages on the forms. What can I say! Dentists don't always know what's best.

Our Suwanee Dental Care New Patient Intake Form asks all of the standard questions plus a few that are not. First, we ask them to include their email address right along with their name, address, zip code, telephone number, etc. It shows our patient that we expect everyone to have one. Soon they all will. Remember also, we first started using this form as far back as the late 1990's when email was rare.

After the first patient's personal information and insurance page, we followed with the dental and medical history page, which was also basically our psychographic patient intake page developed in the 1980's. We did not add the marketing page until 1999. Over time, this page was updated and we reduced the possible number of answers to include only the most frequently answered ones. We found it advantageous to leave places for "other" and "write-in" or "fill-in-the-blank" answers.

ABOVE ALL, HAVE FUN

One goal I had in moving to Suwanee and starting completely over was to have more fun, for myself, my team and my patients. Therefore, I looked for opportunities to add humor to a plethora of otherwise dull tasks… like for patients filling out forms!

As your patients read through your New Patient Intake Form, seriously and dutifully answering the medical and dental questions, what would happen if you hit them with subtle zingers? What if you asked the unexpected or asked a question that was perfectly in sync with what they were thinking, yet one that no one else had ever asked?

In one question, for example, I am asking, "Why are you here?" The choices listed on the form are several but two specifically are the result of actual reasons that I have been told over and over again. I thought them to be novel and humorous, so, I included them on our flexible form. The first is, "I am fleeing managed care" and the second, "I dreamed I should come here." Why not, it's often true! I want to ease the tension, break the ice for patients in their early moments in our confines.

Nothing gets you closer to the instant rapport you need than understanding what motivates your patient, why they are seeking you as their dentist. Questions on your New Patient Intake Form that dig out that question are like veins of gold for your practice to mine.

What better image to portray than one of a light-hearted, happy place where humor is appreciated? Humor is rarely associated with dentistry. You can and will change that perception as you include the unexpected on your New Patient Intake Forms. It's a good first impression to make, once again. So, look for places to inject your personality, even on a health history form.

TRACKING THE MARKETING BEAST

Have you ever seen a marketing question on a dental health history form? If you do, it's likely to be just one, "Who referred you to our office?" On the Suwanee Dental Care form we list 20 potential sources of new patient contact and information. You can easily change this list monthly or quarterly as needed to keep up with your current marketing campaigns. Staying flexible is a good policy.

Tracking your source of new patients and the ROI of each marketing expense is important and the inclusion of all your sources on the New Patient Intake Form is critical for your team to know. Knowing your numbers helps you make better leadership and management decisions and it all starts with gathering the needed data, up front. Since your marketing does and should change on a regular basis, it makes sense to have a tracking form that is customizable and flexible.

ASK THE QUESTION, THE ANSWER TO WHICH IS THE MESSAGE YOU WISH TO SEND

On the last page of the New Patient Intake form, we have the largest departure from the typical dental form. Here on the third page of the New Patient Intake Form, I am expressing to our patients our interest in fresh, alternative ideas and am seeking to match their interests with ours. I am asking them how they first heard about our practice and what influenced them to choose our practice. You will see this page as invaluable as you escalate your practice growth activities and move up to the next level in your marketing action plan.

Do you know if your patients are motivated by the "green movement?" Are they into health and wellness, or cosmetics and beauty, are they more cost-conscious and discount oriented, or are they Type A, get-it-done-at-any-cost patients? Are they from an area of the country where you once lived? Do they work for a company and do a job similar to anyone else you know, are their children at home or in school and do they have any special hobbies they like to do? Answers to these types of questions can help you instigate personal bonding with your patient.

Be careful to not get trapped in the "dental pain story" too early in the new patient interview. To get trapped in that conversation can lead to a less-than-positive relationship. Remember, emotions are tone-setters and memory-makers. The ideal thing to do first is to get a flood of positive feelings going, bond with the patient and then go into why they are there and what is their pain.

One section on our form in the past allowed new patients to check their interest in getting additional information on the following:

(1) vitamin & mineral supplementation,

(2) lowering cholesterol and triglyceride levels,

(3) improving body fat ratios,

(4) homeopathic remedies,

(5) herbal remedies,

(6) healthy longevity and dental wellness,

(7) the best dental care systems, and

(8) Indian sculpture and other art.

You could put anything in this list. Just think of an area you have information to share and list it. I referenced "in the past" in the first sentence above because the form is always changing to suit our needs. We no longer include those exact questions. As times and interests change, we change our form with them.

You may wonder why I would have something such as "Indian sculpture and other art" on the list. Well, the office décor is definitely Southwestern and there are many Indian artifacts around the facility. Patients always ask what the connection is to the Southwest and to native American art. I am proud to tell them that my ancestors on my dad's side were Cherokee Indians.

I have studied nutrition for much of my 36 dental years and am qualified to recommend specific nutritional, herbal and homeopathic remedies. That is why I felt like those questions could lead to some interesting conversations about wellness and health. Patients are looking for doctors who actually know something to help them sort out all of the numerous touting they see on television about nutritional products.

> Each positive response on your check list opens a door for discussion beyond the mundane dental topics of periodontal disease and caries.

Each positive response on your check list opens a door for discussion beyond the mundane dental topics of periodontal disease and caries. You want to be known as more than just the "tooth-fixers" in your community. This request information technique adds to your repertoire of topics to discuss. That personal relationship building can enhance our bottom line, for instance, if you choose to dispense any nutritional or dental care products from our office.

Some of you may be unfamiliar with the economics of veterinary practices, but up to one third of their profitability comes from the sale of pet supplies and medications in the office. Dentistry has never approached that level of commercialization, but we are on the way to that in some areas. Whether that is good or bad, desired or not is up to the individual to decide, but it is a way to serve the public and maintain a profitable practice.

Similarly, I was in a year-long mastermind program and in talking with an audiologist at Lake Tahoe this year, the subject of practice development came up. He shared that his small chain of audio clinics in Dallas, Texas increased its profitability by 150% by implementing efficiency systems and adding products to their mix of services offered. By finding out what people want and giving it to them, you can dramatically improve your bottom line. Ask and you shall receive. The intake form is the beginning of asking.

In my second year of practice in Suwanee, I joined Power Core, a national organization which trains members on getting more referrals, on networking skills and on lead generation. Networking is an extremely important topic and will have an entire chapter in this book dedicated to the reasons to be involved in this activity and how to do it most effectively. Are you involved in any network groups yourself? How do you get leads for other members? You know that it's the person who gives the most leads that also gets the most leads from others. It's the Law of Reciprocity.

So, in that regard, on our Suwanee Dental Care New Patient Intake Form, I added one question, one that is meant to stimulate some discussion and give me insights as to the needs of my client base. In PowerCore, members refer to each other in the community. It's the strategic plan that everyone in the group assists one another in growing their businesses. You would need to know what type leads others may be seeking to be a valuable member of your Power Core team.

SEEK TO SERVE AND YOU WILL BE SERVED

In that same light, you can play a valuable role in your patient's assimilation into the community, even though they may not be a member of a networking team. How do you do that? Your New Patient Intake Form questionnaire could ask if they are new to the community and would like to know who are good attorneys, plumbers, insurance agents, physicians, dry cleaners, painters, etc. in the area. If they check yes, then they are perhaps opening a door to more questions so that you can give them a specific referral. The idea in Power Core is that, "He who gives referrals, receives referrals." It helps build community and connects the new patients to your practice if you are willing to give them a helping hand and make their life easier and don't just confine your role to dental tooth mechanic."

BRINGING GOD INTO THE WORKPLACE

I recently added another question on our Suwanee Dental Care New Patient Intake Form. It is an understated but genuine question to let people know that I am open to speak to them about their spiritual life in addition to their physical and emotional life. I have wrestled with this for many years as to how to incorporate my spirituality into my dental practice. I had not been comfortable witnessing to people about my faith in the past. To me, it's entirely personal.

Lately, however, I have come to realize that the gift of salvation is too dear a gift to keep to just myself and I now find that being uncomfortable is worth the price if I can share with others my faith and belief in Eternal Life through Jesus Christ. So, the question I put on my history form simply goes like this: Would you like information about some good churches in the area? Its easy, non-intrusive, and speaks to a serious need to many in our society. I'd rather be asked about my faith and share that than to be pushy. I never liked "pushy" people myself, and don't want to be that towards any of my patients, staff or friends.

Right now, I would tell you that I am a serious student of the Bible for the first time in my life, only for the past fifteen years. I am seeking answers to my questions that I have harbored all my life. Change and growth is hard for a scientific-minded guy like me. I think all dentists and physicians are that way… at first. But, this I can say, "I am a better person the more I learn and study God's Word." I'll tell you what it is that is most meaningful to me right now. It's that I feel more at peace than ever before because I now, finally, have a way to reach others in my own way about the question of spirituality. That was always a hole in my heart that needed filling.

My New Patient Intake Form, as insignificant as it may seem, helps me feel like I have unlocked a door so that someone in need, someone with a question can walk in and we can talk about their life, their mission on Earth, their faith and eventually their salvation. Have you ever felt the same way I did, that you were not opening the door to let people in?

Why was this a burden for me and why am I sharing this with you? Perhaps because it was a dentist who led me to the Lord, at a conference on TMJ in Washington, D.C. in 1986. I owe him a debt of gratitude. Just after he shared the Lord with me, I walked across the Potomac River. Well, it was on a bridge, not in the way you may have thought. But my feet did not feel like they were touching the ground. I kept that experience private until 1998. Only a couple of people knew about it. But now I want to share. Ask me about it some day! I may not have all the answers, but I know how to get in touch with someone who does.

MAKING THE CONNECTION - BONDING TO YOUR PATIENTS

The last area of your New Patient Intake Form gathers personal facts about the patient's life. Ask things like name of spouse, ages of children, where they used to live or originally came from, occupation and what their specialty is at their job. Ask about the college they attended. All this information is most handy for making a personal connection with the patient, for building rapport. If you've traveled or lived in many areas of this country as well as abroad, you will especially like to know where people come from and the genealogy of their family. Most long-term American families can connect to a common ancestral name by going a few generations back. It's fun to try and discover a common family name, location, city or state with a new patient. It's almost like working with cousins when you can find a tie-in.

Another fun thing to do is the try and play trivia with certain factoids the patient puts on their form. What if you tried to name the school mascot of their college team? Michigan… Wolverines, Presbyterian College… Blue Hose, San Jose State… Spartans. Talk about an ice breaker! What if you attempted to name the top song of the year they graduated from high school? Do you know about the power of music and the areas of the brain that are activated with music? Bring up fond memories and link them with your patients' relationship with you and your dental practice. This will reap huge dividends in the future as you work to build trust and rapport with your new patients.

Before the end of the page is your all-important section on the Internet. First, ask your new patient if they have surfed over to your practice web site—yet! That is an assumptive close technique that all sales savvy marketers know. Give people a reason to go there and also tell them it is okay to share your web site address with their friends.

Next on the New Patient Intake Form ask if they have a web site next, and, if they do, ask for its URL (web address). You'll want to visit it for certain and hopefully create a link to it on your web site. You realize the importance of the local link and the networking potential of that link already.

Finally, ask if they would like to receive your practice newsletter via email. If you send email to people who don't know you, this is called spamming. As time passes, email communication between our practice and our patients becomes more and more necessary. This question identifies the open-minded from the close-minded at our initial interaction, plus now we need a signature on a form to agree to sending that email.

So, by using a new patient intake form similar to ours, what have you gathered? First to note is the concrete psychographic and demographic information which will lead you to better serve your new patient. With the correct information you can now communicate 300% more effectively and efficiently by Internet. Often you know who is ready to move forward and at what speed. You have clarity and can position your actions to best meet their needs in a quicker, more thorough fashion.

The bottom line for our New Patient Intake Form is that we use it to paint a picture of who we are—at the same time we ask who they are. Don't let this statement fall on deaf ears. I'll repeat it here for emphasis: "The bottom line for our New Patient Intake Form is that we use it to paint a picture of who we are, at the same time we ask who they are."

> The bottom line for our New Patient Intake Form is that we use it to paint a picture of who we are—at the same time we ask who they are.

We do this first by speaking to the obvious, by asking questions first, to find out what they think they need before we tell them what they need. All of our questions create a relatively non-judgmental, interesting format for the patient to offer insights into their psyche, their needs and their desires. Its our attempt to communicate in "humanese," as opposed to "dentalese." We paint a visual picture, through positive outcomes of our preferred future and therefore of their preferred future.

If in time, you learn to maximize your communication and behavioral

> Dentistry can be a joy when there are plenty of eager, smiling faces showing up for treatment appointments day after day after day.

skills, take the information gathered from the New Patient Intake Form and combine it with the interview process at the New Patient Experience, you will succeed. If you practice and implement these marketing tools and apply your new-found knowledge as well as you do your tooth carpentry tools and techniques, you will be successful. Dentistry can be a joy when there are plenty of eager, smiling faces showing up for treatment appointments day after day after day.

In the next chapter of *Marketing The Million Dollar Practice,* we will be digging into the details of the Suwanee Dental Care New Patient Experience (NPE). You will not want to miss a single point in this one. The NPE is at the very top of the list of most notable "differentiation devices" that we have ever incorporated into our practice. Since 1988, it has propelled our practice to ever higher levels of predictability, profitability and enjoyment.

TAKE-AWAY POINTS

- Change is Inevitable: Be Prepared
- Build in Flexibility: Use MS Publisher
- Medical History Plus Marketing Data
- Engage, Differentiate, Show Who You Are
- Ask the Important Questions
- Break the Ice and Build Rapport

CHAPTER 13

The New Patient Experience

THE NEW PATIENT EXPERIENCE is at the very top of the list of most notable "differentiation devices" that we have ever incorporated into our practice. The flow, meaning the movement of the patient, is a coordinated, orchestrated event, a play within a play, a strictly constructed score with the potential for improvisation at any point. Each piece of the market-attuned puzzle is linked to another to bring about the desired conclusion.

Marketing switches from external to internal at the moment the patient opens the front door. In the previous two chapters, we exposed the key components of the New Patient Intake Form. Let's pick up the camera and follow the human interactions as the patient arrives for an appointment. First, I will set the scene.

The introduction of the new client to our practice could be called indoctrination into our philosophy of healthy longevity. We immerse our guests into a surrealistic dental event. They cannot navigate through our ocean of sights and sounds, aromas and

> We immerse our guests into a surrealistic dental event. They cannot navigate through our ocean of sights and sounds, aromas and feelings, or possibilities and ideas without coming to the reality of our uniqueness and genuineness, and to the appropriateness of them joining our dental practice.

feelings, or possibilities and ideas without coming to
the reality of our uniqueness and genuineness, and to
the appropriateness of them joining our dental practice.
We believe that most dentistry is optional and can be
accomplished in a patient's own time. Our job as dental
professionals is to assist our patients in telling time.

GREAT BEGINNINGS

The door opens and the aroma of freshly brewed coffee
waifs into their nostrils. Chilled ice water, orange juice and
home baked cookies greet them visually on the sideboard
near the entrance doorway in our smallish reception area.
A welcoming ding sounds as the door closes, announcing
to our receptionist to arrival of Mrs. Vera M. Portante,
a new person with an appointment for our New Patient
Experience.

Angie, our office manager, stands and greets Vera
eye level to eye level, shakes her hand, and says, "Good
morning, you must be Mrs. Portante! Welcome to our
office!" She then invites Vera to partake of the goodies on
the sideboard and asks how everything is going for her this
morning. We are seeking an insight into the mental state of
our new friend. Angie hands her the clear Lucite Suwanee
Dental Care clipboard with the golden apple clip and the
three-page New Patient Intake Form and invites her again
to take her time and fill out the information as best she can.
Many of our patients have downloaded the form from our
web site and we now encourage them to send it in ahead
of time.

While the patient is filling out the forms, which you
know all about by now, we can discuss, among ourselves,
the history of how this new patient experience came to be.

Our exposure to the new patient experience goes back
to circa 1988. Somewhere between the last vestiges of

our Quest training, Dick Barnes style of consultation, the Kendrick Mercer Company's lifestyle-geometric progression program and our fledgling entrée into Napili and Pentegra with Omer Reed, we developed our concept of the New Patient Experience. This term is used to differentiate this interaction from our previous method of introducing a new patient into our practice. The goal of our New Patient Experience was to create a bond of understanding between the new patient, the doctor and the practice. We wanted patients to "experience" a new beginning, a dramatic "Ahh, ha" at this visit.

What did we do prior to the NPE? Probably what most dentists do, what we were taught to do in dental school. Patient signs in, is given a set of forms to fill out in the reception area and waits to be taken back by the hygienist. A quick review of the medical history and some small talk occurs for a few minutes as the hygienist washes hands, gloves up and commences to chart, take x-rays and hurriedly scales and polishes the teeth that are presented to her. At the end of the 45 to 60 minute appointment time, the dentist appears to "meet the new patient," confirm the data gathered and to recommend the next step. Maybe they leave with an idea of needing a few fillings, a crown or with a referral slip to the Periodontist, the oral surgeon or the Endodontist. Sound familiar?

THE PENTEGRA LEGACY

The precipitating factor that germinated the New Patient Experience was our move to "Frontdesklessness," a Reedian phenomena in dentistry. In 1989, as a Pentegra practice, we downsized from 13 to six employees, closed off the front desk and transacted administrative business via work stations in the operatories utilizing cross-trained staff.

It was our plan to have all new patients enter the practice

by having an interview, then an examination, by the dentist, as opposed to seeing the hygienist initially. The idea was to appeal to the discriminating individual. We wanted to distance ourselves as far as possible from the HMO-PPO-Clinic model of dental practice. Breaking the mold of a hygiene-dominated first visit and substituting it with a dentist/patient coordinator interview model was our most difficult barrier. The staff, the hygienist, the dentist and the patients all had expectations that had to be managed. What was efficient had not always been effective in the old model. Now, with the fledgling New Patient Experience being put to use, efficiency was reduced. We were hoping for a monstrous increase in effectiveness.

THE NON-THREATENING ATMOSPHERE IS CREATED

At our large facility in Stone Mountain where we developed this concept, we dedicated an entire room to the New Patient Experience. I ripped out our three chair orthodontic bay, leaving one chair for our comprehensive exam on the far right side of the space. To the left side of this 25 foot by 15 foot room, we placed a couch, a wing back chair, coffee table, bookshelves and lamp to create a virtual living room "home setting." There was a visual separation between the interview area and the exam area, although it was in the same room.

Now, this special room, with its unique purpose, was located at the other end of the 5000-square-foot office. To reach it, a new patient would have to pass by every operatory, the hygienists, the sterilization area, the tomograph x-ray unit, the panoramic x-ray unit, the new ortho room, the TMJ room with its computerized equipment, and finally the laboratory.

THE TOUR

What evolved was a tour. Each new patient was greeted by our patient coordinator and taken on the tour, stopping at each point of interest for an introduction to staff members, an explanation about certificates or plaques on the wall, or a description of a particular device's use in our practice. In this way, the patient became familiar with our capabilities, our expertise in orthodontics, implants and TMJ, our infection control standards, and often met three or four staff members including the dentist before sitting down to fill out their forms.

Jennifer McDonald, our patient coordinator at that time (and who later became a national-level dental speaker and world-class dental consultant with her own company), would offer them a seat on the couch, coffee, tea or juice and a chance to fill out their psychographically oriented New Patient Intake Form. At times, they would be left alone to complete their form. Other times, we would verbally ask the questions and record them on the form ourselves. We were experimenting with suggestions from Omer and others as to whether to complete the questionnaire orally or not. Eventually, we chose to allow our new patients to fill their forms out prior to their tour, for efficiency's sake.

Each step of the New Patient Experience is pre-planned and choreographed. Each staff member has a role and knows it. Developing the traffic flow, the dialogue, the entrances and exits of each staff member and the doctor is done in advance with nothing left to chance. There is flexibility built into the "dance" but everyone knows where each pathway leads and the resulting flow is seamless. The bottom line is that we end up with a patient who is extremely well cared for, listened to, and appreciated by our staff.

What does the client experience? They receive a warm smile and personal greeting by name. They feel special immediately. They feel informed as we take them on the guided tour. They are treated like a guest in our home rather than like a stranger with insurance. They feel acknowledged when we offer them a choice of beverage. As they traversed the hallway, they took in the visual imagery of who we are: Rotary International service poster, Boy Scouts of America merit badges and Eagle Scout award mounted under glass, Fellowship and Mastership award photographs. They saw the diploma from the Medical College of Georgia written in Latin. They listened as Jennifer explained the reason DMD is not written DDM, based on the Latin structure of the doctorate degree. The leisurely tour past framed certificates of endo courses, orthodontic certificates of completion, and plaques from presentations at the Chicago Mid Winter and the Hinman Dental Meetings. What does the patient feel? We hope it is confidence that they have chosen the right dentist. By leading the new patient on a tour, we help dispel their fears and doubts before we ever examine or consult with them—and certainly before we ever initiate treatment.

HOW DO YOU CREATE A SIGNIFICANT EMOTIONAL EVENT

Can we involve the five senses in this experience? Hopefully, we are challenging our new patient up front to experience our work environment. We are not hiding our instruments or operatories behind closed doors. They see comfortable procedures being performed as they pass by; they hear the sounds of Bach, Beethoven, Waylen and Willie or Michael Buble overhead on the in-office music system. The decor is classic but modern as is the equipment. There is no clutter. Dust and debris are strictly verboten.

What is the smell of the office? We like a musky male fragrance. A floral potpourri for the rest room areas is nice as is evergreen and spice. Popcorn is popped and served in the reception area in the morning and afternoon to draw the memories of childhood to the fore, perhaps recalling happy times at the movies. Never will you detect the acrid stench of burning tooth dust or the tell-tale smell of formocreosol and eugenol so prevalent in dental offices. We often hear new folks say that our office doesn't smell like a dental office.

> We often hear new folks say that our office doesn't smell like a dental office.

Did I mention the firm handshake at the beginning of the tour, when the patient coordinator first met the new patient? There is a proper greeting for each age new patient. We meet kids at their level, eye to eye and grip our patient's hand as a friend or businessman would. Shoulders and elbows are touched appropriately to guide or compliment. It is important to us to establish the feeling of our gentle touch before the oral exam occurs.

Walking back to the exam room is pretty much an experience in and of itself for the patient. They are listening to our well-rehearsed spiel, not being asked too many questions at this time. We are inputting data on the fly, if you will. We are building their expectations of their future reality. Jennifer speaks in positive terms about what we do. She is sure to compliment the doctor for his abilities, training, and his most recent spectacular results. She intentionally builds up the doctor and the practice to the new patient in an open and honest manner. This is an important point that must not be forgotten by the patient care coordinator who gives the tour.

I assure you, it takes much longer to tell you about the tour and the new patient experience than to complete it! My total exam time ranges anywhere from 15-30 minutes per patient. Tours take about three to five minutes, the interview by our patient coordinator about 5-10 minutes and my interview about 5-10 minutes. After that, I invite the patient to come on back to the operatory for the exam, Now that we are in our new 9,000-square-foot office space in Suwanee, the New Patient interview room is just a few steps from my exam operatory. Before, in Stone Mountain, we just stepped 10 feet across the room.

THE INCOMPARABLE COMPREHENSIVE EXAM: THEN

The comprehensive exam lasts 10-15 minutes depending on the complexity. Data is gathered, the ground work is laid for whichever of the major dental treatment arenas the new patient will encounter: perio, caries, cosmetics, orthodontics or TMJ. This is the way we did the NPE during the early days in Stone Mountain.

Back to the tour as we currently do it. It's two decades later and thousands of new patients have been through the system. We know it works and works well. We just ended at the couch in the reception room and the New Patient Intake Form is already filled out. Brandy, our new patient coordinator, is introduced to the patient by Linda, our concierge. She conducts the tour just as she has been trained and sits down at 90 degrees to the patient, knee to knee in the Interview Room and continues the process of bonding the patient to the practice. She has familiarized herself with the New Patient Intake Form data and knows a lot about this new person. She has formulated an approach to get the new person to feel at ease, based on her experience and the new patient's social style.

It's nice to have all the information we asked on the forms to give us an insight into who they are. Brandy comments, asks questions and listens. She begins with personal details—original home area, family, occupation, job and move to the medical history, dental history, and why they are here. We take notes and categorizes the important points for the doctor's review.

THE DOCTOR INTERVIEW

At the opportune time, either the dentist walks in or the patient coordinator excuses herself and leaves to get the doctor. That depends on the timing of other patients' treatments in the office. Whichever occurs, Brandy will immediately deliver an executive summary of her findings to the doctor. As the dentist walks to the exam room, he is briefed about any unusual specifics that she has discovered. Brandy formally introduces the doctor again even if they met the patient with a nod or a hand shake during the tour. In our vernacular, when we walk in the door, "It's Show Time!" We are there 100% for and with that new client. Our attention is on their interests, their needs and in the end, their desires.

Imagine you are now that dentist. You are focused on acknowledging this person by commenting on the facts that the patient has written on the new patient intake form and on what Brandy has discovered and noted for you. You also take appropriate notes as the interview progresses. With the sparkling detail of your New Patient Intake Form, you have ample information to find common ground to bond with this new person. You have more than enough data to know what level of exam will be needed. You know from the interview where this relationship will be heading. You know how much time to invest with this person because you already have a sense of the probable outcome.

Most patients tell us that they never had a doctor sit down with them like we do. Most say it's a unique experience and that they are glad they "found us." Those are

> Do you aspire to have more fun, have less stress, and to enjoy your day to the fullest every day? Then adopting this version of the New Patient Experience may just be for you!

their exact words. What would you give for comments like that? Those words are worth millions over a lifetime in dentistry, and anyone can learn this technique to gather them in.

The obvious truth is, this process also is good for a busy dentist. It makes us slow down, allows us to take a breather, to enjoy a few minutes away from the drill and fill. I find myself looking forward to interacting with a truly interesting person, not just performing an exam for my hygienist so she can stay "on time." That's a significant aspect of what our boutique dental concept is all about, enjoying each moment of the day. Do you aspire to have more fun, have less stress, and to enjoy your day to the fullest every day? Then adopting this version of the New Patient Experience may just be for you!

The interview process' goal is to connect on two or three items in each section of my notes and see what "lights up" the patient. You're looking for their interest points or "buttons." The entire gamut of demographic, psychographic, and historical data is open for your review. You, as their new dentist, just want to connect with the patient as another human being at this time. When you sense that they are comfortable, you then move on to the actual dental examination part of their visit. A good segue to the dental operatory is to invite them to have their exam and any necessary radiographs.

THE INCOMPARABLE COMPREHENSIVE EXAM: NOW

Brandy, our new patient coordinator, is usually standing in the wings listening and at this time makes an appearance. What the next step for the new patient is discussed. Brandy then escorts the patient to the exam room and makes them comfortable, bibs them and puts the chair back, chatting all the way. I scrub up, glove up, and pull the light into place as the chair hits 30 degrees reclination. Our exam sequence is consistent with oral cancer screening, charting existing conditions, charting of carious lesions, periodontal probing of six areas per tooth, oral cancer screening, occlusal analysis, ortho and TMJ screening and finally, if warranted, a cosmetic evaluation. We may take a plaque sample from the deeper perio pockets and place it under a glass slide on our phase contrast microscope.

The patient then reviews a two sided diagram/chart showing (1) what normal versus pathological pockets are and (2) drawings of the shapes of spinning rods, gliding rods, spirochetes, amoebae, trichonomads, red and white blood cells as well as plaque matrix. We explain the significance of what is visible in the ceiling TV monitor which is displaying the video image from the microscope's camera.

Perhaps, when significant periodontal disease is discovered, we'll get into a discussion of the oral-systemic connection with the patient and offer advanced diagnostic testing with a combination of Oral DNA pathogen tests, patient inflammation reactivity DNA testing, or various blood tests.

I usually prescribe the type of hygiene/periodontal needs plus the type of next visit, usually a consultation, at this time. I can exit the room with a request to my assistant to take an FMX and/or Panoramic film, intraoral photographs and any additional test that is indicated. I always end the visit acknowledging their decision to complete the oral examination and radiographs and by telling them that I will be reviewing the information we gathered that night and that we will be typing up a consultation report for them which will list my findings and my recommendations, including everything they would want to know about time and cost and how insurance may assist them if they have it.

THE HANDOFF

I then move on to my next patient interaction. The staff completes the prescribed films, study models, or photographs with an intraoral/and or digital SLR camera. The new patient leaves with a good feeling, certainly cared for in a way never before experienced in a dental office. We reappoint them for a consult within a week.

> In conducting new patient examinations like the NPE for the past 25 years or more, we have found that the patients who go through the NPE purchase on average double that which patients who come through the dental hygiene program first. We feel that it is because of the patient's greater understanding of their treatment options and closer connection with us.

THE TREATMENT CONSULT

Upon their return, all new patients complete their consult with our Treatment Coordinator, Angie. She follows my consult notes verbatim,

(1) conditions,

(2) goals, and

(3) treatment recommendations.

Total cost and per tooth costs are estimated for each visit and the financial arrangements are handled at this time. At this point, I usually do not need to appear at the consultation. Angie always asks the patient if they wish to speak with me or ask me any more questions. I will stop in and ask the same question if I am in the area as they are concluding the consultation. Appointments are then made with both the dentist and/or hygienist. This is the end of the New Patient Experience and the beginning of a long and fruitful doctor-patient relationship.

One last note: In conducting new patient examinations like the NPE for the past 25 years or more, we have found that the patients who go through the NPE purchase on average double that which patients who come through the dental hygiene program first. We feel that it is because of the patient's greater understanding of their treatment options and closer connection with us.

In our next chapter, we will develop a case for the use of Direct Email in marketing the dental practice. The use of the new modes of moving information to potential and current clients will be fully explored.

TAKE-AWAY POINTS

- Our NPE is Our #1 Differentiator
- It is Unique and Scripted
- It Follows the Playbook
- The 5-Sense Experience for Patients
- Comments are Always Positive
- Results are Double Other Patient Intake Methods

CHAPTER 14

Direct Email

WHAT IS THE FASTEST GROWING MARKETING TECHNIQUE in America today? Direct email, without a doubt, is the winner. With over 90% of the people in the country now online daily and owning their own email address, the time has now come to access this huge opportunity to make another good first impression.

IN THE BEGINNING

For the first year and a half in my new practice, and every year since, I gathered the email addresses of every patient who entered our practice. On our health history/administrative form I also asked patients if they would like to receive my email newsletter. I developed a solid following of patients who like receiving information from me.

I had a choice, I could send the newsletter to all patients with email capability or just the ones who had "opted-in." I could create my own spam nightmare or could do it right. If you want to wreak havoc, send a direct email to all of the email addresses you can find in your practice area. Its classic spam and results in a 3-5% return on your time. You will also get one or two "bee-in-their-bonnet" Internet Purists who will "flame" you for infringing on "their" cyber "space." I wrote that last line or two quite a few years ago in one of my blogs, and in updating direct email information for this new marketing book, it's now officially illegal to spam someone and it can get you into big trouble. And by trouble I mean that your Internet provider can shut your email down completely.

LEAD GENERATION

The current focus in most marketing circles is now to put most of the effort into Lead Generation. Because of CanSpam laws, the way to get email into the hands of those potential customers whom you want to read it must follow a format that includes their opting-in and requesting information. Resources are available to put together entire campaigns to generate lists of potential new patients to send your marketing message. Of course the best way to get a person's email is to offer a free item they want such as a white paper, eBook, video, a PDF of a blueprint or a link to a free webinar.

Email is used to communicate. You are either trying to get new clients (acquisition) or keep your current ones (retention). With Lead Generation strategies you are working with sophisticated campaigns to build your base, and "fill the top of the sales funnel," so to speak. With email to existing clients, you are increasing sales on the one hand and on retention on the other. How would you use email for retention?

Email to a happy, excited current patient base is a winner. Your newsletter, the Molargram, for instance, can be sent in plain text or it can be formatted in HTML with color and graphics. To save on download time, you may choose to create your Molargram as a web page (in HTML, Java, .php etc.) and save it to a live web site. That way, you would only need to send your patients a link to the URL (uniform resource locator) or web page address for them to access it.

WHAT SHOULD YOU SEND THEM?

What would be the content of your Molargram? Same as a regular newsletter, except more up-to-date, targeted, and with hot links. Hot links are those text words in your document that are active, usually colored blue or some alternative color, different from the surrounding text, that when clicked with the mouse will take you to another Internet site or page. You could send a different version of your newsletter to children, men, women, executives, travelers, certain high school districts. Your only limitation is your imagination and your time. Cutting and pasting is a breeze these days. Your email list can be fractionated for demographic or psychographic effectiveness.

A good newsletter should be relatively short with links to allow a fuller, more detailed experience. Links to valued information is useful and appreciated. People want info #1. That means less hype and more news they can use. Got that? LESS HYPE, MORE NEWS they can use. Dental patients want to read about themselves... who won the stuffed animal (with the digital photo starring the lucky young patient, the stuffed animal in their grasp and the dentist, of course), who was in the No-Cavity Club, who referred the most patients last month, who won a local golf tournament, who won the city council election, etc.

> People want info #1. That means less hype and more news they can use. Got that? LESS HYPE, MORE NEWS they can use.

You could feature an athlete of the month, especially if you sponsor teams in the local area as we do. Do you remember the Local Links chapter? How many kids times how many parents would receive your Molargram? Give them a reason to come back to your web site each month. Return visits, recurring traffic should be one of your goals with your Molargram... increasing the links back to your much larger and informative web site. Each issue of your Molargram should have multiple hot links to pertinent web pages and info on your dental practice web site. Hot links are like spice; they make a dull meal interesting.

Include scientific articles written at a level that your patients can understand. Write articles about the new and improved techniques, services, and equipment that you now offer. Use the articles as an excuse to brag a bit.

A CALL TO ACTION

In every newsletter, include a "call to action." Attempt to "close the sale." Get your patient to see something on the newsletter and make a call to the office. Stimulate their interest. In this way, you monetize your newsletter. And, in business, monetization is what is needed to stay in business.

These are the pyramidal steps that a patient must take to make you successful: Information = Education = Interest = Consideration = Questions = Answers = Appointments = Sales (crowns, recare appointments) = Satisfied Customers = Referrals. The progression of the patient through this formula equals success for your practice. By activating the referral mechanism and lubricating it continually (some call this nurturing your herd), as with a newsletter or direct email campaign to interested patients, you can strongly enhance your bottom line.

Humor is important. Always include humor in your Molargram. Cartoons are best—any dental cartoon is worth a fortune—collect them and use them, if you have secured the rights to republish them. People love dental humor, especially if it's directed at the object of their disdain—the dentist.

If all this sounds like a good idea, start an online or email dental newsletter today! This is your homework, my request, if you do: please put me on your email list!

DIRECT MAIL CAMPAIGNS

Finally, you might attempt the coup de gras : a Direct Email campaign. Set up a systematic, automatic program for marketing your practice. One form of email campaign encourages your current patients to win frequent referral awards outright or at a discount for such items as a trip, a bicycle, a pair of roller blades, a TV, a stereo, a computer, whatever.

REWARDS PROGRAM FOR PATIENTS

Early in my practice in Suwanee, we created our own patient rewards program and gave away a few big trips and items as well as some flowers and movie tickets. Later, I beta-tested and became involved in the Loyal Patient Rewards program. Now, we use that program extensively with both our team and our patients. We have given away rewards each year totaling over $4 million in value. This is a strong loyalty program and I teach about it in depth in the Solstice 5M.

If you dedicate a certain percentage of your marketing budget to such a frequent referral award program, you would want to count both number of new patients referred and dollar volume resulting from those referrals. Your practice management software will track this and break it out for you in most cases. Others are available if not. One reason I like the Loyal Patient Rewards program is its turn-key system and done-for-you approach with no hassle for the doctor or team. All the numbers are presented to you daily. You're likely losing money if you don't know your numbers.

Here's how my original referral program worked. Say Sally Jones referred twelve people within the past year and those folks had $10,000 worth of dentistry completed. She would have a Frequent Referral Award (FRA) total of 22, one point for each of the twelve people she referred and one point for each $1,000 of dentistry you did on that group. Bob Smith referred five people who did $21,000 worth of dentistry, a FRA score of 26. Sam Strange sent fifteen people your way but they only got extractions or prophies for a total dollar value to the practice of $2,250. His FRA is 17. Bob wins the top award because you like working smarter not harder. You reward those best who send you the bigger cases.

My preference is to offer awards to the top three to five referrers. You be the arbiter of the method that you choose to tally the results. Quality and quantity, it all adds up to profits if your fee schedule is properly structured and your technical, behavioral and communicative skills are finely tuned and in daily use.

Here's another idea. You could make a concerted effort to "deliver quality dentistry" to impoverished, needy or out-of-luck individuals or families in the community based on your frequent referrer award program. Often, patients are more inspired if you give away dentistry to a needy person than to themselves. So, you could have a menu of referral numbers that add up to a specific dental service or dollar amount toward dental services that you could offer an individual or group of selected needy persons that your office selects.

This program would work especially well if your choice of the needy patient had email access and a significant group of friends who he or she regularly emails. The good public relations you receive from doing good deeds far outweighs the cost of providing care to them, in my opinion. And the cost of doing good is far outweighed by the benefits to your soul, too.

Still another wrinkle in the rewards program would be to allow the "winner" of the referral award be able to name or send a specific individual to your office for "free" dental care. That lucky individual could be a friend, a family member, a church or local charity-identified needy person to whom the "winner" wished to gift dental services. This could combine charity with good will and involve the community. Having the "rewards program winner" select the actual patient for whom the charity dentistry would be done would make them a double winner.

This line of thinking is exactly what led to the later development of our Deserving Diva Makeovers and the Deserving Diva Foundation. You'll be reading about those programs later in this book.

EXAMPLES OF EMAIL LETTERS YOUR PATIENTS COULD SEND

What would be an example of the proper message that could be sent out by your patients to their friends? Check these out and see if they taste sweet, sour or bitter to your taste buds. You are sure to have varying opinions. In the first set of examples here, imagine that your patients are sending emails along with your dental practice web site's URL.

Dear John,

This is weird. I never thought that I'd be emailing you about my dentist, but I am. I just wanted you to see his web site. We love it there.

<www.atlantagentledental.com>

See you at work,
Clark

Dear Susan,

I had a dream that you asked me who my new dentist was. Dr. Williams at Suwanee Dental Care across from Suwanee Elementary is great. You should look at all the things he does on his web site. <suwaneedental.com>.
Take care,
Robin

Hey Cecil, check this out <suwaneedentist.com>
He's great! He really helped me out in a jam. I can't
believe Dr. Williams came in on a weekend to see me.

Paschal

Hi Tommy, I got my braces on this week at Dr. Williams
office—look at his web site, its cool.

<www.suwaneesmiles.com>

Greg

Dear Mary,

I think we finally found the dentist of our dreams. Jennifer
and I were blown away by how nice Dr. Williams, the entire
staff and their office were. You should go there, too.

Betty
p.s. Great web site, too—<suwaneedental.com

(Now, the next concept to explore changes from a
positive statement and a small call to action to having
your patients sending your Molargram newsletter as an
attachment, forwarding it if you will, to their friends and
associates. Consider this viral method of gaining exposure
for your practice.)

Hey Cliff, here's our dentists newsletter—it's really great!
Tony (forwarded as an attachment)

Hey Barbara—thought you might want a copy
(forwarded as an attachment)

Joe… check this out (forwarded as an attachment)

ASK PATIENTS FOR FAVORS

Try to get your patients in the habit of forwarding your newsletter to as many of their friends as you can. If you are proactive, you can get them to help you build your mailing list just for your Molargram. Everyone has a small group with whom they love to share jokes, interesting stories, etc. Putting humor in your Molargram will insure some send it on and just maybe help it go viral. Just ask them (they must actually give permission) to send it out. If they are playing the frequent referral game, they may even ask you if they can forward your newsletter to their Email list.

Of course, be sure to have an opt-in box on each page of your newsletter so that you can capture the names of all who want to get copies of your newsletter in the future. Remember, too, a small "ethical bribe" such as the newsletter goes a long way to building your list. Include an offer that they can't refuse if you really want to get new opt-in names and addresses.

Direct email is an intriguing phenomenon. It's no longer in its infancy. To run a direct email campaign ranges from extremely inexpensive to free depending on your software program. It therefore has a phenomenal return on invested capital (ROIC). Because it's all digital, the "flip rate" of your marketing promotional piece, i.e. your Molargram, is also outstanding. It can be reproduced in its entirety, 100% perfect, without loss of content, color, or form by an endless string of end viewers. What other advertising medium is so perfectly reproducible? If creating multiple impressions is the key to successful marketing, then direct email is a step up the proverbial ladder.

The winners in Direct Email in dentistry will be the innovators. The first to arrive will not be overcome, if your content creators do quality, creative work from the beginning. The innovators will utilize opt-in boxes and autoresponders in their email and on their web sites. They will get info to potential and current patients within moments or as industry says, JIT (Just In Time). They will have an organized plan of informing their clients by email over a six month or yearly period, all with no effort on their part.

Direct email dentists will offer a video clip of their office on tour, a greeting from the doctor and staff members and even a clip of the Tooth Fairy speaking to kids.

Email postcards from the dentist have become the edge that more than a few dentists now use. How many dentists already have recall cards for hygiene on the net?

RESOURCES WE HAVE USED AND RECOMMEND

How many use email and even text message appointment reminders from Demand Force, Smile Reminder, Lighthouse 360, Yodle or their practice management system? Most in this day and time. The future—is now, it's already the norm in progressive practices.

Let me put a bug in your ear. Look for one of the most innovative companies I work with, Infusionsoft, to put out the ultimate in email campaigns for dentistry. When it arrives, it will be a game changer! As of this printing, the dental plug-in for Infusionsoft has already been released into a beta version in dental offices across the country.

In the next chapter, we will study how to activate your affinity groups in marketing the dental practice. The power of networking your non-dental contacts from years past and times present to manufacture clients will be fully explored.

TAKE-AWAY POINTS

- Build Your Opt-In List
- Write a Quality Newsletter to Keep in Regular Contact
- Have Personal Sharing So Patients Know You Better
- Include News They Can Use and Humor
- Use Loyal Patient Rewards and Savings Programs
- Ask For Referrals
- Be Proactive

CHAPTER 15

Affinity Groups

*M*OST SUCCESSFUL PROFESSIONALS built their practices on hard work and long hours. They maintain those practices on reputation. What better way could there be than to tap into a shared positive reputation by marketing your practice to your own affinity groups? By the end of this chapter, you'll see how to attract these folks to your web site.

MEMBERSHIP HAS ITS PRIVILEGES

An affinity group is one to which you belong, identify with, and hopefully one in which you are active. Marketing the practice is not just about being a dentist. My affinity groups, for instance, are the Boy Scouts of America (I was a Cub Scout, Boy Scout, Explorer Scout, Order of the Arrow and an Eagle Scout and each provides an opportunity for a separate affinity connection), Alpha Phi Omega service fraternity, Beta Theta Pi social fraternity, Auburn University alumni, the Medical College of Georgia alumni, three separate high school alumni groups in Tennessee, Mississippi and Alabama, Rotary International, Amway distributors, Life Plus distributors, Sugar Hill United Methodist Church members, Tucker Youth Football League coaches and players, North Gwinnett Football Boosters group, Collins Hill High School Soccer team, Morningview Civic Association members, PowerCore's North Gwinnett Team, my Bible Study Fellowship group, the Gwinnett Chamber of Commerce Chairman's Club, my Facebook friends, Linked-In connections, my Pinterest followers etc., etc., etc.

Can you make a list of all the important affinity groups in your life? Do you remember who was in each? Do they remember you? Mining your affinity groups for business contacts can happen in a simple and non-threatening way.

CREDIBILITY

Being a part of an affinity group gives you instant credibility in many peoples' eyes because you share common beliefs, goals and aspirations. People feel that they already know you within the group. Belonging raises visibility. Being active assures you of high visibility. This visibility can be a double-edged sword, however, so, be careful. People are watching us as professionals. They expect us to lead. They are critical judges and extrapolate our group interactions to mirror our clinical care, skill and judgment in the dental environment.

I don't think it's necessary to remind you that your MySpace or Facebook persona will be available to your affinity group members and the rest of the world for years to come. Let's hope that you have always acted kind and civil online!

You can establish your presence in an affinity group as a current member or as a previous member from years past. With the Internet, I have re-established connections with scores of individuals who I knew in school as far back as 46 years ago. I went to three 30 year reunions, to high schools I attended in Auburn, Alabama in the 7th and 8th grades, Clinton, Mississippi in the 9th and 10th grades and finally from where I graduated from high school, Bartlett, Tennessee, a suburb of Memphis.

HOW TO BENEFIT FROM BEING A MEMBER

First, to take advantage of affinity marketing, you need a web site. It could be your personal family web site or your practice web site. For instance, on your "Meet the Doctor" page, you can place customized biographical data to include much more than just your dental curriculum vitae. Include family information, membership information, clubs, associations and other business interests there if you are so inclined. Download a logo from your affinity group when possible and create links to those groups located on your personal biography page. Be a resource to those looking to connect.

The inclusion of these affinity groups has two positive results. One, people read the information and see that you are an interesting person who has been around, seen life from several perspectives and hopefully they get a warmth about you before they ever meet you. We receive many patients who identify with me as an Auburn graduate, a member of my fraternity, or a native of a country where we do dental missions each year, etc.

Also, they may be searching the Internet for information on one of those groups and find your link if you submitted it to the 1200 or more search engines on the web. If that occurs, you get a hit on your "Meet the Doctor" web page within the practice web site. Since the average time spent on a page is only one minute, there is the possibility that they will recognize the logo of the affinity group first and then your name, your location, and perhaps remember you if and when their dental antennae goes up and they need some help.

What I am saying is that affinity groups listed on your web site will pull people to your dental practice through carefully planned marketing strategies. I am also indicating that denoting affinity groups to which you belong will create warm fuzzies in those who are evaluating you as

> Trust, quality results, follow through and above-average ability to deliver the goods are the most highly regarded attributes listed in choosing a dentist.

a potential dentist. Membership has its privileges and one of them is certainly trust. Trust, quality results, follow-through and above-average ability to deliver the goods are the most highly regarded attributes listed in choosing a dentist. Where would you rate on these characteristics compared to the other dentists in your locale? What differentiates you from the pack?

How can you become an active member of an affinity group? Join them, go to meetings, post online, contribute to blogs and newsletters, become a leader. Visibility is assured because every group needs workers and leaders, Indians and chiefs. Between fraternal, service, neighborhood, civic, political, sports and recreational groups, there is no shortage of opportunities to be active and be seen.

Don't want to get out that much? Been there, done that? Well, you could cash in on your previous relationships via the Internet and some email. There are plenty of "communities" on the web which are basically both large and small affinity groups. Hang out in several of these communities via chat rooms, mailing lists, email, or forums and you soon develop many new friends based on old associations.

ALTERNATIVE WAYS TO BE PART OF AN AFFINITY GROUP

Chat rooms were hugely popular on AOL, CompuServe, MIRC, and the like back in the 1980's and 1990's. Topics of each "room" range A-Z, colorful to off-color and are most useful if you frequent local chat rooms. I equate them to Cheers, "where everybody knows your name" once you have been there a while.

Early in the practice years, communities like eGroups, Tripod, GeoCities, MyFreeOffice, YahooGroups, etc. offered predefined groups that you could join and participate in at the birth of the Internet. They allowed one to start their own affinity group. Now, Google +, Facebook, and LinkedIn groups give the same opportunity.

Before there was the World Wide Web, there were news groups and Usenet. These are basically the largest collection of affinity groups on the Internet. There are still thousands of groups to browse. You can access them with a news browser like those included in Internet Explorer.

Today, web interaction and affinity groups are changing, and are now dominated by Facebook, Twitter, Instagram, Pinterest and LinkedIn. Google+ is a rising player in the social media networking field, so do not fail to follow its relevance.

As with any group situation, you can decide to be either active or passive. You can send email advice on genealogy. You can attend local political party meetings. You can start a "humor list" and email funny stories/jokes on to your buddies. You can subscribe to many newsletters and contribute to your group with photos, videos, blog posts, status updates and articles yourself.

EXPAND YOUR INFLUENCE

Don't just limit your concept to your own immediate affinity groups. For example, my wife and I have been BSF (Bible Study Fellowship) study leaders and we have received many requests for dental advice and treatment from those who know us from this association.

Also, remember your children's friends, their parents and friends of friends. The circle is ever widening and knows no bounds.My son, Justin, is a re-enactor of Civil War battles. I participate as an observer on the sidelines and am thus a part of that affinity group. Tyler, our youngest son played on the 9th grade football team so we signed up as "Platinum Level Boosters."

For $800 donated to the North Gwinnett Football program, we got four season tickets, a stadium blanket, a full-page advertisement in every home game program, two long sleeve denim shirts with a Bulldog logo, two polo Bulldog shirts and a premium parking pass. Best of all, we got an introduction on the field at the 50-yard line at half time of the first game of the season. That investment has paid for itself over and over again.

Both sons are soccer goalies for different teams. We have performed dental treatment on players from football, baseball, soccer, paint ball, and roller hockey teams over the years due to our sons' participation. It may start with a good deal on a custom mouth guard but over time, there are prophies, fillings, orthodontics, third molars, and bleaching before weddings. Soon enough there are brides and later babies. We have three generations of patients from one family after 36 years in practice. That is certainly one of the joys of being a dentist, seeing families grow.

I have to add another affinity group this year, the Atlanta Braves. On of my little patients has grown up, graduated from high school, and gotten drafted by the Braves. He was the third best pitcher in the rookie leagues this year. Of course he has great teeth, too. Another Atlanta Brave became a patient this year. He plays second base in the majors. I'd tell you who he is, but then I'd have to… well, you know what HIPPA laws say about that. Now I have to add an Atlanta Brave link to my home page. I wonder if the local fan club has a web site?

So, affinity groups should now be very clear in your mind. You can mine this gold on the Internet or out in the community. The choice is yours. Don't ignore this valuable commodity. Let your webmaster know if you need to add affinity groups to your web site.

In the next chapter of *Marketing The Million Dollar Practice*, we explore the value of neighborhood directories. This is a print medium with enormous staying power,

capable of creating numerous visual impressions, the
lifeblood of marketing success.

TAKE AWAY POINTS

- Access Your Affinity Groups
- Look For Connection Points
- Activate the Law Of Attraction
- Join Groups And Participate
- Go Beyond "Dental" Groups
- Enlist Your Whole Team

CHAPTER 16

Neighborhood Directories

VERY LOCAL ADVERTISING

BEAT YOUR COMPETITION to the punch with "VLA" (Very Local Advertising). Speaking of target marketing; this is the niche of all niches to dominate. If you do family dentistry, a two hundred dollar ad can make 1,000 impressions on homeowners in your nearest neighborhood. In a growing, new subdivision, that can mean 100 or more families in a year who choose your practice.

Can you name any other medium that when introduced into a home, is always looked at, thoroughly read, and kept on the den or kitchen desk for a year or longer? Okay, refrigerator magnets may offer a similar profile, but you should already be doing that one. You do need a good deal on magnets, lots of magnets. But, this is a chapter about directories, not magnets.

The ideal way to get into the homes of exclusive subdivisions is with neighborhood directories that are authorized by the neighborhood but sponsored by local businesses. Each current resident and all new residents are given a complete directory of their neighbors, listed by name and by street number. They often list the children's names and

> The ideal way to get into the homes of exclusive subdivisions is with neighborhood directories that are authorized by the neighborhood but sponsored by local businesses.

ages, who does baby sitting, lawn care, pet sitting, and similar info. Being in the directory is actually seen by new residents as an endorsement of sorts. Talk about the power of association, this is it. And often, you will be the only dentist in the entire directory.

COUPONS BRING IN MORE BUSINESS

Here are the specifics on one type of Neighborhood Directory. Advertisers (sponsors) are grouped in the book: retail, medical/dental, restaurants, and services. Tabs make it easy to locate each sponsor group. Tear-out coupons in the back of the directory create additional traffic for those sponsors who wish to utilize this marketing technique. Each sponsor also appears on an index page of all professional practices along with their phone number. So, in this format of neighborhood directory, there are at least three separate and distinct listing areas for the practice's name, their unique message, their web site address and their phone number.

How many large housing developments are within a ten-mile radius of your practice? How many have a neighborhood association? That is how many opportunities are immediately available for this marketing method. Commercial outfits vie for the opportunity to produce these directories. If one has not been developed in your area, there soon will be. Perhaps you could spearhead the effort. Certainly germinating the seeds of their success would be favorable for your practice. The cost of advertising in these types of directories is between $.25 and $.40 per household. That's less than a postage stamp and the results are a whole lot better!

What if your neighborhood does not have an association that is able, willing or is not very well defined? This may be the case in a more urban or more rural setting. We recently had a similar opportunity to place an ad in a "town" directory. The "City of Suwanee" directory was based on our local area, carried interesting data about Suwanee, Georgia, a growing community of 25,000 in the northeastern suburbs of Atlanta. No residents' names or addresses were listed in this directory as in the neighborhood directory, but the spiral bound desk calendar book fills a similar need for many in the community. It has useful governmental and civic information. It has a place for frequently called phone numbers, note-taking areas, local maps, photos, and local business sponsor advertisements. A number of these books are given out free to all sponsors who in turn give them out to their customers. The Suwanee City Hall and the Gwinnett Chamber of Commerce print several thousand books to give to residents and potential residents who are seeking information on the city.

KEEPERS STIMULATE REPEAT BUSINESS

In marketing your practice, look for "keepers." I define keepers, not surprisingly, as "things you give to people that they keep." If a client or potential client keeps an item that has your logo, name, web address, or phone number, that item helps build your familiarity with them. This is called "branding." When they need a dentist, you want them to think of you. Coffee cups, pens and pencils, toothbrushes, refrigerator magnets, calendars, phone books all qualify as keepers. Get your name, phone number and address on these types of items and find a way to get them in use around your community.

The power of personal referral takes over and your requirements for external marketing change once your practice name is branded in the minds of your local community. Remember, external marketing must be your first focus if you do not have a ton of patients yet. Once you have a host of happy clients, internal, referral-based marketing can provide over 50% of your new patients.

In the next chapter we will develop a case for the use of auto-responders and other sophisticated software, like Infusionsoft, in marketing the dental practice. The use of this mode of moving information quickly to potential and current clients will be fully explored.

TAKE-AWAY POINTS

- VLA: Very Local Advertising
- Refrigerator Magnets and Keepers Work
- Be Recommended By Residents
- Branding Pays Off
- Link With Logo to Your Practice Website

CHAPTER 17

Autoresponders

EMBRACING AUTOMATION

*I*N PREVIOUS CHAPTERS I tout direct email, email
letters of introduction, and routine newsletters. Now, I
want to concentrate on a subset of the Internet /
email genre of marketing techniques called the email
autoresponder. We'll explore in this chapter what is on the
forefront of marketing the dental practice that involves
automation. When thinking about an autoresponder, think
in terms of a whole system as opposed to a single reply to
your email.

An email autoresponder system is basically a kind of
"robot" that resides on your web site's server or in the cloud
network waiting for someone to send it an email message. If
you called them webbots, you would be technically accurate.
Webbots stand as sentries watching over your web site, your
business for email and callers from afar. They do not eat and
never sleep. They work overtime without complaining. They
won't ask for a raise or call in sick. Also, they are memory
residents on your server; they work without you having to
turn them on or activate them after you set them up.

How does a webbot sequence get called or started? They
are identified by specified email addresses. Say your web
site domain is smile.com. The email address sendinfo@
smile.com could be locked into the autoresponder webbot's
memory as a signal to wake up and get into action. Once
activated, the action of the autoresponder could be to return
a pre-planned message by return email to the sender. The
autoresponder works by reflecting a new message back to

where the incoming message originated.

An email autoresponder is also sometimes referred to as "mail reflector" or "mailbot." Since it is a software program running on the host server, it can be programmed to receive email from anyone and then automatically and immediately responds by emailing them a pre-programmed message. Email autoresponders were initially used for distributing small text-based information packets or to simply acknowledge that a message was received. (Example: "Your request for an appointment was received. We will review our schedule for the day you requested and call or email you shortly.")

IN THE DENTAL PRACTICE

In a dental practice setting, an autoresponder could be set up to send a basic info piece about the practice, the doctor, or a requested appointment. You could also send an email message of brief, pertinent information on your practice with links to your web site and a link leading to another webbot message. Most autoresponders in your email system send one message from one request. This type of autoresponder is often included free with hosted web site accounts if you want to configure it for your own use.

> More advanced auto responders offer ways to answer email and send messages that lead to a series of options, each tied to another autoresponder. This is essentially a decision tree and can lead a patient to a specific desired outcome.

The simplest autoresponder lets patients know that you are out of contact for a specific period of time and will not be answering email messages. Perhaps you have received some of these when corporate leaders are on vacation. All email accounts use this feature.

More advanced auto responders offer ways to answer email and send messages that lead to a series of options, each tied to another autoresponder. This is essentially a decision tree and can lead a patient to a specific desired outcome. These are the wave of the future in marketing and will become more prominent over the next years. The value of this is that it moves the email from a single event to the level of multichannel, multimedia campaign, the holy grail of marketing.

For the savvy marketer, this special brand of autoresponder makes a series of emails, SMS text messages replies and notifications for the dentist or staff that these events took place. There are continual advancements to make this approach much more useful for follow-up messages. Consider the advantage of a potential dental customer emailing you to request information on a procedure that looked interesting, say tooth bleaching with your Sapphire Whitening System. What if the inquiring patient received an informative reply in their email account within 20 seconds of sending their initial email to you? And, then, what if the same person got another email one day later offering details on another alternative system, Night White? And, what if a third, fourth, fifth and sixth message arrived via email about bonding, veneers, instant orthodontics, and fresh breath products and therapy.

THE VALUE OF FOLLOW-UP

What would it be worth for the practice to automatically be able to send this information to an unlimited number of callers with absolutely no work on your part? What if this hypothetical autoresponder system also emailed videos, PDF's, and text messages to smart phones? Do you see an application for this in your practice or on your web site?

We do much of this with our Lighthouse 360 connection to our patient communications programs in our practice management software right now. We did it years ago with Smile Reminders, Demand Force and the like.

In the chapter on direct email, I mentioned Infusionsoft, a company that I work with in my Solstice Dental Advisors coaching and consulting business. Their's is an integrated client communication and marketing solution that ties all of these factors together and adds the following features to the current autoresponder options:

1. Collect names, email addresses and phone numbers (or whatever you ask for) from multiple opt-in pages related to multiple topics of patient interest on multiple web sites.

2. Push a series of emails to them to get a free consult, video, white paper, eBook, to deploy the Law of Reciprocity.

3. Nurtures the email list that is being built with email management online software like Constant Contact, Mail Chimp, Aweber or iContact.

4. Monitors activity until they either respond by moving forward or the automated system judges them to be a lost cause and drops them from the active system of contacts. They never leave the system or are forgotten until the person actually opts out of the system by telling the system to do that.

5. Appointments can be scheduled and reminders sent. The outcome of the appointment can be gleaned from the system and another series of autoresponder emails can be initiated.

6. New Patient Welcome letters can be sent.

7. Pre-New Patient Appointment letters or packets can be emailed or mailed to the patient by a reminder being sent to the dental team. If a patient has responded to a particular topic, say dental implants,

they can be sent detailed articles and videos on dental implants from your library.

8. Before and after photos and video testimonials can be sent to the new patient using cases similar to theirs.

9. After the consultation appointment, follow up can be sent to reinforce the treatment plan. A regular sales pipeline can be enacted to follow-up on the in-person interview and consult, assuring that no one gets forgotten or falls between the cracks.

10. Email follow-up on specific areas can help overcome objections, such as dealing with phobias, financial issues and time issues.

11. Requests for patient testimonials can be sent.

12. Links to social media sites can increase the footprint of your marketing efforts.

13. All of this is automated and occurs without the dentists or staff inputting new data at each turn.

14. Reports are created at any time and regularly sent automatically to your email inbox for evaluation.

15. A dashboard allows quick and easy assessment of where your campaign is at the moment. You know how many patients have opened their email, how many read it to the end, where they opted-in and who has not opened their email. Tracking the flow of communication is a chief feature of the new automated campaigns from Infusionsoft. The dentist and dental team get a series of reports on how many clients are opting in and accessing their information... at each step of the sequence.

16. Best of all, this setup can be "done-for-you" by trained specialists. All you have to do is to give them the basic content you want in each message. There are templates available using successful campaigns that you can purchase if you do not want to do it yourself.

In our next chapter we will explain the principles behind the success of the group known as PowerCore. As a member of the North Gwinnett PowerCore Group, I have experienced dramatic results from my participation in this local referral networking group in marketing our practice. The best part of it is the strength of the referrals and the low cost.

TAKE-AWAY POINTS

- Employ Robot Autoresponders
- String Messages Together Into Campaigns
- Empower Customers to Make Choices
- Design a Marketing Campaign with Lighthouse 360
- Look For Infusionsoft to Enter the Dental Field

CHAPTER 18

PowerCore: Networking Teams

L EARN HOW TO GENERATE NEW BUSINESS with professional networking organizations. For example, I am a member of PowerCore, a professional networking organization which generates referral business and teaches the follow-through systems to support it. I have been an amateur networker for years, even decades, but this is the first professional networking team that I have joined.

CLOSE-CONTACT NETWORKING

PowerCore is called a lead generation network. The idea is to engage in "close-contact" networking. These kinds of groups are wonderful for small businesses and professionals who survive on leads. Lead network groups are gatherings of individuals of about ten to twenty to a group, who meet with the express purpose of passing qualified leads to the other members. Usually these groups are "category protected," which means that only one person per profession or business category is allowed to join each network group. The groups typically meet on a weekly basis.

PowerCore is one of the largest groups of its kind in the country, with 100 clubs and about 2,000 members. There are at least 23 groups in Atlanta with a total of 500 members. My team is the North Gwinnett team and meets at 7:00 a.m. on Wednesdays.

Statistics show that sixty percent of leads will close

when accompanied by a referral name. That number grows to ninety percent if a third party actually sets up the appointment. Compare that with cold calling, which has a closure rate of approximately one in 100.

POWERCORE MEETING AGENDA

Meetings follow a standardized business-like protocol:
1. Each person, including any guests, have one minute for a company infomercial, ending in the phrase "and a good lead for me is…." The one minute time limit is excellent practice for actual patient consults because research shows that the first minute of a sales presentation is often the most important in attracting a prospect's attention.
2. Two members from each week's group are given seven minutes each for more lengthy self-presentations. This is a time when lots of details can be shared with the group about your profession and your individual skills and abilities.
3. Each member is then given one minute to provide a referral to the group. The meeting is over at 8:30 am sharp.

A GOOD REFERRAL IS…

A good referral results when a team member sets up a meeting between you and the person with whom you can do business. For example, "I'm doing business with this person now. I'll have him call you. Expect his call." Many members give ten to fifteen referrals per month in their team. In the training, there is an opportunity each week to say to your group, "A good referral is someone who….," and you just fill in the blank with the exact type person you want referred to you.

Now, what is specifically interesting about this marketing format as far as dentists are concerned is that the warmth of the referral is very high. They are usually ready to become a patient. The quality of referrals I have received in PowerCore are excellent. The group consists of knowledgeable, committed business people who are actively working to enroll patients into our practices. In PowerCore, when you give, you get. The Golden Rule applies supremely here, "Do unto others as you would have them do unto you."

I noticed, after being a member of Power Core for a year, that the spheres of influence that I began to tap into were much higher than the referrals outside of the group. All of the people in my PowerCore group, are potential clients for me now. And their own business networks, where the majority of their referrals come from, all have dental needs. It is powerful to have a local community referral network of 15 to 20 people out on the streets and in the corridors of business listening for opportunities and looking for leads to pass along to me. That is the method and the goal of Power Core membership.

> All of the people in my PowerCore group, are potential clients for me now. And their own business networks, where the majority of their referrals come from, all have dental needs.

By the nature of our business as dentists we get to know our clients truly "up close and personal." Therefore, we track their comings and goings, their families and their jobs. It is a great way to be of service to refer them to the best people in every category when they have a need, such as an attorney, a landscaper or carpet cleaner, etc. Because of PowerCore, we have excellent referrals for services in our neighborhood and can readily recommend them. We keep a book of business cards in our reception room for such referrals.

Close contact networking may be the right technique at the right time for your practice. Networking face-to-face is a return to the proven, yet oft-neglected, concept of relationship selling. With the increasing clutter of email, direct mail and increasingly larger and more expensive Yellow Page ads, dentists are having to pay for more just to keep up with the competition. Lead networking could be the answer.

To contact the PowerCore team nearest you look on the Internet at www.powercore.net. Much of the information I've passed on to you here is from that site. There you will find the Atlanta web site and an email address to the area director. That is the best resource I know at this time. If you are ready to expand your horizons, consider joining one of the many local network groups.

In our next chapter, we will study the phenomenon of "word-of-mouth referrals" in marketing the practice. The power of networking with your current patients to bring you additional patients will be a topic of high interest to all of you because in a mature practice, this is the number one method of generating new patients.

Ask your team to become involved. Nothing succeeds like an army of marketers canvassing the land. Prepare for the meeting by evaluating how you bring new patients into your practice. Are they generated by leads from others? Again, look to see if you are on a glide path to your goals or do you have to change something to get there. Consider having several members of your team joining different local networking groups. If you do a Google search of the keywords of "networking groups" in "your town," you will come up with a score of them. Don't forget the online groups like MeetUpGroups, too.

TAKE-AWAY POINTS

- Join Local Networking Groups
- Lead Generation is Important to Your Future
- Get Properly Trained to Network
- Follow the Protocol
- Give Referrals to Get Referrals
- Expand Your Sphere of Influence

CHAPTER 19

Word-of-Mouth Advertising

NUGGETS OF GOLD ARE EVERYWHERE

A GRIZZLED, OLD, FLORIDA PANHANDLE FISHING GUIDE taught me to heed this old Apalachicola saying when I was a boy:

"When the wind is from the East, the fishing is the least; when the wind is from the West, the fishing is the best; when the wind is from the North, the fisherman do not go forth; and when the wind is from the South, it blows the hook in the fishs' mouth."

With favorable winds, dentistry is a lot like fishing. Once the proper climate has been established, the magic money machine of marketing, word-of-mouth, can be realized.

KNOW YOUR TERRITORY

Like the points on a compass, our marketing strategies to date have circled the practice in a global approach with, of course, the web site as the center of the magnetic needle. Each strategic point or direction has had a specific purpose, a specific niche to fill in completing the WebCentric Marketing Action Plan.

For instance, the Seven Mountains of Marketing, a strategy we developed to capture territory in our practice area, would be one of the ways of looking at your market and segmenting it into spheres of influence. More on that concept later.

From our previous chapters, you already know that an orderly step-by-step approach was taken to introduce our new practice to our new Suwanee location. Over the first year and a half that the WebCentric MAP was in operation in our practice, we became a thriving, nearly mature, practice. We hired our fourth full-time employee and were into our third six-month recall cycle. Having a strong, if not brief history, a loyal clientele, and a patient base to work from, there are a number of salient features to talk about and show how we implemented a specific "word-of-mouth patient referral" (WOMP) strategy to our marketing mix.

Remember, this is for a startup practice that is only a few years into its business development at this point. This one strategy created 300 of the new patients we have seen in the past 12 months. That is 33% of our total new patients for this time period.

WOMP IS THE BEST MARKETING A PRACTICE CAN HAVE

We believe "WOMP" is like a gentle southeasterly breeze—it is low-key marketing at its best and it blows the hook right in the patient's mouth. WOMP is completely passive in most practices. Your existing patients, or those who know of you through your reputation and your visibility based on your other marketing efforts, create it independently.

Just like yummy bait to a tuna, a southerly word-of-message is swallowed by schools of "patient" fish and , before they know it, they are hooked on your practice. For a new dental practice, this is the blessed west wind. It is marketing at its best. Its free, its easy and its worth more than any other because of its believability.

Jay Levinson and Charles Rubin say this about word-of-mouth value in their book, Online Marketing, "Satisfied customers are the mother lode of marketing, the font of referrals, goodwill and one-to-one promotion of your business. Satisfied customers often buy again, and they also work for you as unpaid members of your marketing team, spreading the good news about your business to friends and relatives." They promote customer satisfaction as the key to this successful tactic and that there are four proven ways to convert satisfied customers into repeat buyers and active promoters of your business:

1. Give them the "high five" by saying thank you. Do it three times: when you see them in the office for their dental visit, when they get home by either a personal hand written note or email, and then whenever they refer someone. Of course the best of all tactics for bonding to your patient is the post-op telephone call.

2. Show your smile: If you are happy around your clients and they know that they are the cause of your happiness, they will try to duplicate their efforts. Show your appreciation for your patients' visits and their referrals by offering special services, discounts, gifts, or extra office hours to repeat buyers and repeat referrers. It's your choice. Remember, people love to be recognized for their efforts.

3. Develop a referral card: Send out promotional information to your current clients to highlight specific services and encourage referrals. For current patients, create a card that they can give to possible patients as a special gift that offers a special discount or service.

4. Offer a referral reward: As we spoke about in the direct email chapter, a frequent referral program is a winner if the people know about it and it is utilized. "One positive comment about your business from one

friend to another is worth thousands of dollars that
you might spend in advertising to reach that same
person," writes Levinson. "Find ways to convert your
satisfied customers into repeaters and promoters, and
you'll be using one of the most powerful weapons at
your disposal."

So far, we have identified what "WOMP" is and what is
the end goal—repeat customers and referrals. But, other
than the reward systems, what are the key ways to stimulate
this vital southeasterly wind?

WHAT'S IN THE ATMOSPHERE?

Start with the atmosphere. What is the atmosphere in
your practice? Is there a detectable odor of unhappiness,
gloom, oppression or even disdain for the patient? Or, is
there an attitude of excitement that greets each patient,
welcomes him or her with open arms?

Attitudes are the superstructure that your marketing
program is built upon. Good attitudes pay and pay well.
Therefore, the work of leadership is to create, stimulate and
maintain good attitudes in the office. They are contagious—
from staff member to staff member, from staff to patient and
hopefully, through WOMP, advertising and referrals, patient
to future patient out in the community.

If attitude is the west wind, then enthusiasm is the
south wind. Enthusiasm about your practice, your services,
your skills, your state-of-the-art equipment, your web site,
your staff, your community will all blow the hook into the
fish's mouth. If your staff is thoroughly trained and highly
knowledgeable about your superior offerings to patients,
then they will be enthusiastic and contagious. If your staff is
rewarded properly for their efforts, they will be enthusiastic.

THE HAPPY, EDUCATED PATIENT

Likewise, if your patients are educated about the exquisite detail and degree of workmanship put into their care, they will be enthusiastic. If your patients perceive your empathy, your gentleness, your confidence and your thoroughness, they will be enthusiastic supporters of the practice.

A happy, educated, enthusiastic patient is a referring dynamo. Give them the tools (such as your business cards, practice brochures, web site address, social media connections) and watch them go. Attitude plus enthusiasm equals a steady southeast wind for years to come. Add in a reward system and the gentle breeze turns into a gale force strong enough to blow away the competition.

WOMP advertising is the lifeblood of the mature practice. It can be generated immediately in the new practice as we have shown, and rapidly build momentum to become the number one referral source of all your marketing efforts. Build it, and they will come.

What ensures that you have maximized word-of-mouth advertising and a constant southeast wind? Survey the attitudes and enthusiasm exhibited in your practice. Implement strategic fixes if needed. Hire more "party animals" is my suggestion, more of the "I" personality types! Work on the nuts and bolts of your patient satisfaction quotient and look into a frequent referrer program such as Loyal Patient Rewards.

Next in *Marketing The Million Dollar Practice* we will dig even deeper into WOMP as a source of

> Survey the attitudes and enthusiasm exhibited in your practice. Implement strategic fixes if needed. Hire more "party animals" is my suggestion, more of the "I" personality types!

practice growth and development.

Why the double emphasis on W-O-M-P...? because it is the best form of marketing you can have. Over 50% of your new patients should be coming from this vital source. Therefore, we all need more W-O-M-P!

TAKE-AWAY POINTS

- Create The Environment For Success
- Promote Word-of-Mouth, WOMP, Activity
- Reward Those Who Do It

CHAPTER 20

Word-of-Mouth Patient Referrals

GENESIS

*I*N THE BEGINNING, there was no Word-of-Mouth, then God said, "Let there be W-O-M," and He saw that it was good. Then He created Dental Patients and said, "Go into all the world and proclaim the Good Word." So, then, W-O-M-P was in the world and began as the first marketing activity.

I don't know where you stand on the evolution versus creation debate, but I do know that taking a proactive role in your practice to create a successful word-of-mouth marketing campaign is far better than just letting it evolve from that primordial soup kitchen called "the new practice." Mature practices get the majority of their new patients from Word-of-Mouth Patient (WOMP) referrals. The goal of a new practice is to get as quickly as possible to a self-sustaining level of new patients through WOMP.

WHY WOMP WINS

There are three reasons WOMP referrals are superior to all other referrals:
1. They are basically cost-free to you
2. They are more powerful than other methods because of their third-party credibility

3. They are capable of growing geometrically with no
    huge effort on your part.

The power of geometric progression assures the
competent quality dentist a steady stream of new patients.
Once the pump is primed, it flows. You've heard that every
satisfied patient tells an average of seven people. You've also
heard that every dissatisfied customer is more vocal and tells
20 people their sad tale. The key to building positive vibes
in the community is to do everything necessary to keep
people happy, even at the expense of eating some crow or
re-doing some dentistry.

With the help of geometric progression, it takes time
for the WOMP Referral Team to become the number-one
referral source in a practice—a couple of years on average.
Fully one third of our referrals were due to WOMP referrals
after two years in Suwanee. That means 20-25 patients a
month are from patients' referrals. One interesting point
of note is that not all of the people who refer us are our
patients. Reputation and branding have created a group of
referrers who are not yet patients in our practice.

The power of WOMP referral marketing is its credibility.
When a third person recommends you, it adds to the belief
of the referee that you are a doctor worth seeing. The secret
of WOMP referral marketing is to leverage it against your
other marketing efforts such as the web presence in all its
activities, direct mail, your sign and your social media. If
WOMP referral marketing is the third or fourth impression,
it translates into the "hundredth monkey." (Get the small
book, *The Hundredth Monkey,* to understand the power of
knowledge and paradigm shifts.) In that book, as soon as
the group dynamics decided that a new idea was good for
the majority, all of the primates decided to move in unison.
Marketing is like that. When critical mass is reached in your
community, outstanding results, such as a sudden influx of
new patients, just miraculously happen.

FREE IS GOOD

Another terrific aspect of WOMP referral marketing is that it is FREE. Sure you can encourage it with campaigns that have a cost, but the actual method of referral is generally dependent on others and is done at their whim at no cost to you. The flip side is that it's also done with no obligation to you. Thus, the trade-off for free is lack of control. The trade for lack of control is more credibility for you. That's more than fair if you promote this good will with your gratitude for their efforts to support you and your practice.

PROMOTIONS TO STIMULATE REFERRALS

How do you promote WOMP referrals? First of all, you need to know why people refer. You need to know your sales psychology. Your patients who actually refer to you are satisfied, impressed, excited, or rewarded. Create that situation and you increase your WOMP referrals. Patients are satisfied when their treatment is on time and a good value. They are impressed when their treatment is painless, of higher than usual quality and naturalness, and when the practice is high tech and state-of-the-art. And finally, patients are excited when the doctor and staff treat them like real, important people who are valued as customers.

You don't need to reward your clients to get them to refer, but it does help. We've done it for over 25 years, ever since our computer could track the number of referrals per patient. Small gifts go a long way to recognize their efforts. Movie tickets are a winner. We buy bulk movie ticket packages for 40% off.

Some dentists don't get as many referrals as other dentists and wonder why. Some dentists need to manage their own bad breath better. Some need to cultivate a pleasant personality and the ability to listen to their patients. Others need to learn a painless injection technique. Do you know any other specifics that some dentists need to learn? The list is likely to be quite long. When a dentist is his or her own worst enemy, someone needs to tell them the hard truth.

Another reason some dentists don't get many referrals is that they don't ask for them. The old saying is, "If you don't have, it's because you haven't asked."

W-O-M-P referrals are the MVP of referrals, so make it easy for your patients to connect people to your practice. Give them the tools and make your practice memorable. With a good practice name, your business cards in their hands, an easily found Yellow Page ad and an in-depth web site, Facebook page, Google+ page and Twitter setup, your patients can become first class referrers.

You must train them to know your web address. Make it easy. We just added another URL to suwaneedental.com, the main domain name we use, to make it easier for our patients to remember and also easy to refer. Think about it, which is easier to remember, wbwilliams.com or suwaneedental.com or atlantagentledental.com? Which one tells what and where? Which one is the best to promote "out there?"

> In the beginning, I did a dumb thing. I used my name, wbwilliams.com as my web site name.

Let's look at domain names for a second. In the beginning, I did a dumb thing. I used my name, wbwilliams.com as my web site name. I could have done much worse, but my name was not good for a dental practice web URL. Now, if I had added Dr to the URL and had it become DrWBWilliams.com, that could have been more likely to let patients know what the site was about. A little over a year later, I realized this error and purchased the URL SuwaneeDental.com. That has been the practice web URL for the past 12 years.

Through the years since then I have added a

number of additional URL's that all point to the same web site: SuwaneeSmiles.com, SuwaneeDentist.com, SuwaneeDentalCare.us and AtlantaGentleDental.com have all been added to the list of URL's we own.

Marketing guru, Michel Fortin, suggested the AtlantaGentleDental.com name when we updated our practice website to Word Press in 2010 so that we could draw from a wider territory. Most people in metro Atlanta know where Suwanee is located, but folks outside of Atlanta may not. With Atlanta being an international city, expanding our web presence URL to include that name offers an expanded option to appeal to the out-of-state and out-of country clients. As of today, we have had clients fly in from as far away as Kuwait, London, Brisbane, Bermuda and Alaska.

Now, thinking about it that way, what is your domain name? Is it doing the job you want? Would another one do more, add to the results you are getting? Getting an additional URL is as easy as paying a domain name registration company (such as DirectNic, GoDaddy, Internic) a registration fee for a two-year period for its use then $100 or more a year for an ISP (Internet Service Provider, such as Bluehost and Earthlink) to host the domain and forward hits to your main domain name.

> Now, thinking about it that way, what is your domain name? Is it doing the job you want? Would another one do more, add to the results you are getting?

Here are three action items you can do to enhance your WOMP referrals. Review your marketing funnel data and see how many come in from this category. List the three reasons your patients would be excited enough to refer patients to you. List the three reasons why the public would come to you for dental care.

In the next chapter, our focus in *Marketing The Million*

Dollar Practice will highlight how to develop an E-Based practice. For those who want to tap the advanced Internet features, don't miss our next marketing tip.

TAKE-AWAY POINTS

- WOMP is Your Low or NO Cost Best Option
- WOMP is Your Strongest Recommendation
- WOMP's Credibility Is Tops
- WOMP Grows by Geometric Progression

CHAPTER 21

Developing the E-Based Practice

STATE-OF-THE-ART

BY NATURE OF HAVING AN ONLINE PRESENCE, a blog, a web site, email connections to your patients, sending out newsletters, a social media footprint and marketing through other online vehicles, you are already an e-based practice. Having a Facebook fan page for your practice, your own YouTube Channel means that you are an even cooler, more market-savvy, cutting-edge marketer. What is the chance that you are the only dentist with a Pinterest account for your practice in your community?

So, the follow-up questions to ask yourself are, "Is your edge getting dull? Have you sharpened your e-skills lately, does your team have e-tools to use to push social media in your practice and how does your e-savvy measure up compared to your competition?"

HOW FAR WE HAVE COME TO DATE

What valuable strategies have you seen, so far, that can be developed and activated in your own practice to promote and grow your business via the Internet? Let's look at the list of what has been discussed so far in *Marketing The Million Dollar Practice*:

1. Personalized domain name
2. Multiple URL's

3. Direct email and online patient newsletters
4. Marketing your web and email address
5. Auto responders
6. Affinity groups
7. Web site design
8. Frequent referrer program
9. New patient offers on your website

Here are some additional ways to increase your Internet exposure:

1. Internet store and e-commerce on your website
2. Guest book for patients and visitors
3. Opt-in boxes for free reports, surveys, free gifts and samples
4. Search Engine Optimization (SEO)
5. E-Connects (FAQ, before and after photos, Q&A sessions, training videos, "how to" blogs)
6. Facebook pages for the practice
7. Blogs on dentistry
8. Twitter strategies for the practice
9. Link-back strategy
10. Membership on LinkedIn, Blogger, Picasa, Orkut, BranchOut, Namz, Stik, Ecademy, UNYK, StumbleUpon, Digger, Google +, and Flickr… just to scratch the surface of possibility
11. Groupon and LivingSocial
12. Facebook Places, Gowalla, FourSquare and Google Places

Another way to improve your web site is to add content and update the look, making it more user-friendly, and more interactive. The use of online patient surveys is an excellent way of garnering patient feedback and of enhancing interactivity.

Some of the online survey tools that are free for your use with limited capability are:

Zoomerang—KwikSurvey—SurveyMonkey
LimeSurvey—SurveyPirate—SurveyGizmo
ESurveysPro—CoolSurveys—FreeSurveyTools

You may find that the simple free version is plenty adequate for your sampling needs. If you require a more robust solution, each of these systems has a higher-end version that answers those needs with good customer support. For those who use the Word Press web site systems, there are a number of these above that are already compatible, plus:

PollDaddy—Word Press Simple Survey
Survey Me—WP Survey And Quiz Tool
Rationale Survey—WP-Polls

WordPress Easy Polling Plug-in is one that is cheap and very functional with graphs and interactivity.

UPGRADING YOUR WEB SITE TO MORE PAGES

A basic 10-page website can be upgraded to a 20, 30 or 40 page site. New logos, colors, site designs can create a fresh look. Content we have added over time includes:

1. Dental stores
2. Dental wizards
3. Office tours—photos and video
4. Specialist areas
5. Dry mouth pages
6. Scleroderma pages (and other dental structure-affecting diseases)
7. Google Business photo panoramic tour inside our facility

8. Sleep apnea pages
9. Snoring pages
10. Tooth fairy links
11. Kids pages
12. Orthodontic pages
13. Implant pages
14. Wisdom tooth pages
15. Fresh breath pages
16. Intraoral video pages
17. Doctor CV pages
18. TMJ pages
19. Migraine headache pages
20. Neuromuscular dentistry pages
21. Interactive maps
22. Autoresponders
23. Guest books
24. Web rings
25. Local web and email links
26. Mission trip photo pages
27. Awards page
28. Vision—Mission—Philosophy—Culture page
29. Gwinnett Gladiators page
30. Deserving Diva Makeovers page
31. Sedation dentistry page

> **Continually updating the look and content of your web site is one way to keep your patients interested and excited about revisiting it.**

All of these pages have been a part of our web site for the past decade or longer. Some have been updated, some removed. As times change, so too does your web site need to change. A static website is a low-ranking web site. Google rewards those websites that add new content on a regular basis.

Continually updating the look and content of your web site is one way to keep your patients interested and excited about revisiting it. New content also gives your staff a reason to talk about the web site with patients—a marketing need. Updated content also raises your score in the search engines and improves your Google placement.

This chapter reminds those who have web sites to re-evaluate them on a regular basis. Don't get caught by your competitors. Stay ahead of the pack. Ask yourself: Were you once on the leading edge with your web site? Are you still there? Has anyone in your community by-passed you? Are you getting results from your Internet presence? How do you know? Are you measuring it? What is your M.A.P. for the new year? You should be writing your plan now to become the premier E-Based practice in your locale. The longer you give others a chance to surpass you in your social media outreach, the closer you are to falling by the wayside as just another "me-to" practice. Change always happens and the leading edge marketers have to stay in front of the wave.

Next in *Marketing The Million Dollar Practice* we will cover why some dentists do not succeed as well as others. It can be traced directly to visibility, and visibility is linked directly to signage. It's a "sign of the times." Now, you may think, "Whoa, that's old school; that's not high-tech or important." But let me tell you this. The "sign" is the third most important aspect of your dental practice marketing. Pay close attention to the next chapter.

> The longer you give others a chance to surpass you in your social media outreach, the closer you are to falling by the wayside as just another dental "me-to" practice. Change always happens and the leading edge marketers have to stay in front of the wave.

TAKE-AWAY POINTS

- Do Not Be a Luddite
- Be Net Savvy
- Increase Your Net Exposure
- Involve Patients in Surveys and Polls
- Continually Update and Improve Your Web Content

CHAPTER 22

A Sign of the Times

A COMMON SCENARIO:

Telephone: "Ring, ring, ring, ring...."

Receptionist: "Hold please............................Hello, Dr. Smiley's office, Mrs. Tick D. Awff speaking."

Inquiring Patient: "This is Mr. Snarlie. I had an appointment at ten o'clock."

Receptionist: "Where are you Mr. Snarlie, don't you know you are 30 minutes late already for your first visit to see Dr. Smiley?"

Inquiring Patient: "Where am I? The question is where are you? I have been driving up and down Singleton Road for 25 minutes looking for your office. Your Yellow Page ad has 3562 as the street number but I can't find it on any building. There is no map and there is no sign on the road. What kind of dental office is this, anyway?"

Receptionist: "We're very select on who we see, Mr. Snarlie, very select. We are right behind the Acme Exterminating Company building, down the alley to the right. You can come on in if you want, Dr. Smiley doesn't have anyone here right now anyway."

*N*OTICE ANYTHING FAMILIAR in that conversation? Hope not, but if you have people getting lost on the way to your office, showing up late, or you have very few new patients come in as a result of seeing your sign as they drive or walk by the practice location, then you need to STOP and reevaluate your signage or even your location.

FOR LACK OF A NAIL, THE KINGDOM WAS LOST

Signage, as defined by our broad terms, is the visible picture your office projects to the road. Don't be caught without one that can be found, seen and read. You might extrapolate that to include the actual sign, with your name, your logo, phone number, slogan, picture, etc. It could include the face of your building—its illumination, street frontage, and visibility from the road to passersby. You could say that it's the architectural style, the unique image you portray to the outside world. It's your "signature in full" at the physical location you call your practice.

It's the "sign of the times" that a dental practice has retail visibility. There is a ranking of good, better and best that we can aspire to as market-minded dentists in terms of facility. Number one is your own magnificent building at or near the corner of a busy intersection—much like what I had in our Stone Mountain practice and now occupy in Suwanee.

Next, is a highly visible space in a highly trafficked strip shopping center in the burbs. That described my first location which I practiced in for nine years. Finally, it's the primo practice location in a professional building with other doctors. Are you planning expansion into one of these types of facilities anytime soon? Anything less is now undesirable, in my opinion. In any case, a carefully and specifically designed sign identifying the practice facility is essential.

Signage is how people know where you are. It's the way they locate you as they drive or walk by your office. Hopefully, your signage not only identifies your office to those coming in today, but also creates an image such that it makes people want to become associated with your practice. In other words, it becomes a draw unto itself.

WHAT DOES IT LOOK LIKE?

First, a sign must be as big as possible—within reason. It must be able to be read while driving by, have enough information to allow someone to reach you by phone or through your web site. It must create a positive impression and be memorable. And finally, it must fit within your image.

A sign must have letters big enough to be read, colors and backgrounds which are clear, complimentary and do not clash, with dimensions large enough to hold your logo, your name, your web site address, your phone number and perhaps your slogan. A sign should be visible and lit, day and night. A dark, unlit sign misses 50% of the potential traffic when both ends of drive-time rush hour are in the dark. A truly great sign should be colorful and well designed. No expense should be spared in creating the perfect sign, because once created, it bears fruit forever—at no expense. Your sign becomes your cheapest form of advertising the day after it is installed.

A sign, too busy with too fancy a font, or with too much tightly packed information is a marketing faux paux . The test of a good professional sign is if it can be read fully in five seconds or less. A sign facing the wrong direction reduces its usefulness. Having only one sign for a corner lot may reduce your patient attraction results. Signage on both streets of a crossroads location will allow visibility to both directions of traffic. A well designed sign should face traffic coming and going. If you have street traffic, its better to turn the sign perpendicular to the road and have it read from each direction. Better yet, have a sign "on the road" and a sign parallel to your street on the building.

Don't forget a sign on the door if you are in a multi-use building. Put the practice name and the doctor's name there (i.e. Suwanee Dental Care above with William B. Williams, DMD below). What may be appropriate is additional information such as hours of operation, web site address, and phone or fax numbers on a glass front window or door. In a retail setting, the use of window space for marketing can significantly enhance your traffic. There are many types of smile photos, posters, and dental art that can signify what we as dentists sell (hopefully benefits, not features only). Perhaps you carry some unique oral care products such as ClO-Sys that you wish to highlight with a window poster that promotes fresh breath.

IMAGE IS EVERYTHING

Signs speak to your image and have so much to do with the initial impression people have of you and your practice. Seek out a quality sign company and produce one that you are proud to see day in and day out. Ideally, your sign is a continuation of your total package.

Want to see if your sign is effective? Take a photo of it with a digital camera from the middle of the road and see if you can easily read the entire sign when the photo is enlarged to 81/2 x 11. It's the sign of your times.

Negotiate with your landlord to allow space for everything you need on your sign. Color catches the eye, as does an image. Use your logo for achieving both. While green and blue may be soothing to the eye, it is the reds, oranges and yellows that catch the attention of the eye. The purpose of marketing is to catch the public's eye so that they read your message.

What if you are limited in your sign size and can only place half of what is preferred? First, include the practice name with logo. If it includes the word dental or dentistry, that is most ideal. Second, the dentist's name and degree should be included. Next, the phone number is important. Lastly, place your web site address in its short form, i.e. suwaneedental.com.

Nowadays, the universal meaning of the .com precludes the inclusion of the http://www as a prefix to web addresses.

Want to see if your sign is effective? Take a photo of it with a digital camera from the middle of the road and see if you can easily read the entire sign when the photo is enlarged to 81/2 x 11. It's the sign of your times.

The next chapter of *Marketing The Million Dollar Practice* will explore the benefits of adding "warm fuzzies" to your web site and your office. We are trying to capture the emotional center stage of our patients' hearts. Look for Impressions: The Name Game coming in the next chapter. We want to make many, many good impressions on our patients from a variety of angles. See if you can identify how many approaches are mentioned.

TAKE-AWAY POINTS

- Be Visible—Be Found
- Best, Least Expensive, Marketing Tool
- Make It Big But Fit Your Image
- Make It Easy to See and Read

CHAPTER 23

Impressions: The Name Game

WHAT'S IN A NAME?

*H*OW MANY DENTISTS does it take to restore a difficult restorative case with multiple implants in B and C bone?

The answer is 106!

Three to interview you for a place in the dental school class, twenty to teach you the basic sciences, 33 to guide you through dental school to get your DMD degree, three to critique you on the state board practical and clinical exam, one to be your mentor as a rookie associate, 25 more to teach you the basic CE needed to advance from a neophyte to a competent diagnostician and operator, five more to give you valuable insights in communication and behavioral techniques important to being a successful dentist, eight fellow study club members to support and motivate you to continue your dental education, six implantologists who guide you through a rigorous hands-on surgical course in implant dentistry, one dentist to refer that difficult case to you, and finally one, you, to place and restore those implants.

And you thought you did it all by yourself!

Well, marketing a practice successfully is just as dependent upon a constellation of many stars as the successful training of an implant dentist. Just as with implant dentistry, marketing a practice must apply principles from many diverse areas of business to achieve the total package. A lot of the parts and pieces of a marketing plan are foreign to a dentist, just like sinus lifts, bone augmentation and Bicon implants may at one time have been for me.

Dentists are not commonly trained to know how to engage a PR firm, to hire an ad agency or to film a TV segment. Ignore any one major aspect of your Marketing Action Plan and you can expect unpredictable, and likely, poor results. In the end, it is the integration of the pieces and the normal function of the whole that is the measure of success in both marketing and implant dentistry.

To be truly successful in the implant field, you need an over-arching unification of ideas to focus your methodologies. You need a strong examination, treatment planning, and implementation strategy to place dental implants. Strong, reliable, beautiful teeth that patients can easily use are the goals of dental implant therapy.

Building into the treatment plan a backup system, a safety net is ideal. A redundancy in your systems means that if one part fails, the whole plan does not fail. Think of the Apollo moon shot and how it succeeded because of its backup systems that, when called upon, worked to get our astronauts back home safely. A haphazard approach to dental implants that cannot satisfy these goals is not recommended. If there is not enough bone, you need to know how to get more bone.

Likewise, neither is a haphazard approach a good idea for marketing your practice. If there are not enough patients to stabilize your practice, you need to know how, or know somebody who knows how, to get more new patients.

PLANNING TO SUCCEED: A FUTURE OF CHOICE, NOT CHANCE

The correlation between marketing a practice and providing implant dentistry is clearly visible. A coherently, well-designed plan which accounts for all possible contingencies is the best MAP of all. The goal for a marketing campaign has to be to get results. You get results by putting out into the public arena a lot of pertinent impressions that people see and act upon. A good result is called "many new patients" in marketing for a practice. Results are also called "sales" to new and existing clients. The purpose of marketing is to drive revenue to your practice.

What is your Name Game? What do you want to be known for, known as, stand for, be recognized in your city, town or state as? As you begin to create your MAP, you want to identify your core beliefs, your practice focus, and be sure they are congruent with your practice vision, mission and philosophy. If you are starting out, creating a new practice or reinventing your current practice, you will want to be certain that your vision can be successfully implemented into your community. Being congruent with your community is as important as being congruent with your own core beliefs.

DESIGN YOUR PREFERRED FUTURE

As you begin to paint the clear picture of your preferred future and MAP out your growth, you will want to pay particular attention to what impressions your marketing message will leave behind. You will certainly want to evaluate the effect that your day-to-day dental activities have on your patients who already know you and come to you for dental services. After all, it's your current patient base that is your greatest sales force for your future practice growth, if you can activate and mold them into that positive force.

Just like the number of dentists (106) involved in bringing an implant case to fruition, the actual number of impressions you may need to create and then send out into the market to bring a dental patient into your practice and then to actually get them to complete their entire treatment plan can amount to scores of impressions over a period of months and years.

Impressions are any interactions, views, or dealings with your dental practice by a person. An impression could be your practice name, logo, sign, website page, phone call, email, appointment, treatment, etc. You never know which impression will be the one that motivates an individual to act, to pick up the phone for an appointment, reschedule for that bridge, or make the call for their son's wisdom tooth removal. What we do know is that a high number of impressions are necessary for success in your marketing campaign.

Perhaps it was the refrigerator magnet you sent last spring in the "Welcome to the Neighborhood" letter. Or, it could have been the neighbor next door saying that they just got braces put on at Dr. Williams' office (word-of-mouth blowing south). Some people need a confirmation from a third party ("Dr. Williams is a really gentle dentist who gives shots you can't even feel!"). We recently signed up to put our Suwanee Dental Care ad on pharmacy bags (12,000 over a year for just $416). As a part of this campaign, the pharmacists will have our cards and brochures at the pharmacy window and plug our office when they receive an inquiry. At every turn, in every space in the community, you want to be seen, to make a good impression to the public and to your existing patients.

In an earlier chapter of *Marketing The Million Dollar Practice,* I identified that marketing research has shown that it takes about 30 attempts (the number of opportunities to be seen) to create nine impressions (those attempts that are actually seen by patients, for instance). Once nine impressions are visualized—in a sense, internalized—the sale is usually completed. In your case with dentistry, the patient decides by this time that you are the dental practice for them. But that is only the beginning.

The real test, where the rubber meets the road, comes when all the other sights, smells, feelings, inklings, implications, associations and even hallucinations that patients get from visiting your dental practice confront them! We spoke about the importance of image in one of the first chapters of *Marketing The Million Dollar Practice*. We discussed smells in the office, sights along the way down the hall, what patients hear, how you reassuringly touch them. Yes, eyes, noses and noises matter in creating your office "image."

You never know what will turn on, or turn off, a patient. I have had people tell me that they came to us because the office of their previous office "looked dirty." This is actually a pretty common statement. We have, ourselves, lost a patient in the middle of an exam appointment because my dental assistant touched a Rhinn holder before putting gloves on. It goes both ways and we have to be vigilant in the impression we are creating—across the board, from our web site design to our staff's telephone attitude. It all shows through; it all gets noticed. It's all creating impressions in the patients' minds about who you are and for what you stand.

Does it matter which impression makes a difference? No, the final impression they see may not be the one that makes the biggest difference. It may be that the final impression just confirms a belief that they already formed from other impressions. It's not really critical to analyze all of your impressions, as long as the necessary total occurs and a result is achieved. Bottom-line thinking always beats over-analyzing. Analysis paralysis is sometimes the reason for stagnation. Activity, campaigns and testing and measuring make more sense than endless study of data.

> **Does it matter which impression makes a difference? No, the final impression they see may not be the one that makes the biggest difference.**

MULTIPLE EXPOSURES

Multiplying your effort by providing many media exposures will give you a better chance for success in attracting new patients. You also need to thoroughly plan the experience your patients will "enjoy" with their five senses in your office. You have a wide array of opportunities to create good impressions that make a difference—both in quality and quantity of referrals.

The best ways of achieving a huge number of impressions is with:

1. Local direct mail: The initial personal letter and practice brochure (tri-fold, five total pages of targeted information along with a personal letter which is hand signed and addressed), followed up with post cards.
2. A search-engine friendly web site (10-20-30-40 or more pages of interesting, specific info, including patient testimonials, before and after photos).
3. Strategically placed local billboards that differentiate your practice
4. Activated patient base: personal referrals, references, testimonials, and reviews from your current patients.

QUALITY OF YOUR IMPRESSIONS

Let's talk about the quality of the impression for a moment. What kinds of things make you feel "warm and fuzzy?" What kinds of things make your patients feel that way, too? Find out what they are and develop a Marketing Action Plan that included a number of "warm and fuzzy makers."

We implemented two "warm fuzzies" into our Suwanee Dental Care practice in 1999. Positive, up-tempo innovations come either in a moment of brilliance or from just copying someone else's great idea. It does not matter where an idea comes from. What matters is if it's useful, if it's easy to implement and if it's cost-effective to do.

INNOVATION NUMBER ONE: SUWANEE DENTAL CARE BEARS: CUSTOM CRITTERS, INC.

We bought these from my refrigerator magnet source, Paul Buck of the Promo Shop and PowerCore. He makes a cute line of Beanie Baby-like animals to your specifications and dresses them in advertising garb. We chose a "workout" sweatshirt that says, "Suwanee Dental Care Bear—visit us—@ SuwaneeDental.com. I ordered 300 and gave them away for special patients, to secretaries in busy, well-trafficked, local business offices, to 5-10 year old children who win the "why I love my dentist" art contest, to winners of the monthly stuffed animal drawing, and for outstanding referrals.

How do cute little teddy bears make you feel? How does making a kid's day warm your heart? What would a kid do with a new unique custom critter in his neighborhood that is just right for carrying around? Do you think he might show it off—with the workout shirt on, of course? What do the ladies talk about at the school bus stop as they wait with their small children in the mornings?

INNOVATION NUMBER TWO: ANNOUNCEMENT WEB SITES FOR BABIES

Proud mamas and papas crow loudest and longest when they have a new arrival. Why not celebrate life with them? Why not employ the tooth fairy to be your agent, your goodwill ambassador, to wish the newborn into the world?

Talk about making a connection early in life! Nice baby, nice tooth fairy, nice practice, nice doctor—it's a virtual love fest! We make the web site and put up some of babies first photos for the family to share around town and across the nation. (We did this early in the life of the Internet, before Facebook, Picaso, and other photo friendly sites.)

Here's how we did it. Offer a free web site for a new baby in or around the practice. Why limit it to your patients? Expand your thinking to incorporate every new baby in your practice sphere. All you need to do is to get the word out and contract with a web designer to do the pages very simply.

THE PHOTOS

On our front page at SuwaneeDental.com, there was a link to babysite.htm, the "baby" landing page for our site. On that page, the details of what we would do for free were explained. The baby page was one page of pure fun—goo-goo (audio) sounds, photos of the proud papa, mama holding the newborn, video of baby's first bath, etc. (no actual live births please) were just a few of the possibilities. You get the picture! They get the picture, a picture sent around the world—with your practice name on it. I'll explain that in a moment.

What do you think happened to these baby web pages? They were shared with mom, pop, brother, sister, aunt, uncle, cousin, cousin-in-law, all in-laws, neighbors up and down the street, the office, the friends from college, the Kiwanis Club, The Bible Study group, the email list on any computer in the house! And, the impression starts with the web address—SuwaneeDental.com/baby. Do you see any benefit to these aforementioned people getting that web address? Therefore, the best way to market the address is to spell it out so they must type it in:

SuwaneeDental.com/etc./etc.

THE TOOTH FAIRY

Next, there is a tooth fairy graphic image on the baby's page—in a prominent site, as a sort of Mistress of Ceremonies—leading the celebration. And, over on the left margin is a link to the tooth fairy's web site. It could be the ubiquitous www.toothfairy.org or it could be the more closely held SuwaneeDental.com toothfairy page.

THE BLESSING

Finally, the credits below the baby site state, "This site is dedicated to Jennifer and her parents by Dr. Bill Williams and the staff at Suwanee Dental Care as celebration of her coming into this world on 12/31/99. May God bless her and guide her all through a long and fruitful life because she is God's very special gift to us all."

Think how nice a color print of this page would look in Baby Jennifer's baby book. Think about the number of impressions your practice gets from a baby web site. Are these the kinds of warm fuzzies you want to create?

These two examples of "warm fuzzies" were in place and used as tools for marketing for years in our practice. One still remains intact, in use. The other, with proper testing and measuring, fell by the wayside of good ideas that did not bring in a large number of new clients or grow the practice compared to the effort to run the campaign.

> I included the description of "the baby pages" in this chapter because I wanted you to see that not everything we try works as well as we imagine. It may sound good, but have a poor ROI. Being bold, trying and then failing is better than not trying at all. Remember, test and measure!

Can you imagine which one was scrapped and which still continues with some success? The message here is that you need to be proactive, to constantly be trying new things, to continue to stretch your boundaries, but to test and measure the results as you proceed and to continue doing what works for you and to cull out those loser strategies that bog you and your practice down.

I included the description of "the baby pages" in this chapter because I wanted you to see that not everything we try works as well as we imagine. It may sound good, but have a poor ROI. Being bold, trying and then failing is better than not trying at all. Remember, test and measure!

Next in *Marketing The Million Dollar Practice* we will highlight a marketing method called the *Coffee News,* a franchised exclusive newspaper for retail establishments, as an example of local print advertising that shows up in well-trafficked spaces with captive audiences.

Here are a couple of action items you may want to complete now that you have read this chapter. Take a tour of your parking lot, walk in the front door of your office, walk down every hallway, into every operatory, sit in the dental chairs, lie back in treatment position, visit the patient restroom, and stand at the checkout counter… experience exactly what a patient in your practice experiences. Gather a list of the impressions you got from your tour of your own office, from your experiences from a patient's perspective. Are they all as good as you would like them to be? What improvements do you see needed?

TAKE-AWAY POINTS

- Public Relations Matters
- Generate Positive Impressions on All Fronts
- Map Out Your Future
- You Create The Image You Want in Your Community
- Test and Measure Everything

CHAPTER 24

Coffee News

WHEN IS IT MAXWELL HOUSE TIME?

*H*ERE'S A MARKETING NICHE you may never have heard of... restaurant air space. What do people do when they come into a dental-medical-veterinary office? They look for something to read to while away the time. There is always a wait (except in mine and your offices, right?). In many busy restaurants, there is a longer wait than in doctors' offices. Therefore, there is a wait worth exploring in the restaurant business.

COFFEE NEWS

Enter the *Coffee News,* a franchised newsletter with local advertising set in prominent places in restaurants, auto repair waiting areas, professional offices, hair salons, and the like. This 33-year-old company based in Canada sells ad space around the border of their mocha-hued, newsy, artsy, lighthearted communiqué.

As a company, they build the *Coffee News* name brand, develop a loyal readership and rotate the businesses' ads around the page to keep the look fresh. Local representatives replenish the issues of *Coffee News* weekly with new generic topics of interest and a section (20% of the news space) on local news. All news is positive and interesting; you'll see no reports on how many homicides, burglaries, crashes or arrests in *Coffee News.*

The purpose of *Coffee News* is to entertain the customers

during that time between their arrival and seating at the table (or auto servicing, dog washing, kid's hair cut, etc.). The "news" in *Coffee News* is always good, informative, humorous or upbeat.

One unique factor of the *Coffee News* is that its artwork ties into the text of the communiqué via subliminal guided pathways. That means that the reader automatically shifts his or her focus from the news text to the adjacent ad because of the flow of the artwork, the eye-catching open borders, the purposely broken lines, the intentionally curved lines, the art design and the fonts of the ads. *Coffee News* uses the psychology of sales to its advantage by combining good copy with good graphic design.

> **Coffee News uses the psychology of sales to its advantage by combining good copy with good graphic design.**

MARKETING IS AN INVESTMENT, NOT AN EXPENSE

What about the cost per impression for *Coffee News?* A year's worth of ad space cost about $1200, about what value comes from one new patient in a year. *Coffee News* sells ad space by the quarter and half year also. In our case, they place *Coffee News* in 70 restaurants and shops in the Lawrenceville-Suwanee area. Each advertiser in the newsletter has an industry exclusive for the *Coffee News* edition in which they advertise. Restaurants may do 100-500 meals per day.

One issue of the *Coffee News* may be taken home for family members to read. The next may be read and left for the next person. If 70 restaurants or other outlets times 100 meals times 300 days a year times only one half of the people taking the time to actually look at the *Coffee News* in the 12 minutes they are waiting on their food see the ad, then that equals

1,050,000 impressions of your dental practice and better yet, your web site address in a year. The only thing I can think that would be better for you than that is to have you install a web surfing kiosk in each of those same restaurants that ties in directly, and only, to your web site.

So, if we can get flashing lights or balloons tied to the *Coffee News'* acrylic display stands, we could probably get up to 2 million impressions a year from our $1,200 investment— that would be 1,666 impressions per advertising dollar, or 16 impressions per penny, or six one hundredths of a cent per impression. Dang, that's nearly free! Maybe I'm beginning to see why mass media (radio, television, newspaper) advertising works so well. No matter how much you spend, it's nearly free on a cost per person count!

Like the proverbial bottomless pit, the endless night sky or the enigmatic mathematical symbol Pi, there is no end to it, to the benefits of making that many good impressions. Many good impressions equal lots of new patients over a given period of time. That sounds like a formula.

BY THE NUMBERS

Going by the numbers, it takes 30 impressions to equal a customer—in your case, a patient. Your $1200 investment would thereby equal one million conservatively counted impressions. Divided by 30, that would equal 33,333 patients beating down your door if the numbers don't lie. Now, if you don't live in the midst of one million people, don't fear, this marketing method works in small towns just as well.

It takes 30 impressions sent in the vicinity of just one person to get them to see scarcely a few of them. Over time, if you give them enough reasons, they should all come around. By logic then, you should eventually—perhaps as soon as in a year or two—have nearly every person in a town of about 30,000 as your patient of record. Thank heavens for expanded duty assistants and dental hygienists!

Well, I know you don't want to work that hard, but you do, by now, see the benefit of putting your marketing dollars to work in a variety of venues. And, WebCentric Marketing Action Plans all point to the practice website to lock in those referrals.

Next in *Marketing The Million Dollar Practice,* we will highlight a marketing concept called: If I could put Time in a Bottle—time management in dentistry. How do we do twice the volume of dentistry as some offices in the same amount of time, with the same or less staff? In the next chapter, I will explore some of the ways we do it.

Here are a few action items you could do. As you and your team are out and about in your local shops, restaurants, and professional offices, do some comparison shopping for advertising opportunities in them. What magazines, newsletters, and other media formats do they use to get their brands across? See who is cross-promoting each others' products and services. Dig deeper and find out more about the opportunity to participate with them. Look into whether *Coffee News* comes to your location.

TAKE-AWAY POINTS

- Be Everywhere With Your Marketing Message
- Capture People Where They Are
- Entertain—Inform—Call To Action
- Make An Attractive Offer
- *Coffee News* is Worth It

CHAPTER 25

Time in a Bottle

THE HOUR GLASS

E CAN'T BANK IT, save it, or get more of it. We can't stretch it or condense it. Time passes and time is consistent. No one has more of it than anyone else in a day. Since, it's been said that time is the most precious thing we have, how can you use time to your advantage in marketing your practice.

There are two types of time: Patient Time and Practice Time. Focus on saving patient and practice time by doing more dentistry today. We get many new patients because of what we do related to "time."

> There are two types of time: Patient Time and Practice Time. Focus on saving patient and practice time by doing more dentistry today. We get many new patients because of what we do related to "time."

SAVING TIME

One excellent goal would be to market "saving time" as a benefit to your patients. "How do you do that?" you ask. Well there is the "Get'er Done" philosophy, the Same-Day Dentistry Model of Care. In this model, the patient is given the chance to:

1. **Come in Today**—when they call for a New Patient Appointment—whether it's for an exam, exam and

prophy, or an emergency visit. If they want it—we accommodate. We make heaven and earth move for the New Patient and the Emergency Patient.

2. **Stay for Additional Dentistry**—when they are in the doctor or hygiene room. This is a classic upsell technique that doctors and patients both love because it saves time for the patient, fills an empty hole in the doctors' schedule and increases practice profitability.

As the recession rattled on and dentists began to feel the effects, many went to the Same-Day dentistry model, striking while the iron was hot, doing dentistry on a warm body, rather than sending them home to await a consultation appointment scheduled a week or two down the road. Better control of the appointment book often occurs when this model is used because more dentistry is done on people already in the office and there are less opportunities for broken or failed appointments. Saving time for those emergencies and same-day add-ins will make for a smoother day in many cases.

Once word gets around town that you are available for Same-Day dentistry and emergency visits, you will see a significant uptick in calls for treatment today. It's important to be able to meet the needs of those with immediate problems. Being a decathalon dentist (one who can perform all ten dental specialty services well), like we talk about in the 5th module of the Solstice 5M, means you can perform endo, oral surgery, crown and bridge, restorative, as well as other services.

Being the comprehensive dentist in town is one concept I always promote: becoming a MAGD and taking many advanced courses in implants, third molar removal and such. One of the main reasons I teach dentists the Implant Efficiency Institutes' technique of immediate implant placement after extractions is to enable them to capitalize handsomely on Same-Day Dentistry. The ability to remove and then replace a tooth in its entirety in one appointment is dramatic. Eliminating the waiting time between appointments for socket healing, bone grafting, abutment placement and temporization is a true "time-saver" and a certain practice builder.

SCRIPTS TO SAVE TIME

Let me give you a few scripts I use to get patients to stay and have more dentistry done. This one is easy and fast and it gets about 50% success that day to stay. When I notice a patient who has generally been in the practice for a while, has had all or most of their needed dentistry completed, I'll sit back from the hygiene exam and say, "Mary you are really doing well, no cavities and no signs of any other problems. The only thing I can help you with from here on are elective services and procedures. Things like orthodontics, bleaching your teeth and such. There is one other thing that I can do that you may be interested in. Would you mind if I shared with you what I'm thinking?"

(Wait for their agreement, of course.)

"How would you like me to be able to take 10 years off your smile in ten minutes for very little cost and no pain or shots?"

(Again, wait for their answer, Doc)

"I can do what's called coronoplasty, or smoothing the sharp and uneven edges of your front teeth, making them appear more youthful and a lot straighter. You'll look and feel 10 years younger when you smile and when you speak. I can do that in about 5-10 minutes now if you'd like."

(Wait for their question of how much it costs)

"The cost is just $125 and I'll smooth those broken and chipped edges just like you polish your broken nails. You'll look like you just had orthodontics, a smooth, straight, perfectly even smile."

How's that for an easy script to say 3-4 times a day. Wouldn't you like to add a few into your schedule like that. Just one a day over a year equals an unplanned bonus of $25,000 to your practice. Now that's saving time in a bottle.

How about the script to get a patient to do more dentistry than is scheduled in their restorative appointment. We try to upgrade and upsell our patients every day to fill the time available to do fine dentistry. For instance, when they have a single crown scheduled in the lower left quadrant, we look for all other needs in their mouth and say, "Mrs. Ratcliff, you have a small filling that is planned to be done in the tooth next to the crown scheduled today. If you can work that into your budget, would you like to get that done today while you are here and you are numb anyway? It'll save you a visit to the dentist later on." We get 95% acceptance on those small upsells.

UPSELLING IS GOOD

If you think of it, each and every upsell you or your team makes is pure profit in these types of cases. The time was open, the time would have been lost and the overhead is negligible. There is no way a single filling, sealant, or coronoplasty can be profitable unless done in conjunction with some other more profitable procedure. That's why we look to combine all small items with a large item or a whole mouth of small items. We save our time, our patient's time and we make more profits per hour than with any other system.

Let's take it to the ultimate timesaving script. "Mr. Roscoe, we have a lot of dentistry to do to get your mouth where you said you want to be and how you want it to look. I can do this in four major appointments with sedation as you indicated you prefer, or in two major appointments, one for the upper and one for the lower, it's your choice.

But the best way to do your dentistry is to do it in one main appointment. You'll be sedated, you won't really remember being here and doing it. How does that sound to you?"

I use a variation of a script like that on all of my cases, not just the big reconstructions. We get a lot of patients who want to "get'er done!" If you open your mind to same-day dentistry, full-mouth dentistry, and saying "Yes!" more often, you too will reap the benefits of saving time in a bottle.

Here are some action items you may want to employ. Have a mindset shift team meeting to create new awareness and focus on the opportunity of "Saving Time In A Bottle." Reserve emergency time on your schedule daily for those Same-Day calls that will come in. Create, learn and use multiple upsell scripts daily. Discuss in your morning meeting the undone dentistry in your scheduled patients charts and who will be asking what questions to upsell each and every patient on todays schedule, both in the doctor's book and the hygiene book.

Next in *Marketing The Million Dollar Practice,* we will highlight a marketing concept called: The Experience Economy and how the expectations of consumers are changing the way professional services are seen by the public and rendered by dentists.

TAKE-AWAY POINTS

- Time is Your Most Important Commodity
- Save Patient Time to Win Friends
- Save Practice Time to be Profitable
- Do it Today at Every Position in the Practice
- Same Day Dentistry is a Key Play

CHAPTER 26

The Experience Economy

IT'S A NEW DAY

W E HAVE CHANGED AS CONSUMERS. The Experience Economy details what best-selling American author Joe Pine calls a major evolution in consumer marketing. It's experience that we now seek as shoppers.

To summon consumers (patients) in droves and at a profit, you (the dental practice) need a little something extra. You need to engage them with an experience that leads them to purchase. The dental practices that really get it are the practices that can get the public to pay them for the opportunity to sell them items or services, i.e. (1) consumables while at the dental office for a prophy or fillings (2) preventive services such as sealants, fluoride and home care supplies, (3) specialty services such as bone grafting, third molar removal, molar endo, dental implants, and (4) elective services such as bleaching, veneers, coronoplasty, orthodontics and laser gingival recontouring.

Think about the difference in buying toothpaste from the grocery store shelf, picking one out of 75 confusing brands of toothpaste and mouth rinses versus buying them during your three-month checkup that your dentist recommends because it eliminates mouth odor and kills bacteria. People want to experience a reason for making choices, and the dentist's choice, the dentist's recommendation is a large factor in their decision. The education that accompanies the purchase of a tube of toothpaste like CloSys is a part of the experience that patients are craving in the experience economy.

CONVENIENCE COUNTS

Why not let the patient capitalize on the convenience of your carrying the product in the office? Why not make a nice profit for delivering this "value-added" service to your patients? Soft selling oral care products can mean a child's college tuition for an entire year for the owner of the practice... or a cruise on the Caribbean for the entire dental team. Think about it, "There's gold in them thar hills!"

What patients want today are customizable treatment options such as menu-driven cosmetics. They want to know they can look as good as the next guy or gal. They want to be in control of the process and have a say-so about the timing and duration of treatment. They want to manage their dentistry on their own terms if they can. They want to reduce the pain and increase the gain. They also want someone else (like the insurance companies) to pay for the routine dentistry. They are more likely to pay for the extras, the cosmetics, themselves, out-of-pocket.

WOW EXPERIENCES MATTER

What patients also want today are experiences that impress them. They want to be made to feel special. They want to be remembered. Photographs on the chart or now digitally in the computer help us know our patients. Personal data sheets in the their file keep family and personal details at finger-tip readiness so that we can be as tuned-in to each individual as possible. Apply the Ritz-Carlton concept of recording a customer's preferences, for example, classical music, decaffeinated coffee with sugar but no cream, NuCalm sedation, the fact that they appreciate a rubber dam while removing mercury-laden amalgam, and their specific staff member preferences. This is an important way to customize their dental experience with an eye towards the future. This kind of experience virtually guarantees customer loyalty. The goal is to heighten the dental experience, take it out of the pain zone and, instead, to draw the patient into a comfort zone for more business opportunities.

> The goal is to heighten the dental experience, take it out of the pain zone and, instead, to draw the patient into a comfort zone for more business opportunities.

Dental practices that truly understand this new experience economy appreciate the need to retain staff and get everybody on the same page, all committed to focusing on the entertainment/educational process. In the experience economy, work is really theater, just like we explained in the New Patient Experience. Imagine the impact if your staff always said the right thing at the right time! That's the goal of making dental interactions a communication via theater. The lines are scripted, learned and delivered by professionals. When we walk through the operatory or consult room door, "It's Showtime!" The audience is waiting to be entertained, so do your best to win an Oscar every day, every time.

> When we walk through the operatory or consult room door, "It's Showtime!" The audience is waiting to be entertained, so do your best to win an Oscar every day, every time.

IT'S SHOWTIME
AT THE DENTAL PRACTICE

Using the acting analogy a step further, remember that there are lead actors, supporting actors, musical scores, a director, a producer and one or more special effects people, to name a few. What if your staff had parts to play, some, as actors, some as technicians, and some as pre-production staff? Who is the director of your team (the office manager), the producer (the dentist), and the engineer (the appointment coordinator)? Who is the person in charge of special effects such as image enhancement, digital radiology, etc. (the dental assistant)? Assign the roles and give your crew members their scripts to put on a successful production.

Could you come up with a scenario whereby everyone on the staff knows his or her place and their lines before each and every common event that occurs in the dental practice? The way to do that is to first make a list of the patient-centered events that take place in a dental practice. Write down what you ideally say each time. Then, print it out and give each staff member a copy. That is what is called a script, your specific dental script for that scene in the event, and each of you is an actor.

We learned about the front desk and consultation scripting in Dick Barnes' Arrowhead seminars in the 1980's. A stack of flash cards for each scenario served as cues, as learning tools. Dr. Bill Blatchford promoted a similar approach to excellence in communication, each staff member knowing his or her lines. With this technique, all successful practices can guarantee a clear, consistent, and streamlined patient interaction and a less stressful transition when staff changes occur. The secret is to operate with written guidelines and scripts for these vital patient interactions.

RESOURCES YOU CAN USE

There are many good resources to consider. I mentioned Barnes and Blatchford, some of my favorites. We learned and condensed much of what is good and what has worked well for us over the past 25 years into our Solstice 5M training by attending hundreds of hours of classes with dental speakers like Linda Drevenstedt, Jennifer McDonald, Kathy Jameson, Paul Bass, Gary Takacs, Paul Homoly, Brad Durham, and Linda Miles. Office Magic Productions with Dr. Patrick Wahl and Lorraine Hollett, has a good scripting program for financial and other front desk persons.

It's not always necessary for your entire team to spend thousands of dollars traveling and attending live courses. Solstice Dental Advisors has webinars, teleseminars, MP3 audio files, CD's, DVD's, office manuals, eBooks and printed books for training available that may do the job for you in your office. That seems to be one of the new frontiers of dentistry in this decade. Online training is rapidly replacing many of the hotel seminar sessions and getting much more dental training into the dental practices at a deeper level, more often, to a greater number of staff members.

Many people will tell you that the main reason for digital rather than on-site training is the savings on travel and lodging costs from an overhead standpoint. I believe the greatest benefit from online training is the ability to access the information anywhere, anytime. The more team members can review and study the material at home, during lunch periods and on weekends, the better they will assimilate the CE material. Flexibility is the key to learning in the digital age.

THE NEW PATIENT EXPERIENCE

In a previous chapter, I detailed the traffic flow of the New Patient Experience and the concept behind it. Outlining some of the verbiage to use in the interview, the tour and the comprehensive exam, you saw how this process elevates the dental practice and the doctor in the eyes of the patient. It is imperative that the team be able to operate interchangeably in each of these situations with the utmost efficiency and efficacy to achieve ideal results. "Seamlessly" is a word that should describe the way one staff member fits into the part they play that day, that time, in that office. Each part, each role in the play also needs an understudy, a pinch hitter, just in case the main actor or ball player is out.

DENTAL THEATER

Theater happens in the initial entry of the patient into the practice. Theater happens in the hygiene room. Theater happens in the orthodontic screening exam with mom watching the reaction of the doctor to the child and the child to the doctor. Theater happens in the reception room as the guests sit and wait their turn in the doc's play or they wait for family members attending a prophy "playtime" or "happy visit." This is where your long-term patients are introduced to your newer patients and given the "green light" to share their experiences. By doing this, you harness the power of their good will and their "experience."

Your goal in this "experience economy" is to make each encounter your patients have with your office a happy comedy, not a sad tragedy. You want to make people laugh... not cry. Having fun, creating positive memories, impressing people with your "viva la difference" type of dentistry is what you seek to do. Every positive event, experience, or treatment builds your reputation and your base of loyal patients. It is very possible to erase a fearful patient's bad memories, the ones that caused their phobias in the first place. This, in turn, tends, to keep people coming back to the dental practice on a more routine basis.

When you hire happy people, professionals who know the value of a good attitude, a warm smile, and a comforting hand on the shoulder, you can confidently delegate the duties of communication and guidance to improved health. With all this in mind, you create a lasting memory in the "experience economy." You remain in the forefront of your patient's minds as being a good place to go for dental care and a doctor to whom they can confidently refer friends. And after all, that is the bottom line, isn't it?

TAKE-AWAY POINTS

- Patients Want a Positive Experience
- Patients Want a Reason to Buy From You
- Patients Want to Belong to Something Bigger
- Patients Want a Branded Process

CHAPTER 27

Daycare Dynamite and the Tooth Fairy

DO IT FOR THE CHILDREN!

E VERYBODY KNOWS that parents tend to take care of their children even before they spend money on themselves, especially when it comes to health care. Dental practices that cater to the entire family are also known to be more recession-proof than those who limit themselves to working in smaller niches. In a down economy, the place to be is "family-friendly."

> Dental practices that cater to the entire family are also known to be more recession-proof than those who limit themselves to working in smaller niches.

BIPPO THE HIPPO

So, how does a dental practice appeal to families, children in particular? One of the early methods we used to employ was Bippo the Hippo, a character costume that my staff would dress up in and visit kids at the office and around the community. Bippo was young and didn't yet talk but he did bring coloring books when he was let out of his pen and he was usually accompanied by The Tooth Fairy!

Bippo the Hippo is a franchise that any dentist can check out online at www.bipposplace.com. In 1971, Navy pediatric dentist, Dr. Edward L. Donaldson created the idea of our Bippo while he was stationed in Cuba. He generated a whole legend of Bippo and his first visit to the dentist that dental teams have been sharing with little ones ever since.

We would send Bippo the Hippo and The Tooth Fairy to elementary schools, daycare centers and health fairs to represent the Stone Mountain Dental Group or Suwanee Dental Care. What we noticed was that we had scores of referrals from the teachers of those places and children who actually looked forward to meeting Bippo and the Tooth Fairy at our office during their visits.

February is Dental Health Month and there is always an opportunity for the dental team to fan out across the community of schools and daycare facilities to do dental education seminars to young people. On our team there is always a young lady or two who love to play the role of The Tooth Fairy. They dress up in a pink fairy outfit… it's a combination of prom dress, ballet costume and party clothes. They always bring with them a magic wand and fairy dust! Kids love to have their picture taken with The Tooth Fairy and Bippo the Hippo… don't your young patients?

Part of our plan in doing these school visits is to leave something with the youth that their parents will notice about your practice. Give the kids a special kid-appropriate toy or toothbrush with your practice name on it. Remember one of our slogans… ABM… Always Be Marketing. When you have someone's attention, be sure to close the deal, finish the drill, get the name, add to your list. Find out how you can get your marketing information into the hands of the mother and how you can get the mother's name and other info into your database.

SUWANEE DENTAL CARE BEARS

One marketing item we enjoyed giving the kids and the adults was a Suwanee Dental Care Bear, which I mentioned in a previous chapter. We dressed the seven-inch tall stuffed bears in a tee-shirt emblazoned with the Suwanee Dental Care logo and name. You cannot give a better gift than a lovable stuffed bear.

The care bears proved to be so popular that we expanded our thinking the next year and created an African menagerie: Leo the Lion, Gertrude the Giraffe, Rocky the Rhino and Ellie the Elephant joined the Suwanee Dental Care Bear as gifts to our patients and, dare we tell, their parents! Yes, the adults wanted the stuffed animals just as much as their children. We had been going to Kenya on our mission for a number of years and the addition of the additional animals was a natural. As an added touch, our African menagerie wore the Kenya Medical Outreach tee shirt.

One effective tactic to gather names, addresses and phone numbers for building our practice marketing list is to offer to send one of the Suwanee Dental Care Bears or Kenya Medical Outreach's zoo animals to anyone who fills out a form, or opts-in on our special registration web site.

THE BOTTOM LINE

Let's think about the bottom line on why you market: to get more exposure, so you get more new patients, so you make more sales, so you make more profits. One of the important tenants of WebCentric Marketing is to cover all bases. You want to capture a certain number of patients from all categories, demographics, ages, and localities. You want to dominate your competition.

> Going where the little people are, schools and day care, is part of the marketing plan. Giving them something that is just for them is part of the strategy.

Going where the little people are, schools and day care, is part of the marketing plan. Giving them something that is just for them is part of the strategy. Put your contact info on the gift so that the parents of the little ones know you were there and that you are interested enough to invest time in their children. Nothing happens by accident; you are successful because you planned it.

Here are a few action items to try: Call the Tooth Fairy hotline and see if you can arrange a special visit to your office. This would then be "news-worthy" and would be something to let your patients know to come and be a participant. Better yet, get an official Tooth Fairy to reside in your very own office location (can you say "team member?"). Create a marketing plan to be kid-friendly and parent-attracting. Have plenty of toys and goodies on hand, because everyone likes the Toy Chest.

Just as it is essential to give a gift to your little pediatric patients, it is crucial to be seen by your community as a generous, giving dental practice. That is why I want to share with you about the Sugar Hill Dental Mission and other charitable events connected to our dental practice. Perhaps this will spark some interest in your heart to go beyond the norm of what most dentists do and are all about.

But next, we will delve into the spiritual realm and see how knowledge and acknowledgment go hand in hand to lend a helping hand to you and your practice. Those who want a good and wise sidekick, a Tonto, on their side should read this next chapter!

TAKE-AWAY POINTS

- Be Known as Family Friendly
- Cater to Kids
- Catering to Cowards Means You Treat Adults As Kids
- Prizes Work in Many Ways

CHAPTER 28

The Prayer of Jabez

E VERY NOW AND THEN a seminal event occurs to change the way the world, as we know it, works. I invite you to read this particular chapter of *Marketing The Million Dollar Practice,* to travel down a personal pathway with me and see how such an event occurred for my family and me and how it could possibly happen for you, too. This is about the impact of God in our lives and the rewards God bestows upon us when we follow His wishes. Answers to prayer happen and this specific prayer being discussed here is very, very meaningful. It's called...

THE PRAYER OF JABEZ

Praying for the Right Stuff - God wants you to live beyond your limits. So pray that you will have an extraordinary life.

The Opening Excerpts from <u>The Prayer of Jabez,</u> a book by Bruce Wilkerson:

"My own story starts in a kitchen with yellow counters and Texas-sized raindrops pelting the window. It was my senior year of seminary in Dallas. Darlene, my wife, and I were finding ourselves spending more and more time thinking and praying about what would come next. Where should I throw my energy, passion, and training? What did God want for us as a couple? I stood in our kitchen thinking again about a challenge I'd heard from the seminary chaplain, Dr. Richard Seume. "Want a bigger vision for your life?" he had asked earlier that week.

"Sign up to be a gimper for God."

A gimper, as Seume explained it, was someone who always does a little more than what's required or expected. In the furniture business, for example, gimping is putting the finishing touches on the upholstery, patiently applying the ornamental extras that are a mark of quality and value.

Dr. Seume took as his text the briefest of Bible biographies: "Now Jabez was more honorable than his brothers" (1 Chronicles 4:9). Jabez wanted to be more and do more for God, and—as we discover by the end of verse 10—God granted him his request. End of verse. End of Bible story.

"Lord, I think I want to be a gimper for you," I prayed as I looked out the window at the blustery spring rain. But I was puzzled. What exactly did Jabez do to rise above the rest? Why did God answer his prayer? I wondered. For that matter, why did God even include Jabez's mini-profile in the Bible?

Maybe it was the raindrops running down the window panes. Suddenly my thoughts ran past verse nine. I picked up my Bible and read verse ten—the prayer of Jabez. Something in his prayer would explain the mystery. It had to. Pulling a chair up to the yellow counter, I bent over my Bible, and reading the prayer over and over, I searched with all my heart for the future God had for someone as ordinary as I.

The next morning, I prayed Jabez's prayer word for word. And the next.

And the next.

Thirty years later, I haven't stopped.

If you were to ask me what sentence—other than my prayer for salvation—has revolutionized my life and ministry the most, I would tell you that it was the cry of a gimper named Jabez, who is still remembered not for what he did, but for what he prayed—and for what happened next."

—Dr. Bruce Wilkinson

WHO IS BRUCE WILKINSON?

Dr. Bruce Wilkinson, president of Walk Thru the Bible Ministries, takes readers to 1 Chronicles 4:10 to discover how they can release God's miraculous power and experience the blessings God longs to give each of us. The life of Jabez, one of the Bible's most overlooked heroes of the faith, bursts from unbroken pages of genealogies in an audacious, four-part prayer that brings him an extraordinary measure of divine favor, anointing, and protection. Readers who commit to offering the same prayer on a regular basis will find themselves extravagantly blessed by God, and agents of His miraculous power in everyday life.

What was the importance of Jabez in history?

Jabez was listed in the genealogies of the Old Testament, the Hebrew Bible.

Many places in the Scriptures contain very long lists of names. We do not know much about most of them; they merely lived, had a wife or child also named in the Scriptures and then died. Today, it's not very much different. Of the billions of people in the world, only a relatively few leave an indelible mark upon the earth; far fewer will impact eternity!

WHAT ABOUT YOU AND I?

A decade beyond our death, will we have made a difference? Will we be remembered for something inspiring or important? Or will we perhaps be just one name among thousands on a list in some newspaper obituary or long-lost genealogical report? The way it was is not always the way it has to be!

> A decade beyond our death, will we have made a difference? Will we be remembered for something inspiring or important?

The name Jabez was significant because of its inclusion in "the list." Otherwise, Jabez was insignificant.

> *He was not a famous prophet or powerful preacher.*
> *He was not a king who ruled many nations.*
> *He was not a glorious general of the battle field.*
> *He was a man that was "more honorable than his brothers."*
> *… He now lives on in world history because of his prayer!*
> —*The Prayer of Jabez*

Dr. Williams' note: Just like Bruce, I prayed this prayer daily. What was in the book that produced wonders upon wonders? I have created a synopsis here and put a commentary at the end. Living life wholistically, there is no separation between work, play, self, family and worship. L.D. Pankey's cross of life is a life in balance and we subscribe to that philosophy wholeheartedly.

The Prayer of Jabez   1 Chronicles 4:9,10

Jabez was more honorable than his brothers. His mother had named him Jabez saying "I gave birth to him in pain." Jabez cried out to the God of Israel "Oh that you would bless me and enlarge my territory! Let your hand be with me and keep me from harm so that I will be free from pain." And God granted his request. (New King James Version)

Jabez prayed for spiritual prosperity.

"Oh, that you would bless me"

He was not satisfied with his lot in life… he wanted God's true blessings to fulfill his life. He understood what was most important in life.—God's blessings. Jabez wasn't seeking money, fame, or possessions here, though he may have achieved some measure of those—he was seeking God's best for his life.

He prayed for widened horizons.
"Enlarge my territory"

COMFORT ZONES

We all have our comfort zones. When we are in them we may relax more and be contented with the status quo. Such things could include our friends, our careers, our way of worship. When things begin to happen that are outside of our "comfort zone" we may become worried, suspicious or nervous. That is a natural protective behavior. The danger of being over-protective with our comfort zone is that we can grow stagnant spiritually. If that occurs we begin to give God reason to feel grief over us.

There is then the danger of becoming like the church of Laodecia. (lukewarm)—Revelations 3:16 says, "So, because you are lukewarm—neither hot nor cold—I am about to spit you out of my mouth... ." Jabez prayed a prayer that would lead to the avoidance of just such a tragedy.

He didn't want to merely stay in the "comfort zone!" The word 'enlarge' means simply to make larger, extend in limits or dimensions, to extend to more purposes or uses. 'Territory' here refers to boundaries and borders. His wish was to reach out beyond himself... to magnify his sphere of influence.

He prayed that the hand of God would be with him.
"Let your hand be with me."

In Hebrew the word used here means an open hand. It indicates power, means, and direction. Jabez prayed that God's open hand of direction and power would be with him.

We are comforted knowing that God, with His open hand, will gladly take ours and pull us up when we are low, and encourage us when we are weak.

He prayed for deliverance from sin.
"Keep me from harm."

The power of evil existed in Jabez's time, just as it does today, and he was no stranger to that fact. He also knew that God could deliver him. Could it be that he had seen others who were grieved. For whatever reason, Jabez did pray and seek God's help in overcoming sin in his life.

God answered his prayers.
"And God granted his request."

We may feel safe staying inside the circle we call our comfort zone. We may grow complacent when our beliefs and habits go unchallenged and unstimulated. So as we go forward, perhaps we will be prompted to open our minds and seek Divine guidance as a part of the strategic plan we are developing for our lives. Pray that God would truly bless us with great spiritual prosperity, that He would widen our horizons, that His hand would be upon us, and that He would keep us from evil.

Know that God WILL grant your request!!

THE FINAL ASSURANCE

If we begin to pray the prayer of Jabez and if we live an honorable life like Jabez, then we can hope and even expect, as did Jabez…" and God granted his request."

Now God makes many promises and is well known to keep them all. For instance, this one from the New Testament below is similar to the promise made to Jabez.

God does grant our requests if we are honorable, if we are living within His will.

> *"If you abide in me, and my words abide in you, you shall ask what you will, and it shall be done unto you."*
> —John 15:7

Now, where, you ask, does this all fit in with dentistry? Certainly, this is not a technical dental matter, nor your standard marketing treatise. But, it is about personal growth and being connected to The Source. If one grows personally and spiritually, the benefits pour down in torrents to the professional being we all are as dentists. Let me expand on that by way of a personal explanation, with your permission.

> **If one grows personally and spiritually, the benefits pour down in torrents to the professional being we all are as dentists.**

MY STORY

I grew up in a traditional Christian home, fell away in my college years and drifted for awhile. Getting married to a fine Christian woman who put up with my wandering spirit was the only thing that kept me in the ball park. She finally saw my transformation take hold in 1987 as I came to accept Jesus as my personal savior as an adult.

For many years, I have considered personal growth to be about being a better communicator, a problem solver, mediator or salesman. I studied the Norman Vincent Peals and Zig Zigglers of the world. I went to Quest and Napili, did EST and other New Age development programs.

Now, however, I have a different focus on personal growth. I seek growth through the Holy Spirit, my personal

Counselor, not just through the teachings of men. We know from reading Exodus 11:10 that God hardened Pharaoh's heart and that Pharaoh therefore did not listen to Moses in his direction. Likewise, unless your heart has been hardened, you still have the opportunity to learn God's lesson for your life by inviting and then listening to the Holy Spirit.

I know that you may internalize all of this, the Prayer of Jabez and my commentary on it, in many different ways. My Christian and Jewish friends will look into the Old Testament verse and see the same message. But my Jewish friends may be hard-pressed to see beyond that into the New Testament truths sprinkled throughout the text and especially in these few concluding paragraphs. But, I have an extra special burden in my heart for my Jewish and non-Christian friends specifically because of this. My hope is that those out there who do not yet know Jesus personally will look into the fulfillment of Messianic prophecy spoken throughout the Old Testament and examine the truths in the book of Matthew and beyond. It's just too important to ignore.

My burden also extends to my Buddhist, Muslim, and Hindu friends who have not read or studied the Words of the Bible. I am hoping for them to adopt curiosity, just enough to get to the point of looking and asking questions.

My study of the books of Isaiah, Matthew, John, Romans and Revelations, for instance, leads me to want to warn all who do not know Christ to get to know Him. Why? Because I do not want any of you to be left behind, to be eternally lost. I treat in my dental practice daily, as you do, the earthly gnashing of teeth and, if all indications and promises are correct, the eternal gnashing of teeth will be much worse than the common garden variety we see in our practices.

All questions concerning who is to be saved and who isn't are addressed in the second half of the Holy Bible. My concern is for those who have not even read it yet. Matthew

13:9 says, "Let him who has ears, hear." Forget about what other men say, even me, even your Priest, preacher, Imam or Rabbi and do some Bible study on your own. You know, the Great Reformation occurred when The Bible first became a printed book and with mass production the common man could read it in English, or German or French... for himself. Let God speak to you personally. Its just too important to let men keep you from knowing. We are no longer bound as people were in the Dark Ages.

The best selling book series, *Left Behind,* has been made into several movies. To get a feel for how this will all turn out, you can start out reading and viewing this fictionalized novel of the book of Revelation. Many are now hearing this for the first time. Of course the main source of inspired information is the Holy Bible and if you read one thing, just one thing, go to the parable of the weeds and, with your inner being, study the spiritual message of this incredible passage in Matthew 13:24-30 and its explanation by Jesus a few passages later in Matthew 13:36-43.

I think that the Holy Spirit in you will discern the significance of what Jesus describes as God's plan to allow many to grow up unscathed, unwitting, unknowing and without knowing Christ but that He will not select them for ascension into heaven. Many of you will recognize that God says that only a remnant will be saved (Isaiah 6:9-13 and Romans 9:27-29). This must make you curious as to how to avoid being "left behind."

If one is to grow and be more, be better, be as one is ultimately supposed to be, then one needs a pattern to follow. There is no better guide than the Holy Bible and the Word of God, both in the Old and the New Testament. As I mentioned, I grew up in a Christian household all my life, thought I was a Christian, but did not make sure until 1987, when I was 37 years old. I only started serious study of the Word of God in 1998. And that is when the transformation that leads me to write this particular chapter began. I now know that the reason I did not get more involved in Bible Study until 1998 was that I was thinking of myself, developing my career, my practice, my teaching and lecturing.

Reading and studying the Word is the one thing I urge all to do. I would not go by what someone else says about God's Word. I would read it myself, knowing what I now know. The personal, professional and family growth from this activity has been phenomenal. Praying the Prayer of Jabez, for instance, has produced results that only God could deliver! Thank you for allowing me to share with you my personal journey.

DENTISTRY COMES BACK INTO FOCUS

Now, back to something we can all sink our teeth into and agree upon without any consternation! God did expand our territory (70 to 100 to 120 to 170 new patients a month and among them patients from Alaska, Bermuda, England, Africa and Australia).

God did expand our influence (as a board member of the Suwanee Business Alliance, chairman of the capital growth committee at our church, by having the *Atlanta Journal* newspaper call me for an interview on BriteSmile; by my appearances on the cable television network TBN where I teach Doctor to Doctor segments on their broadcasts world wide, by being named Small Business Person of the Year, and by winning the Ron Lamb Award from the Christian Dental Society as the top missions dentist in North America).

> We are being protected from the pain that inflicts much of dentistry because of our prayers and our preparation for the storms that come our way.

God did expand our missions (Solstice Dental Advisors is booming as we teach other dentists, we're doing free dentistry for local Suwanee indigent in our Deserving Diva local dental mission program and we have built medical clinics, schools, churches, grain silos, water storage tanks and houses in Kenya).

God is guiding our methods and our actions because we have asked Him to do so (adding new staff and a new associates). We are being given opportunities to serve our patients and our community as never before (our "best months ever" keep coming year after year after year.) We are being protected from the pain that inflicts much of dentistry because of our prayers and our preparation for the storms that come our way.

So, there you have it. You have seen several reasons why I feel led to share with you about the results of prayer and this specific prayer of Jabez. My friends with whom I share this prayer also seem to be having similar results after praying to God in the manner of Jabez. We are truly blessed and we wish for all of you to be so blessed. God is good to those who follow his ways. Those who have ears should listen.

> My friends with whom I share this prayer also seem to be having similar results after praying to God in the manner of Jabez.

Thanks for your attention and indulgence as we drifted away from dentistry but, in my opinion, opened a much more important door for your consideration. If you would like to continue this dialogue, just email me personally for some answers to your questions or to discuss comments I have made. Don't let the birds of the air steal the seeds that have been sown here.

Previously, in our chapter about the Daycare Dynamite and the Tooth Fairy, we said we would share with you about our local dental mission projects and giving back to the community. I interceded with this topic, the Prayer of Jabez, ahead of that topic because it was the reason that the dental mission project was conceived. Now you know the rest of the story! Stay tuned for the Sugar Hill Dental Mission Project and what grew from it in the next chapter.

TAKE-AWAY POINTS

- Get Your Own Copy of the Holy Bible and Study it
- Pray the Prayer of Jabez to Expand Your Territory
- Read Select Passages and Ask That God Show You Their Meaning
- Bible Study Fellowship as a Formal Program with Over 1100 Classes Around the World and I Highly Recommend It

CHAPTER 29

Sugar Hill Mission Project and the Deserving Diva Makeovers

BLESSED ARE THE MERCIFUL

THE SUGAR HILL DENTAL MISSION serves indigent patients who have limited ability to access dental care. The purpose of this local, church-based program was to serve a need by offering the community a way to refer needy patients to local dental practices who would donate their services.

As we initially designed the program, a group of six Gwinnett County dentists volunteered to serve by seeing a maximum of one patient per month in their private practices. Our church, Sugar Hill United Methodist, would screen the applicants through their counseling and community relief center, the Haven of Hope. In order to be considered for the program, a patient had to be nominated by a pastor of one of the local churches in the area.

The announcement to the congregations in the area assured that the Sugar Hill Dental Mission had a steady stream of applicants for charity dentistry. Over time we expanded the number of dentists to a maximum of eight before the number of practices participating in the program began to wane. This particular mission lasted for a number of years and helped a significant number of people.

PROVERBS CARRIES
THE WISDOM OF THE AGES

"A generous man will himself be blessed, for he shares his food with the poor." Proverbs 22:9 In all, there are over 100 references to how we should treat the poor in The Bible. Repetition is one of God's ways of calling things that matter the most to our attention.

> Goodwill, known as cause marketing, flows downhill and influences the opinions and actions of the community.

Why are we discussing a local charitable program in a marketing book? The answer is obvious, to serve those in need, do good works and to establish good will in the community. Goodwill, known as cause marketing, flows downhill and influences the opinions and actions of the community. Cause marketing has been a staple of our dental business in the last 20 years. Every business, whether it's in the medical field or not, needs to be identified as a supporter of one or more causes. And that's just because it's just good business to be charitable and support local causes. When God adds His blessing to that, you see why we focus on it clearly and openly here in our treatise on marketing.

Causes elicit an emotional response from many patients who see sponsors as good corporate citizens and therefore worthy of consideration when choosing a place to shop and do business. I cannot emphasize this strong enough! What cause do you and your practice openly support?

> What cause do you and your practice openly support?

Is it one tied to your brand and identity or one tied to some charity outside your arena? There is a message here that you should hear as a dental team.

Over the years, the volunteering dentists we had

assembled began to drop out of the Sugar Hill Mission team. We continued for a few years on our own and then decided to change the direction of the local mission. It was the era of the Extreme Dental Makeover shows on television featuring our friend and fellow AACD members Drs. Bill Dorfman and Deborah King.

THE DESERVING DIVA PROGRAM

The Deserving Diva Makeovers were started in 2006 with one or two unannounced makeovers for especially deserving patients. That is, they were not selected by putting out a call for applications to the makeover program; they were just selected based on need from within our practice. Their treatment usually involved an extreme makeover of dramatic proportions, something that the individuals could never have afforded in their normal life. What we began to look for in our charity program was need and a special degree of deservedness, a quality of giving back to the community through selfless service.

Two years later, in 2008 we designed a dramatic upswing in the scope of the Deserving Diva Makeovers by adding a few of the successful features of the Sugar Hill Dental Mission to elements of ABC's Extreme Makeovers.

ELEMENTS OF THE DESERVING DIVA MAKEOVER:

1. Nominations would be sought from the public
2. Magazine ads offering the Deserving Diva Makeovers were placed in Gwinnett Magazine, the main county news source
3. Radio ads were played requesting nominations on 104.7 The Fish FM across metro Atlanta

4. Our entire patient database of 7,000 was emailed a special edition newsletter and given the opportunity to nominate a candidate.

5. A potential Deserving Diva could not nominate herself; she had to be nominated by her family, peers, co-workers or friends.

6. Our staff would take the nominations and review them, selecting the top 25 for the doctors to review.

7. Application forms would need to be filled out by ten finalists that included their personal story, recommendations by several references and a full dental examination to formulate a treatment plan by the doctors of Suwanee Dental Care.

8. We recruited other vendors to participate in the process, too. Sugarloaf Eye Care, Revival Salon, Advanced Ceramics, Pittman Dental Laboratory and Suwanee's Ambience Design & Interiors all donated to the cause.

9. We hired Marietta Video Productions to video the entire nomination, planning and selection process. When the time came to notify the winner, it was all caught on camera as a huge surprise. Because we have three or four dentists on our staff, we ended up choosing one Deserving Diva patient per dentist.

10. As their treatment progressed throughout each year, the video crew documented the progress, creating two five-minute videos per Diva. They were highlighted throughout the year on Atlanta Home & Style TV. This lifestyle television show is seen on local and cable TV around the city, state, nation and globe. In all, 55 million people had access to view the makeovers.

11. Once the makeovers are completed there is a Big Red Carpet Reveal Party. We have held these in conjunction with the United Way Kickoff Dinner in Gwinnett

and at the Top Gun Conference Awards Dinner at Lake Lanier Islands.

12. The completed cases are displayed in our magazine ads as well as on the TV shows and on our practice website, SuwaneeDental.com, the practice Facebook page and on our YouTube account.

13. One of the best rewards of being involved in the Deserving Diva program is the gratitude we receive from our Divas and their sharing on Facebook and our Deserving Diva blog about their good fortune of being selected and then their beautiful result once we have completed their makeovers.

In this chapter, Sugar Hill Dental Mission and Deserving Diva Makeovers, you see the progression of a cause marketing program from one concept and its metamorphosis into a real powerful force for generating good will and positive public vibes. The lesson is, don't be afraid to try something that can benefit your patients and your practice. But, don't stay wedded to an idea whose time has passed. The future belongs to those who are nimble andwho take stock of current

> One of the best rewards of being involved in the Deserving Diva program is the gratitude we receive from our Divas and their sharing on Facebook and our Deserving Diva blog about their good fortune of being selected and then their beautiful result once we have completed their makeovers.

> The future belongs to those who are nimble and who take stock of current trends and events and find a way to stay topical and relevant.

trends and events and find a way to stay topical and relevant.

GUERRILLA MARKETING FOCUS

My feeling is that guerrilla marketing should be low key at times and high profile at times. The focus on the practice or the doctor need not be the main point. In the Deserving Diva Makeovers, we have low doctor focus, low practice focus and high patient focus. The star of the show is the patient and their personal story of overcoming their life circumstance, making a difference in their community, being recognized for their contribution and being nominated by their friends or family.

Certainly the magazine, radio and TV presence is high profile, but their cost is minimal compared to the good public relationships developed as a result. I'll give you a hint here, the fact that we chose non-profit stations, were operating as a charitable event gave us a reason to get discounted media rates from some of the magazine, radio and TV stations and free donations from our generous vendor partners.

If you go to our YouTube channel at SolsticeDental, you can view many of our Deserving Diva Makeovers, our other Cosmetic Makeovers video taped in completeness by our producer, Donna Davis of Marietta Video Productions and our videographer, Daniel Trumble.

Action items to consider are: Consider the role of "cause marketing" in your practice and establish a game plan to offer support to that cause. Create a Public Relations Campaign around your "cause." Enjoy the process by involving your team, your patients and your entire community.

In our next chapter we will bring the two edges of dentistry together: high tech and soft touch. We present the Ying and Yang, the Alpha and the Omega. The focus is on being the best at both worlds, meeting a patient where they are, and understanding the psychological hot buttons of each.

TAKE-AWAY POINTS

- Serving Others Improves Focus
- Missions Matter to Many
- Local Missions Allow Local Participation
- Never Negate the Impact of Local Involvement

CHAPTER 30

High Tech —
Soft Touch Perception

EYES OF THE BEHOLDER

T HE FRONT PAGE of our practice brochure for over ten years had the words, High Tech—Soft Touch right under the name of the practice, Suwanee Dental Care. Why do you think I put that slogan in such a prominent place? Could it be that I am trying to set the stage, create an impression, or lock in a mindset?

High tech or old equipment? Soft touch or heavy handed? What do your patients perceive? I have asked our dental team, "Which is more ideal for a dental practice—to offer excellent dentistry and high tech services or being perceived as offering excellent dental care and high tech services?" The answers were divided down the middle. A hot debate ensued where one side said that being good had to be superior to being perceived as good since perceived did not mean that, in all actuality, it was good.

This last point is legitimate, but a dental practice could go out of business with excellent services that are not perceived so by its patients. Dental patients must perceive value that equates to being good for them. In today's world, high tech is often thought of as up-to-date and defines excellence. Modern equipment means the practice is financially able to provide the latest for its patients. It means

> Dental patients must perceive value that equates to being good for them.

that the dentist is usually in step with the leading edge technology and services. Patients like to go to the most successful dentist in town.

REALITY IS WHAT IS PERCEIVED BY THE PATIENT

Have you experienced this in your office? You delivered what you thought was an outstanding experience to a patient with your perception of the correct periodontal diagnosis with your high-tech Florida probe and your recommended treatment being totally appropriate. Then you later found out that the patient did not schedule for a return appointment because the perio probing was too painful, the appointment coordinator was rude at checkout and there was no offer to make any financial arrangements to pay for the $2,500 treatment recommendation.

> Soft touch occurs not just with the hands but with the psyche.

What was that patient's perception? Was the Law of Soft Touch violated? Soft touch occurs not just with the hands but with the psyche. We have to handle our patients with kid gloves at all times, lest they walk away and never come back.

Now just think about that custom-tailored suit you purchased that went beyond your expectations, which exceeded your perception. Isn't this just the same as a finely-crafted set of custom-stained porcelain veneers? This would equate to a Ritz Carlton or a Nordstrom's experience. In both instances, the reason to purchase should have been quite similar from a patient's viewpoint. The difference is that you would not return for another dental visit if the perception were negatively impacted by what was, in fact, received. A poor experience will quickly overcome the perception that excellence is the rule, not the exception.

Here is the crux of the matter: the perception of excellence or of offering a superior service makes a significant difference when it comes to turning a potential patient into an actual patient in your practice. The key is to insure that the service rendered can reinforce, then match or exceed, the patient's preconceived notion of how it should be. How many times do we go into a doctor's office with an expectation of how it will be and come out disappointed? The answer is, "All too often." Our goal, then, if we want to be successful in building a bridge to the person who presents to us for care, is to find out what the expectations are before we begin our care for that patient.

> Our goal, then, if we want to be successful in building a bridge to the person who presents to us for care, is to find out what the expectations are before we begin our care for that patient.

For those dental practices that are financially stable, the use of intelligent marketing sets them far ahead of all of their competitors. Their ability to develop and foster a "preferred" perception is faster and broader with continuous reinforcement potential. This mirrors the techniques we employ at Solstice Dental Advisors in our Marketing Action Plan with all direct mail, brochures, advertising and patient-on-hold messages pointing to our web site.

HOW TO MAKE THE RIGHT IMPRESSION

You may have to "fake it before you make it," as we all know. For those practices the presentation is the key. In this case, it's the high tech look, the online presence, the information flowing from the internal practice environment, the dental staff and even the literature racks and posters on the wall that can make the difference. Stepping up a notch, it's the practice web site, the Smile Channel, and Caesy patient education in-operatory video that creates the perception of excellence. Perhaps it's the Fotana LightWalker Erbium-YAG laser in the corner of the operatory, the Diagnodent in the hygiene room, or the Dexis Digital Radiography that is pointed out during the new patient tour that causes the new patient to give you a high credibility rating. Patient testimonials are also important armamentaria in the perception game, a most important tool for your success.

In the best of all worlds your dental practice will have a perceived worthiness and value that is substantiated by the dental services that are being offered. If it looks like a duck and quacks like a duck, it must be a duck. There may be nothing worse for your business in the local community than being perceived as the rough, careless or out-of-date dentist.

SOFT TOUCH

Now, let's talk about the concept of "soft touch." What patients want is a painless, on-time dentist. If you can only be one of those, the painless guy is still preferred, compared to the "Swiss watch" "time-is-money," "don't-have-time-to-wait" dentist. I have made it a perceived value that we are the painless dentists in town. We all know that dentistry and pain are not synonyms but that they well could be. We also know that no one gives 100% painless injections or always performs painless extractions or root canals. What we also know is that patients will sing your praises if you are perceived by them to be more empathetic, more careful, more gentle, more painless than their last dentist.

We start with the clear statement on our web site:

"You want Dentistry to be a gentle, positive experience. At Suwanee Dental Care we strive to provide excellent, comprehensive, gentle dentistry to discriminating individuals." Focus is on what the patient wants, not on what we want, gentle and positive, not a dental service, procedure or thing that they associate with pain... and negativity.

Next we tell prospective or current patients on our home page: "Serving patients who are our friends in a warm, Southwestern home-style environment is the goal of our well-trained dental team." Focus here is on being their servant, bringing them into our home and treating them as human beings, as friends, as family... not a number. Also notice that the team is treated as an object of high esteem here, not just an appendage.

Now on the web site we employ the clincher, the strengths of the doctor, compassion and experience. We inform the patients that, "Dr. Bill Williams (see bio) has served his patients with compassion and understanding since 1975. Experience does make a difference."

Can you see "soft touch" oozing through the computer screen into the keyboard, out the wire, to the mouse and onto the fingertips of the patients as they peck, click, and scroll? From the very first impression, we're forming an impression that *this* is the place they want to be, that *this* is the dentist for them.

PAINT THE PATIENT A PICTURE

The last paragraph of the opening page creates the vision of their preferred future: "You will find that we work to involve all of our patients in an active program to prevent dental disease. We combine high tech solutions with a soft touch. Simply put, we want to be the best dental office you've ever had!"

As you can see, the perception precedes the actual. We're reaching out and touching the mind of the patient before they ever enter the practice. We create believers before they have an actual experience. Then we have to make good on our promises. If seeing is believing, then we want our potential patients to "see" themselves as having a good dental experience with us by taking a vicarious dental visit while on our web site or on our on-hold messaging system.

We also want them to hear testimonials of our patients on our television special makeover features and read about them on Kudzu.com, Google and Yelp. Positive impressions of others having successful experiences are part of the sensitization of people considering who to chose as their dentist.

> Positive impressions of others having successful experiences are part of the sensitization of people considering who to chose as their dentist.

One thing I have found is it that the mental state of the patient improves the outcome for the patient. If I can plant seeds before, during and after the patients' visits, they are happier and easier to deal with. Our "We Cater to Cowards" sign is worth its weight in gold every year without fail. We get lots of referrals from it because wives or husbands send their "chicken" spouses. Who doesn't know five or ten dental phobics? They announce themselves with regularity.

Being a sedation dentist in a land of phobics is like being a duck hunter hiding in a duck blind in a lake full of mallards. Glowing testimonials are like duck decoys on the pond, attracting other phobic ducks. Dentistry can be your own personal Duck Dynasty!

In our preliminary interview and the new patient tour, our staff emphasizes the care, skill and judgment of the doctors. In our exam we are gentle but thorough. As we

place patients in the chair before their first treatment, their
first injection, we reassure them that we will be easy and
painless. We use topical on the oral mucosa. And, most
importantly, we developed the San Francisco technique for
our injections.

THE "SAN FRANCISCO" TECHNIQUE

As I approach, needle unseen, I perform a quick
movement: the pull of the tissue into the needle. Then I
begin "the shake," i.e. The San Francisco Technique. Of
course, I'm talking to them, usually asking a question…
and, all the while my assistant is patting their shoulder.
We're doing as many distractions at once as we can. All
this while, the patient is thinking about the answer to the
question that I just asked them… just before the injection.

You ask, "What is the San Francisco technique?"
Sometimes I'll ask my patients what it reminds them
of, what I'm doing as I give the injection. Distraction is
increased. I'm getting them to think about something rather
than about what is going on in their mouth. When they link
the shaking with the term San Francisco Technique, they
usually laugh and it's a good feeling we have generated. If
you know much about NLP, neurolinguistic programming,
you'll see how making a potentially bad experience such as
an injection be associated with laughter and good feelings
is a positive step in overcoming dental phobia and anxiety.
We know it's the shaking that is the best distraction and it
reminds me of an earthquake, the shaking of the shelves,
the rattling of the teacups in the cupboard, ergo, The San
Francisco Technique!

By the time the patient figures it out, I am finished with
the injection and they are laughing. Quite a change from
the usual and we have a friend for life. How many patients
finish their shot and laugh?

Action items to consider today could be: Evaluate the

perceptions your patients have of your practice. A patient survey is a good way to do this. Review the elements of "soft touch" and see if your doctors and your dental hygienists are known for being gentle or rough, compassionate or callous. Make a plan to modify behavior in any instance that fall short of your protocols and office policies.

Author's Note: As I write this chapter, it's the 4th of July here in Suwanee, Georgia in 29 minutes. Thank God for America and for the legacy that our forefathers have given us. We certainly have much to celebrate in this great nation. We have been blessed as a nation under God. In the next chapter of *Marketing The Million Dollar Practice,* you'll be examining the impact of community work on the dental practice. I'll share experiences that we encountered as we saw our growth double in two years. Our marketing needs changed as we transitioned from a startup practice to a maintenance practice that was fully mature.

TAKE-AWAY POINTS

- High Tech Means Up-To-Date
- Soft Touch Means You Care
- Perception Matters Most
- Create the Reality You Want
- Establish Your Future of Choice, Not Chance

CHAPTER 31

Dental Missions Fallout

CONSEQUENCES

*A*S I CLOSED OUT OUR PREVIOUS *MARKETING THE MILLION DOLLAR PRACTICE* chapter on local missions, I said we would be examining the dentist's role of doing good works in the community at large and its impact on the dental practice next. So, I'll share my experiences that occurred in the third and fourth years of our new practice startup. It's a truly amazing story and one that I hope you can see is our gift from the Lord to share with you. And, this story is one that has replayed itself every year since… for the past 13 years.

Our growth doubled in those two years. Our marketing needs changed with the transition from a startup practice to a maintenance practice that was fully mature. We had been averaging 100 new patients a month by our second year in Suwanee and we were cutting down on our external marketing quite a bit, moving to the softer, gentler internal marketing methods that are the earmarks of a successful practice. We had already moved into our new 3,000-square-foot facility and taken in our first associate dentist. In order to balance our professional position in our community, I formed two dental charity events, the Sugar Hill Dental Mission and Kenya Dental Mission.

At that time, our marketing was done with the purpose of creating a positive image of the practice in a

> We wanted to be seen as the people who care, who know and can deliver quality dentistry.

low-key way. We were looking to develop the niche in our area as the high tech-soft touch practice. We wanted to be seen as the people who care, who know and can deliver quality dentistry.

What I want you all to know and feel confident in is that the reason for doing dental missions is not related to the marketing result that one gets from doing the mission. We do dental missions to fulfill God's great commission to serve others in need and to spread the word about God's saving grace through Jesus Christ, His Son. We feel that God rewards those who have a pure heart and act according to His purposes.

> **People who hear about our practice as a result of our mission trips are His blessing and we are thankful to God for sending them to us.**

People who hear about our practice as a result of our mission trips are His blessing and we are thankful to God for sending them to us. Therefore, I call this article Dental Missions Fallout because our dental office receives a blessing or unintended "fallout" from the missions work we do.

LOCAL MISSIONS

An earlier chapter detailed our successful local dental mission, the Sugar Hill Dental Mission. "Giving Back to Those Less Able" was about the six area dentists volunteering to see indigent patients in pain or with debilitating cosmetic needs in their respective offices. I'm happy to report that the number of dentists participating grew to eight.

The focus of this chapter, then, is to correlate the effects of these two types of dental mission projects, one local and one international, and to see how they had a positive impact on our dental practice, our overall patient population and the potential patient pool all across the Atlanta area.

I believe nothing happens in a vacuum. Life is a wholistic event whereby one action impacts many other actions. It's one of the laws of nature, the Law of Cause and Effect. Think of it as a chain reaction in chemistry or as a cue ball breaking up the rack of billiard balls. When you let God be the one in charge and you follow His will, good things happen.

As I discussed earlier, the number of impressions that get sent out by a practice, that get noticed by the potential patient population and that eventually get acted upon, measures marketing success. Dental missions, while implemented for altruistic purposes, do get noticed, do get talked about, and do create favorable impressions in the public eye. They are another form of impressions being made, good impressions.

CASE STUDY: WOMP IN ACTION

For example, here is how the word travels, the story goes around and the legend builds. I wrote the chapter on local charitable works and giving back to those less able. Well, after I had started that program in our area, one of my dental mission patient's stories about finding pain relief for TMJ after 10 years and nine

> When you let God be the one in charge and you follow His will, good things happen.

> Dental missions, while implemented for altruistic purposes, do get noticed, do get talked about, and do create favorable impressions in the public eye. They are another form of impressions being made, good impressions.

doctors (but no dentists) was to be featured in our church newsletter. This newsletter, called Coming Home, goes out to 5,000 local residents of our community. In addition to her story, the editor of Coming Home asked me to describe our local dental mission project for an accompanying article to the patient's story. The editor wanted to know how the TMJ patient came to be one of our patients. I sent her an article called "Giving Back to Those Less Able." She essentially printed it in its entirety.

The good "fallout" from that combination of two dental mission articles has been that hundreds of my current patients and thousands of people in our community who I have not met who now have a good impression of our practice. They will need a dentist or will be making a dental purchasing decision within the next year or two. These articles will favorably impact the decision as to where they will spend their dental dollars. They will also favorably impact the public's perception of the entire dental profession.

KENYA MEDICAL OUTREACH

Another dental mission success story for the practice has been the Kenya Dental Mission. Upon return from Kenya, I busily scanned scores of photographs into my computer. Twenty web pages of the 80 or so photos of the people, places and animals of Kenya went online in the summer of 2001. I updated the website every year for the next ten or twelve years as we completed more and more mission trips to Kenya and beyond. I told the story of the trips in pictures with captions. Our trip sponsors received a link to this page with a grateful acknowledgment to them for their support.

Once the Kenya web pages were completed, I emailed the link to hundreds of people on my email list, many of which, as I mentioned, had supported us in the dental mission with their prayers, their equipment and supply donations and their financial contributions. Many of them were locals in the community. The website about Kenya is very interesting so it gets lots of hits, thousands each year. The people who were directed by our email to view it had to go to the link via the front page of my dental practice web site (suwaneedental.com) to access the Kenya Dental Mission pages. So you see, the number of impressions we get for the dental office as well as the mission projects was dramatically increased.

After I finished the arduous task of building the web presence for the 2001 Kenya Dental Mission trip, I began to build my Kenya Power Point presentation. For this new project, I had to rescan my photos because I had made my initial scans too small for good projection on a wall (but good for a web site). I hope you learn from my mistakes here. Too large a file shuts down a Power Point presentation (I did that, too!) and too few pixels in a photo file makes for a fuzzy projected photo.

Once the Power Point presentation was complete, I printed a CD of it, bought a small LCD projector and had a portable show ready to roll. Over the next six months, I shared the presentation to the following groups: my family, of course, our Georgia AGD Mastertrack class of 25 dentists, our Iron Men's class of 35 men at our church, our Sunday night Praise and Worship Service at church, the Sugar Hill UMC Health Fair and the couples Sunday morning class of 30 folks. Later that next year, as 2002 dawned, we made a showing to the singles class at church and to the Suwanee Business Alliance, which were 100 of the movers and shakers in our local business community.

Over the past decade, thousands of local Atlanta area residents have seen our live presentations. Many more have seen the television features on Atlanta Home & Style and on Good Morning Atlanta local network shows. Five local radio interviews have featured our latest practice news and allowed us to talk about the mission to Kenya as well.

Because the show can be tailored from 15 to 60 minutes in length, it is adaptable to a number of programs and events. I can also send the CD out to others if they wish to view the presentation or show the presentation themselves to a group. Very often, the people who see the presentation wish their spouse or children had been there to see the Power Point show. I tell them that they can show their family the show on the web site by clicking on the Kenya Dental Mission link on my web site at Suwaneedental.com. I'm sure you see the logic in the placement of these links on the dental web site that is a part of who we are and what we represent.

BE PREPARED—NOT JUST A MOTTO FOR BOY SCOUTS

Now, just about everywhere I go, there is a person who comes up to me at church or around town and says they saw or heard about the patients we are treating, the mission we went on to Africa or some other project we have been involved with in the community (see the previous chapters on PowerCore, Sponsoring Community Events, and Day Care Dynamite). They usually ask if we are still taking new patients. They usually ask for a business card.

I carry a stack of cards with me in my wallet or coat pocket. Thankfully, we are winning the hearts and minds of the community and doing a lot of dentistry along the way. Again, praise be to God for his generosity and faithfulness.

OUR FIRST KENYA MISSION REPORT

Here is one of our Kenya Dental Mission reports. We compile a report each year and send them to various supporters and patients who request them:

June 26, 2001 (our first mission trip to Kenya)
Greetings from back in Atlanta,

After a week back in the office and a week scanning photos then uploading them onto the web site, I am now getting on with the task of reporting to you, my wonderful support team, all about our two weeks in Kenya. As time passes, the magnitude of what has been accomplished grows. In the retelling of the stories, the scope and depth of this mission are revealed to me, even though I did not realize it while we were in the midst of the trip.

We took seven in our group: a dentist (that would be me), two dental assistants (my wife Sheila and Karin, 25, from Virginia), my son Tyler, 17; his friend Jeremiah, 17; from school; Paul, 23, from Brad's church; and my brother Brad, a minister and the founder of KMO. You should all know that each of them played a vital role in the success of our trip, in both the dental and film missions. We needed all of their help in the dental clinics at one time or another. And, they did an excellent job.

There was also another U.S. citizen who worked the two weeks before us in building a church in Olmekenyu. We each took two duffle bags of 70 lb. each plus our carry on knapsacks full of medical supplies, food and a few clothes. Where we were in Kenya is 5,000 to 6,000 feet above sea level. We were just south of the equator and the weather was cool in the evenings and mornings, perfect in the daytime, much like Atlanta in the Spring.

You are now able to see the places and major events on the web site as well as the major players in this mission. We flew into London, spent the day sightseeing before taking the late plane into Nairobi. We were picked up in a Toyota Land Cruiser by our excellent driver Jeffrey. We immediately headed for the supermarket then out into the bush to Olmekenyu where the medical/dental clinic building has been built. The drive was over good roads, and then fair roads, then dirt roads, then muddy roads.

Driving in Kenya is hazardous to your timetable. You never know if you will be stuck in the mud or not. This is especially true in rainy season. We were on the end of such a rainy season. A four-wheel drive is essential and I prefer the Land Cruiser over the mini-buses there. We by-passed quite a few stuck mini-buses over the two weeks there. We only got stuck once and that was only for ten minutes. Its worth the extra money to hire a Land Cruiser in my opinion.

We stopped off in Narok, at the hospital, to pick up our Community Dental Health Specialist, Dr. Daniel Chepygon, a three-year graduate of the British system in Kenya. He can do anesthesia, fillings, extractions, partials, dentures and root canals. There are additionally trained (four more years) dentists in Kenya, but there were none in Narok or the entire district we visited. Daniel was our legal means of practicing dentistry in Kenya without going through lots of red tape, plus he was invaluable as far as diagnosis, translation and in giving anesthesia.

The clinic building that Brad and our team are building in Olmekenyu is nearly complete. We were able to hold the first dental clinic in it this trip. Brad had rigged up two ingenious wooden dental chairs for us. Our first afternoon, we saw 46 patients, working until 8 p.m. with flashlights as the rain darkened the sky by 6 p.m. The next day, we worked two shifts, morning and afternoon, and saw 112 patients, all for extractions. You have to see the photos to appreciate seeing that many patients in the clinic.

In between sessions, we visited a local primary school and presented them with books, musical instruments and other gifts from the United States. We only brought 300 toothbrushes and those were given to the 6th, 7th and 8th grade students. I gave them oral hygiene instructions in English and the headmaster translated into Swahili.

After two days in Olmekenyu, which is in Kipsigi territory, we trucked over to a distant region called Morijo where the Masai live. This is an area seldom visited by outsiders. We were the first dentists to be in both Olmekenyu and Morijo. Our extractions with xylocaine were the first done in these regions with such comfort. John, our guide and host told us that they usually cut out teeth with a knife with no anesthetic.

In Morijo, we held three clinics, one in the afternoon in the "downtown area," one the next afternoon at a local nurse's office. We trained the nurse to do extractions and left some good dental instruments for him to use. Then we held a clinic at John's home where we stayed. You'll notice from the pictures on the web site that the conditions went from difficult to more difficult with each succeeding clinic. We were standing doing extractions with the patients sitting on a bucket the last morning at John's.

All in all, we saw 252 patients and removed 600 teeth. Daniel diagnosed and anesthetized 90% of them and I extracted 90% of the teeth. Many broke off at the bony crest and had to be elevated. A handful of them each took a half hour to remove, especially the impacted third molars that we found ourselves tackling. We used the international tooth numbering system and it got to be a joke on our side of the clinic that we did not want to see #38 or #48 teeth any more.

I certainly learned a thing or two about what can be done with each of the many strange dental exodontia instruments that I had donated to the cause by many of you. I am proud to have left only one root tip in the entire 600. The lack of suction (we used 2x2 gauze to enable us to see, once the roots broke off and the blood covered the tooth in the socket). I got good at packing gauze with an elevator then removing it to see, for a moment, where to elevate.

We worked at the hospital in Narok for one afternoon's

clinic. That was our only time in a real "normal" dental setting. However, the instrumentation and equipment was not in good working order so our ability was hindered. At this, the only dental clinic in the region, there was not one working dental high speed or slow speed hand piece. Additionally, the suction was not functional. I did have the use of an operatory light and a cavitron. On two hospital employees, I excavated a class five lesion with an excavator and the cavitron and placed a glass ionomer restoration.

We had donated by many of you (most notably my dental school instructor, Dr. Arun Nayyar) a total of 50 extraction forceps, 25 elevators, and many hemostats, mirrors, syringes, etc, . I also had about 800 carpules of anesthetic. After the first two clinics where we saw 158 patients in about 17 hours, I was worried about running our of anesthetic. As it turned out, we did not see as many people per day after the second day. I was able to donate the remaining supplies and equipment to the three areas where we did clinics.

The Narok hospital dental clinic was given 20% of the instruments, Daniel was given five forceps for his private clinic in Narok, the nurse in Morijo was given a couple of instruments and the bulk of the donated instruments went to our budding dental clinic in Olmekenyu. Daniel will use them if he can get up there one day a month. (Author's note in 2013: Dr. Daniel has been going to Olmekenyu every year on his own in the winter time to do charity dentistry in KMO's name since 2001, in addition to being with us when we travel there in the summer.)

You'll be interested to know that we have built the clinic, the pastor's home and the church so far. Plans include building a physician's home and two nurses' homes plus a hotel. All this goes on the 11 acres that were either donated or purchased by Kenya Medical Outreach, Inc. and donated back to the community to be run by their board of commissioners. Another trip is being planned for 2002, either in Feb, April, or the summer, perhaps in two of those times.

In addition to doing dental mission work, we spent our evenings on six nights showing the Jesus film in either Swahili or Masai languages. We carried a VCR, video projector, sound system and a generator to remote churches in the areas where we did dental clinics. All in all, we had over 2000 attend these inspirational sessions. Many saw a movie for the first time in their lives. Many came to know Christ as their personal savior during our invitations. The talks by the people, their witnesses, were inspiring to us.

After the dental missions, we went into the Masai Mara National Game Reserve to see the greatest natural resource in Kenya, its wild animals. Everyone going to Kenya needs to experience the variety and habitat of the native fauna. We stayed first at Fig Tree Camp then at Mara Serena Lodge. This is what Kenya shares with the world and it is unique, a bucket list experience!

I want to again thank the many of you who donated your time, money, equipment, supplies, and prayers to this worthy cause. We impacted many hundreds this trip and will impact many thousands, as the clinic becomes fully operational over time. This clinic will be the major medical and dental center for perhaps 300,000 people in the coming years.

I'll be getting more info out about our 2002 trip in time for you to either join us or support the mission again. I want to send a few items to our main support team still in Kenya, Daniel, our dentist, John, our guide, and Jeffrey, our driver. If any of you have used 4-hole hand pieces for Daniel at the Narok hospital, I want to send some over immediately. If any of you have a used camera, I want to send one to John. And If anyone has (another) used Pentium laptop, I want to get one for Jeffrey. We had five *laptops donated for the hospital and the clinic this time.*

Over the next six months, I will stockpile anything any of you wish to donate for the next trip. Boxes continue to come in periodically even as I type this letter. In addition to the things dental, there is always a need in the local schools for teaching aids, books, musical instruments and the like. If you ever join us, you'll get as much joy in presenting these gifts to the school kids as anything related to teeth and our profession.

Please visit the web site for a real look at the way it was, June 1-13, 2001 in Kenya.

Sincerely,
Bill Williams, DMD, FAGD
www.suwaneedental.com
follow this link to the Kenya web site
(Author's note: We now have another site where we keep information available www.kenyamo.com)
p.s. Many thanks are due Dr. Sarah Roberts who kept the Suwanee Dental office going while we were on our first mission trip to Africa.

Now, stay tuned for some dynamic marketing lessons in the next chapter from the hot book, Differentiate or Die by Jack Trout. I have synopsized the major passages and will be relating them to the practice of dentistry.

TAKE-AWAY POINTS

- Belief And Faith in Jesus as Savior is the Key
- Good Works are Blessed by God
- Being Known as the Missions Dentist Has Been Very Positive in Our Community, to Those We Serve and to Our Own Selves
- Missions Fallout is a Real Blessing to Our Practice

CHAPTER 32

The 12 Differentors: A Marketing Treatise on Dental Practices

Based on the Book, "Differentiate or Die,"
by Jack Trout with Steve Rivkin
Quoted, Summarized and Adapted
by Dr. Bill Williams

*A*S YOU READ THIS, consider the state of marketing in your practice. Consider if you have a marketing action plan in place and who is in charge of it. What is the growth rate of your practice over the past two years? To what do you attribute this rate?

1. Too Many Choices and the Havok It Causes

The Fork in the Road: When setting up your marketing action plan, the path can be viewed as an ever-expanding sea of options. Just when you think you have arrived at your final destination, there is another decision to make, another option to consider. It's endless. Not only is it a long and winding road but one filled with high roads, low roads, left turns and right turns, rabbit holes and dead ends. What is a dentist to do?

Right now, we can go down two roads with this discussion: one when speaking about how a dentist chooses a marketing action plan, and two, how a dentist puts together a treatment plan for a patient so that they understand it and move forward. Both are sales processes with the same end goal. I call it looking at the BIG picture (your practice MAP) and at the SMALL picture (an individual patient's treatment plan, your PTP). Both are important so, in this chapter, we'll give some examples of both as we go through the key points.

The Choices: The Internet is a sea full of dot coms and dot nets that can give us unlimited information, education and opportunity. Consumer psychologists say this plethora of choices is driving us off the deep end. So many choices, offering instant fulfillment. People are stymied, they lose their ability to decide, they hesitate, they pull back and resist change all because of over-stimulation. In a sense, they get bored.

The takeaway point is to reduce choices for your patients to two or three, perhaps to even just one. Consider this in treatment planning and giving multiple options. Give informed choices, yes, but don't overwhelm the patient with endless options. What we have found is that patients want your highly informed PTP recommendation most of all.

A note about specialization: In the past, specialization was considered a good approach in almost every case. Now, the trend has changed from being a specialist to being more of the Super Generalist, the Specialist of the Entire Mouth. In our teaching of the Solstice 5M, I call it being the Decathlon Dentist. Patients want it and in this economic climate, the rewards of being comprehensive are dramatic. Therefore, spend the time to learn each facet of dentistry well before forging ahead to the next discipline. Be good at being the comprehensive dentist to your patients or don't try it at all.

2. Unique Selling Proposition—Your USP

Know the Reason They Should Choose You: USP is being different in the eyes of the consumer: In advertising any product or service, you need to give a potential patient a good reason to choose you to perform.

Find your USP: Realize that you can't be all things to all people. If you disregard your uniqueness and attempt to serve everybody at every level, you may soon weaken your brand and all that makes you special. If you stay in the shadow of your larger competitors and never establish your different-ness, you will always be weak. In Suwanee, we say that we love our competition. For the most part they are all invisible. Of the 50 dental practices within a ten-mile radius of our practice only about three of them are effective marketers.

> Find your USP.
> Realize that you
> can't be all things
> to all people.

Branding takes time for a dental practice and is expensive to create. But, once it is set up it separates the little players from the big players. What is your preference? Do you aspire to be big or to stay little in your community?

> Branding takes
> time for a dental
> practice and is
> expensive to
> create. But, once
> it is set up it
> separates the little
> players from the
> big players. What
> is your preference?
> Do you aspire
> to be big or to
> stay little in your
> community?

Entertaining with the ad at the same time is extra, it is not the reason for your ad. Too many ads these days focus on being cute, artsy or politically correct. The better ads will be the ones that get results, not entertain.

Each ad, email, postcard or letter must make a proposition to the buying public. Consumers look for specific benefits, solutions to their problems. You must make a proposition that other dentists are not, will not or cannot make. Uniqueness is a highly desired ingredient for differentiation: such as a 70-page dental web site, comprehensive dentistry for the entire family so that they don't have to go anywhere else, 25 years of dental implant experience, or an e-commerce shopping cart on your web site to purchase products and services, pay dental bills and check on insurance status.

How do you attract the new patient when there are so many personality styles and variations? The question begs an answer: The left-brain types are creative and emotional; the right-brain are factual and rational. The concept of being unique or different is far more important in the year 2013 than it was in 1960. Marketer dentists need to be talented in recognizing that there must be balance in their approach, appealing to many personality types in each ad is ideal.

In a campaign, speaking to all personality types is essential. Think of the DISC profile and the Drivers, the Influencers, the Steady and the Careful. Give each type a reason to choose you in your ad copy and in your email campaigns. Make a separate USP to fit each personality style. Another unique system divides the personality types into Intuitives, Thinkers, Feelers and Sensors.

Differentiation with the personality types is the key to life or death of a brand. In dentistry, think of your brand as the image the public has of your line of services. Imagine the marketing of those services and your practice as a whole as the magnet that draws them to you. Yet, you need to attract the four personality types each with a different message.

Differentiating with Intuitives: People who use intuition concentrate on the possibilities. Next generation products could be cosmetics, high tech, and leading edge. They love to be shown the whole picture in an overview from 40,000 feet so they can understand how it fits in the whole scheme of things. They gather information to process it quickly.

Differentiating with Thinkers: Use details, logic, cost… the argument of facts. As they move forward, they need to understand each detail and how it fits into the plan specifically. They don't show or relate to emotional pulls as much as feelers. Two thirds of males are thinkers.

Differentiating with Feelers: They are relationship seekers. They need to fit in, avoid conflict and to decide if their point of view will cause any strife before voicing it. Their strength is that they get along well with most others, but their weakness is that they are easily led by stronger types.

Differentiating with Sensors: They want all the details, the explanations, the how-tos and the processes before they get their dentistry. Sensors are slower to process information, but when they do they move ahead steadily. 70% of Americans are sensors. Use the CAESY patient education software program in treatment consults with them.

The Diamond Rule of Marketing: Just as the many facets on a priceless cut diamond reflect brilliance, anything can be differentiated, made different from its original look, use or purpose, and become more valuable. Your practice can be enhanced by offering patients more than they think they need or have come to expect. Remember the story of the baker's dozen and the little extra he added to over-fill the order by just one more. Going beyond what is normal or expected generates a feeling of gratitude, very positive vibes and actually creates a desire to return the favor, invoking the Law of Reciprocity.

In the end, it's all about the reinvention of your USP. Get a trained professional's opinion to be sure you get it right. Spending time to hone your message and create your MAP is critical to your success in marketing.

How do most people select their USP? By listening to others and copying it if it resonates. That is called "me-too ism." You'll be more successful if you upgrade or reinvent your USP. Those who shoot for the moon will at least reach the stars. Create a dental office unlike any other. What if your USP were, "America's Most Sought-After Dentist." It's okay to have to say, "Due to overwhelming demand, please allow 4-6 weeks for a dental appointment." This works as long as the wait is worth the wait and "the experience" is a big enough payoff.

3. Quality and customer service are not differentiating ideas

Quality is a Given: Quality should be a given these days, not a difference. Knowing and loving your patient is a given, not a difference, or at least it should be a given. In the old days it was an easy win just having decent customer service and a measure of quality. Not now because everyone tries to make that a cornerstone of their practice. You can still rise above the masses of "quality" dentists if you are really good at focusing on the patient. The New Patient Experience that I teach in the Solstice 5M and which is covered in detail in this book with its ten stations along the route to success is a very patient-friendly differentiator.

Giving more than expected is a winner, too. A patient loyalty program that rewards multiple good behaviors is one example of differentiation that sets you apart in dentistry. There are not many of them yet, so now would be a good time to jump onto that band wagon, while you can still be on the leading edge of that guerrilla marketing attack tactic. Loyal Patient Savings and Rewards is a program that my practice, Suwanee Dental Care, has used for over five years very successfully.

A marketing campaign consists of holding on to your current patients while at the same time attracting new patients who now use your competitors, if anyone at all. That means finding a point of differentiation unique and meaningful within the dental industry. We believe the best strategy is focusing on taking a different path because it's the one you can predetermine to win. For instance, procedure mix combined with quality and customer satisfaction can be huge. Focus on filling your seats with crowns, wisdom teeth, endo and implants instead of just single fillings, simple extractions, denture adjustments. Service can be used as a differentiator; it can be your big strategy... but only if your competition is foolish enough to allow you to dominate this niche. Fortunately in dentistry, there are a lot of not so marketing-savvy competitors. So we suggest you go for this differentiator in a big way.

4. Price is Rarely a Differentiating Idea Unless Tagged to a Formula

Price is Often the Enemy of Differentiation: By definition, being different should be worth something. It's the reason that supports the case for paying a little more—or at least the same—for a product or service. Focusing on price exclusively to get new patients or more sales is unhealthy and leads to commoditization of your services.

Michael Dell rewrote the computer hardware industry. His method was to avoid retailers and go directly to users through Dell's online commerce sites. Dentistry's lesson: go to the Internet to buy direct for dental supplies and other commodities. Look for "me too" products that are generic but can be had at 25% of premium prices. Join buyer's groups to save. They are out there and allow you to cut your cost of production so that you can be profitable even in your fee-based formula promotions. If you knew where to get an implant system that included the implant, abutment, cover screw all for under $100 wouldn't you use it?

Use Ameritrade's approach: Both Dell and Ameritrade start with price. But without a structural advantage, you can't win the game with price only. Moving up the food chain is critical to profitability. Our lesson was that young dentists may open with PPO membership as a feature of their practices, but they eventually dump them because they often lose money serving their patients. At the very least, negotiating better rates and only keeping the best of the PPO's is the name of the game.

Make pricing work for you. Do something unique and meaningful for the customer to cause them to refocus on your offer. Mess with their mind a bit. If you can throw them off their skeptical mindset and cause them to consider your argument, then you have solved half of your marketing problem. Make the offer so attractive that it cannot be refused; add in bonuses instead of cutting prices severely. Tie your price to a formula to arrive at a handsome profit in the end. Know the lifetime value of a new patient and be willing to spend a lot to get them laser-locked into your practice. You may want to give a steep discount to get a patient in the door but you don't have to continue giving away your farm from that point on. That is why specials are special, not the normal day-to-day price.

Promotions: Promotions do not seem to leave memory traces. The bigger the promotional blip, the bigger the loss. Any dummy can offer a deal, but it takes genius, courage, faith and perseverance to build a trusted brand. Dentists who dedicate their advertising to creating a favorable image, the most sharply defined identity for their brand, are the ones who will achieve market dominance and be able to command the highest prices. If you are choosing to be the high-priced dentist in town, you have to back it up with expert status and authority. That would be "your branding."

Again, your formula, if you are seeking the high end of the market may look something like this: smooth, classic ads featuring quality, luxury, and exclusivity. You'll get a few clients but the ones who do come will spend a lot. Then, the other end of the spectrum is those dentists who enjoy and seek the large majority of the public who want basic to good dentistry at a reasonable price. They use low promotional fees and get many new patients to come to their practice, to kick the tires and perhaps continue with them in the future. What is key to measure here is the total lifetime patient value created by multiple treatments at higher fees versus lower fees.

People will pay for quality, perceived quality and position. If you are not working on your public relations, building your reputation and adding to your resume all the time, you may not be able to command the fees you wish. And, speaking of low-priced dentists, don't get the reputation for being the low-priced guy in town. You don't want this conversation overheard about you, "That guy is really cheap, but not the one to go to when you want really good dental care."

Differentiating with high price can pay big dividends. Patients who can afford the best are more impressed with dentists who employ the high price differentiator.

1. High-end dentistry should be more expensive. Patients expect to pay more for excellence, but the quality should be notably better than the average dentist can create in some way the patient can experience.

2. High-end dentistry offers prestige and lends status to the purchaser. There is a segment of the population that looks for and appreciates this benefit.

3. When dentistry carries a high price it says the service is worth what you have to pay for it. When a practice, a doctor is obviously successful, this is social proof that others feel the same way. High price does differentiate.

5. The Stepping Stones to Differentiation

Step 1. Understand the Context: Start with what the community thinks and feels about other neighbor dentists. What marketing message have they sent forth? Make a list of how they are perceived by the community and create your Marketing Action Plan to attack those areas in which they are most vulnerable.

Step 2. Find the "One Big Thing," the Differentiating Idea: Separate yourself from those dentists by understanding that the secret is that it does not have to be feature-related such as in offering crowns, whitening, implants and or free exams. The key is to find your USP, your unique selling proposition, your special difference, and then use it to establish a benefit for your patient. This could be "lifetime whitening" as a guarantee or "Six-Month Braces" as a time-savings focus point in your marketing.

Step 3. Earn the Credentials and Communicate Them: Expert status, unique selling proposition and social proof of your ability to produce excellent dentistry must be communicated in ways that reach your target market. Your story may be the best in town but if no one hears it, it is of little value. Developing a Marketing Action Plan and having a Guerrilla Marketing Attack Plan to enact it are crucial. This involves the outlay of time and money. It takes a lot of one or both to win patients over.

Advertising is costly. Ideas without dollars don't create results. You have to spend money to make money in dentistry just as in any other business. Be prepared to give in order to receive. You must spend your first dollars on marketing to stay in the profit side of the equation. You can't save your way into prosperity, but you can spend your way there.

The one with the most dollars will nearly always win. In marketing, dollars drive results. Having the resources to drive your ideas into the minds of your potential clients is the key to market domination. If you dedicate 4% on marketing, you can readily see why those who can and will spend 4% of $3,000,000 do better at dominating the market than the dentist who can spend only 4% of $500,000. $120,000 is six times $20,000 and buys a lot more ads, ad words, SEO, TV time, articles, radio spots, flyers, postcards, email blasts and impressions in the community. That is why a practice with associates, i.e. a group practice, can overtake a solo practice by size alone. Economy of scale is a big thing in marketing. Joining others in what is termed "fusion marketing" is one way to compete with these larger practices.

6. Differentiation Occurs in the Mind

Simple is Superb; Complex is Clumsy: Confusion seems to be everywhere; we are all "over-communicated." The information age has overtaken us in its sheer volume and frequency. Jack Trout calls it, "Electronic Bombardment." Therefore, dentists, to be effective marketers must stay "on differentiation."

There is only so much a person can comprehend; we tend to weed out extra info that is not relevant or needed when it arrives. The number one and number two dental practices in the community have a tremendous psychological edge over the later arrivals. You must work to be number one in your community or your niche.

The secret to being remembered is getting to the core of the problem. Develop a thorough understanding of your competition and their position in the mind of your prospective patients. Don't focus on what you want; instead, dig deeper into what your competition will allow you to do. Find the weak chink in their armor and use it to your advantage.

The Power of Easy: The number one way to avoid the psychological mine fields of over-communication, electronic bombardment, complexity and hyper-stimulation is to make it easy, simplifying your core message. The lesson here is not to try to tell your entire story. Just focus on one powerful differentiating idea and fire it into the mind of the patient. i.e. high tech, soft touch. If there is any trick to finding that simple set of words, it's one of being ruthless about how you edit your story. Anything that others could claim just as well as you can, eliminate. Anything that does not fit your customers' perceptions, avoid.

Overcoming Uncertainty and Anxiety: Most patients don't know why they make certain choices or react in ways that may sabotage their future. They may be insecure or fearful. They may have had childhood events that cloud their thinking. They may not even know what motivates them to react a certain (usually harmful as in dental phobia) way. It is a scientific fact that the brain tends to remember and is influenced by things from the past that no longer exist. The dentist and team that study this psychology of the mind and understand the sales psychology that goes with each personality style and reactionary type of patient will serve those patients better in the long run.

Be the Authority: Considering that most patients struggle to put all of this together and to navigate the medical-dental waters tranquilly, being in a position of authority and being seen as the expert has a distinct advantage here. Recognition of who's number one in the minds of the community and the power of being first is the evidence. Foster your image in your local area as the best dentist, the top dentist. Allay their insecurity and anxiety by being who they want you to be. Fill the role of their caring, compassionate caretaker. This is what people want—a Dr. Marcus Welby-like DDS.

People Buy What Others Buy: More often than not, people buy what the think they should have. They're sort of like sheep, following the flock. The main reason for this kind of behavior is insecurity. If you've been around a long time, people trust you more and feel secure in their purchase. This is why heritage is a good differentiator. Capitalize on it. That's why we say, "Doesn't everyone use ClO-Sys?" This is why people buy from perceived leaders. They say, "If everyone else is buying it, I should be buying it, too."

The Power of the Specialist: When you study the market-ing battles between companies, the well-differentiated specialist tends to be the winner. That is not to mean as a dental specialist necessarily , but as an expert provider of the service being marketed (like orthodontics, implants, cosmetic makeovers or neuromuscular dentistry), one that the dentist has particular expertise in performing. How about being a specialist in High Tech-Soft Touch or being the Internet-Savvy Dentist? How about the dentist like Paddi Lund of Australia and his dental buns, tea ceremony, relaxed yet comprehensive dentistry style of practice. What if your web site address were the de facto "brand name" for dentists in your home town (i.e. SuwaneeDental.com and AtlantaGentleDental.com)

7. Being First is a Differentiating Idea (#1 idea to emulate, in my opinion)

Be First in the Minds of New Residents: Getting into their mind with a new idea or product or benefit is an enormous advantage because minds don't like to change. They like to "keep on keeping on." It's the magnetic attraction of the status quo. If you're there first, when your competitor tries to copy you, all they will be doing is reinforcing your idea. Its much easier to get into the mind first than to try to convince someone you have a better product than the one that did get there first.

Be first and you will automatically be different. If you can hang in there and fight off the imitators, the challengers, you will be very successful. Being first to offer neuromuscular dentistry in Atlanta is a big differentiator for our practice. Being a founder of the Atlanta Craniomandibular Society and of TMJ Framework, a teaching group, created an aura of authority that still exists today, some 30 years later.

> **Be first and you will automatically be different.**

First on the Internet: It's good to be first, i.e. Since 1997, the website at suwaneedental.com has lead the Atlanta metropolitan area in having an Internet presence. But, the competition is fierce and to stay on top is always a challenge.

> **Dedicate to missions all profits on sales of specific items or services, i.e. hats, T-shirts, bleachings, etc.**

A Do-Good First: An interesting difference—How about the story of Nika, a company that blesses others… 100% of all profits of this bottled water company go to charity, to help peoplehave better drinking water. The differentiating idea is on every bottle of water they sell. All their profits go to charity.

Dedicate Your Profits: Likewise, dental work and charity work are a good combination. Giving away all your profits to do good sure is a unique selling proposition. It's also one that doesn't attract many imitators. Dedicate to missions all profits on sales of specific items or services, i.e. hats, T-shirts, bleachings, etc. In other chapters of this book you read about cause marketing and charities like Kenya Medical Outreach and the Deserving Diva Foundation. There are a multitude of ways to capitalize on being seen as a difference-maker.

A Borrowed First: Being first in one part of the world doesn't preclude someone from borrowing that idea and launching a "first" in his own part of the world. Make it a habit to keep on the lookout for novel and interesting ideas that others have used successfully. In other words, being first often means being observant. Who says you can't have your own dental extreme makeover show! Bill Dorfman would approve!

8.   Expert Status and Authority are Ways to Differentiate

Leadership is the Most Powerful Way to Differentiate a Practice: It's the most ideal way to create credentials and credentials are the collateral you put up to guarantee the performance of your practice. When I teach the 12 Points of the Solstice Compass in the Solstice 5M, I always lead off with Expert Status and Becoming Seen as the Authority. As our consultants work with practices, one of the main implementation strategies is to train leadership skills from the top to the bottom of the organization. This training alone can lead to doubling of the dental business.

Don't Be Afraid to Brag: A leader who doesn't brag is the best thing that can happen to the competition. If you don't take credit for your achievement, the one right behind you will find a way to claim what is rightfully yours. Bragging should not be confused with being egocentric or boastful or prideful. Bragging here means putting the facts on display. The main purpose of 'the tour" in the New Patient Experience is to show your expert status, your community footprint and the high-tech positioning of your practice.

9. Heritage is a Differentiating Idea

Minds are Insecure: There appears to be a naturally psychological importance in having a long history, one that makes people secure in their choice. Even if not the industry leader, having good heritage is a substitute for leadership and gives prospects the feeling that they are dealing with an industry leader. The key is to sound very impressive and different. It's never too late to sell your heritage story. There are times when you have to change to survive.

Locational Heritage: An important aspect of heritage is where you come from. Speaking personally, being a local Atlanta native does not hurt me in Atlanta. Neither does being part Cherokee Indian, which is one reason we did our office decor in an Indian theme. It certainly creates a differentiation among the other dentists in the area. Did you know that Suwanee was the beginning point of the Trail of Tears that led the Cherokees to Oklahoma from 1831 to 1838? It's no accident that we are in Suwanee, our name is Suwanee Dental Care and that the Indian theme is our heritage trademark.

Anti-Competitor Heritage: "The dentist that dentists go to." Turn a narrowing factor into a marketing virtue. What lay person wouldn't like to know that other dentists choose their dentist to do important dental work for themselves!

Family Heritage: An effective way to separate yourself from the striving herd is to stay a family business, especially in dentistry. People appear to feel more kindly toward a family-run business as opposed to a cold, impersonal public clinic that's beholden to a bunch of non-dental shareholders. They get high marks for community involvement because they live there, are involved, and they treat their employees like family. Dramatize your family heritage by slogans such as, "We care for our patients like only a family can." In today's competitive world, a family company is in a better position to serve its patients.

10. Preference is a Differentiating Idea

Following the Herd: One of our experiences is that people don't always know what they want, especially when it comes to their dentistry. They follow the herd mainly. The main reason for this kind of behavior is insecurity. Perhaps dentists are like that too when it comes to choosing that marketing plan to follow.

Social Proof: The principle of social proof is a potent weapon of influence. For instance, "Everybody's bleaching their teeth" is a workable phrase in building a case for your treatment plans. The principle states that we determine what is correct by finding out what other people think is correct, or what constitutes correct behavior. The tendency to see an action as appropriate when others are doing it works quite well normally. Right now, you would be hard-pressed to find a dentist without a web site. It has become a commodity and is no longer a technological marvel.

No Preference Overlooked: There is no doubt who is the most preferred dentist in Suwanee. Overcome the competition early and often. Maintain your lead at all costs. The closer you get to authenticity, the more you separate yourself from your competition. Separating is a big problem on the Internet, where it's easy to get overwhelmed by all the choices. A big weapon you can use on your web site is an endorsement, an exclusive partnership, an emblem, or an award-winning notice. Such a piece of social proof is telling the world, "Now here is a herd worth following." My advice is to use upscale image as a way to differentiate with the upmarket segment as well as those who aspire to be part of this group. This preference is expressed in a simple way, "Suwanee Dental Care is preferred by people who know the difference."

A Legitimate Preference: What other people think is correct. The principle of social proof gets stronger when your claim stands up to scrutiny. The more legitimate it is, the better. Understand the power of the press: five times as many people will read an article than will read an advertisement.

The Ethical Preference: Patients don't have the sophistication to make complicated medical decisions. So how are they supposed to wade through the multiple, confusing options and pick the right professional? Once again, what informed people think can carry the day. Ratings by others gets high praise from people who worry about things like the ethics of doctors advertising. Doctors' medical techniques could be rated by neutral parties, much like the Barron's guide rates colleges. Patients' opinions of bedside manner could be correlated into a kind of Dental J.D. Power ratings scale. Neither of these preference lists puts the doctor in a questionable ethics position.

11. New Items, New Products and New Services Can Be Differentiating Ideas

Find the Magic Ingredients: Often we find a powerful differentiating idea that has been ignored. CloSys for example has chlorine dioxide. Marketing people tend to dismiss these same elements as too complex or too confusing to explain to people. They say people don't care what things are made of, only what they can do for them. But for differentiation, this is the why we like to focus on the product and locate that unique piece of technology, give that design element a name and package it as a unique magic ingredient that makes the product different. And, if it's a patented magic ingredient, all the better.

Find the Magic Tools: The more complex a procedure, the more you need a magic tool to differentiate it from its competitors. i.e. the airbrush, air abrasion, the LightWalker Erbium-YAG laser, or Cone Beam 3D CT Scanner. In studying them discover the "patented prism technology" and spout it out. Does anyone understand what it is? Nope. Did it matter? Nope. It just sounds very impressive. It's what makes your practice not only better, but different.

> ## Dramatize the Difference:
> ## When you've got it, flaunt it.

Dramatize the Difference: When you've got it, flaunt it. If you come up with an innovation, make sure you dramatize it, get credit for it in the minds of the public. If you have the first of a new product or diagnostic device in your area, don't let the fact go unnoticed. Put it on the web site and promote it, i.e., "We have the Diagnodent from Kavo, a new device that detects dental cavities at 98% accuracy, a 43% improvement over traditional methods." Doing things like your biggest competitor is how to get killed in the marketing battle out there. There is no advantage to being seen as a distant fourth or fifth in the race. It only serves to draw attention to the front runner and highlight their marketing focus as being correct. Be different, be bold.

Employ System Innovation: There are opportunities to be different by coming up with something that connects to your product as part of the system. Our use of periodontal protocols has evolved over more than 25 years to now include the LightWalker LPT protocol developed by Dr.

Robert Barr using the combination Erbium and YAG lasers with the Perio PIPS tip. This has dramatically improved our patient's periodontal health. .

Make it the Old-Fashioned Way: If you go to Suwanee Dental Care's web site, it is obvious that the company knows what the difference is all about. Here's what we say, "Why is Suwanee Dental Care different from other dentists? Because Dr. Williams is the high tech—soft touch dentist in Suwanee

Charge a Little More: If you have a "better-made" story, there is a valid reason to charge a little more for your service. It just goes to show that sometimes the way you make a product can be a way to say your special. Years of training and education added to vast experience translates to your having the ability, and the right, to charge higher fees than your not-so-blessed or capable competitors.

NEWNESS, IN AND OF ITSELF, CAN BE A DIFFERENTIATING IDEA

Obsolete is "Out": Rather than try to be better, we advise practices to try to have the "next." The psychology is obvious. No one is comfortable buying what could be perceived as an obsolete product. So the way to leapfrog your competition is to position yourself as what's new and better (with the emphasis on new). Provide new drugs for treatment as they come out. Use that as a marketing advantage, i.e. Perio Chip, PerioStat, and Actisite all for periodontal pocket treatment. Now, most of those have been replaced by Arestin. Keeping on the leading edge is important for growth and profitability. Oral DNA bacteria , HPV and HbA1c glucose testing are the new kids on the block in periodontal care that bear watching and using.

Break with the Past: It's important that this "break" be established so as to convince the prospect that this is indeed a new technology. The more the separation, the easier the sale. You can do this most easily by incorporating things into your New Patient Experience that are new: instead of only the "dental pick" use the Diagnodent, instead of culturing bacteria, use a salivary sample Oral DNA testing, instead of articulating paper alone use the T-Scan, instead of a 2D panoramic for dental implants use a 3D Cone Beam CT and for TMJ and neuromuscular dentistry, instead of only gnathological approaches use the K7 kinesiograph, sonograph and electromyograph to aid in diagnosing pathology and the ideal mandibular position.

Add Another Technology: This is an effective way to create a difference, as people will quickly see this as an improvement. Milestone Scientific did just this when they added computer technology to, of all things, the very simple hypodermic needle. They created the Wand, which was billed as the first computer-controlled injection system. They even had a magic ingredient called SloFlo technology.

12. Hotness is a Way to Differentiate

People Love Hot: When you're hot, the world should know you're hot. People love to know what's hot and what's not. It's also why word-of-mouth is such a powerful force in marketing. That word-of-mouth is usually one person telling another person what's hot. With social media, especially with Facebook, Pinterest and Twitter right now, the word-of-mouth travels about a really good or really bad dental visit within hours. Words that influence countless others will likely hit the status bars and tweets on hundreds of smart phones and tablet devices.

> Many dentists are shy about telling about their success.

Don't be Afraid to Boast: Many dentists are shy about telling about their success. Being hot or experiencing practice growth beyond that of your competition can give you the thrust you need to get your brand up to altitude.

Once there, you need to figure out something else to maintain your position. Remember, you aren't in business to make your competitors like you. This is a business and the strong and bold win the game.

Spread Your Hot Messages: Post complimentary quotes about your practice—from newspapers, from industry and business magazines, from customers, etc.—in obvious places patients go, both inside and outside your facility. End advertisements with a tag line like this, "Suwanee Dental Care Winner of Best of Gwinnett for the Ninth Year in a Row." If you put out the message, everyone will know that your office seems to be the hot dental practice and must be doing something different, something right.

WHO IS IN CHARGE OF DIFFERENTIATION?

You are in Charge: Top management, the dentist, has to be in charge of differentiation and messaging. All too often, the "right strategy" is assumed, but not analyzed. Superior strategy and superior execution equal superior results. Most problems start at the strategy stage, not at the execution stage. So the success of your campaign starts with you, the leader.

Put First Things First: Gather great ideas first, then assemble your team, and then put the facility and equipment in place to make the idea a reality. The strategic idea—the differentiating idea—is easily half the battle, not to mention the more important half.

What Really Went Wrong? Dentists have to understand what's on the table and what their options are, if any. Most big moves forward will often challenge old ways of doing things. This is what a paradigm shift is all about. The result is a reluctance to foster the new ideas. Peter Drucker calls this "slaughtering tomorrow's opportunity on the altar of yesterday."

Why the Dentist Must Be Involved: Staff can have a personal agenda. They may make decisions based not on what is best for the practice, but on what's best for their career, or, make decisions trying to avoid mistakes that could put their career in peril.

A SUCCESSFUL VIEW FROM THE TOP:

1. Trust your instincts. Have your own strategy.
2. Have a strong visual identity. Your practice should be different.
3. Throw a party. A new practice needs all the help it can get. It is a big city. You need to reach a lot of people. Differentiate yourself in their minds.
4. Be creative with spending. Find new ideas and package your practice in a different way. If you don't have a large budget, you have to have a point of view. This is why Guerrilla Marketing the WebCentric way works.
5. Utilize your existing idea in different ways. Be different in all things.

The foundation of effective leadership is thinking through the practice's difference, defining it, and establishing it, clearly and visibly.

TAKE-AWAY POINTS

*   Too Many Choices Confuse
*   Your USP is Critical
*   Study Ways to Differentiate
*   Implement Your Differentiation Strategy for Success

CHAPTER 33

The Seven Mountain Marketing Strategy

W HAT ARE AND HOW DO YOU CLIMB the Seven Mountains of Marketing to ensure practice success. That is one of the systems I implemented when I founded my new dental practice in 1997. Because we were able to grow it a half million dollar a year for ten straight years, the lesson I'm going to share with you today is one of significance. A growing practice cannot afford to ignore the Seven Mountain Strategy. Whereas in our Decathlon Dentistry model of practice, the dentist is trained and has high expertise in all ten disciplines of dentistry, in the Seven Mountains of Marketing a practice focuses on the seven key elements of society that have influence and cause it to become the de rigueur professional practice in their region. This strategy is all about gaining influence.

The Seven Mountains of Marketing are:

(1) Government,

(2) Education,

(3) Media,

(4) Economy,

(5) Family,

(6) Celebration, and

(7) Religion.

Included in **government** are the entries into the professions, the regulations and requirements of practice as well as those who work in and for the government. You see, opportunity is given by government to practice and there are barriers to overcome to enjoy success with this mountain. Plus, think of all the governmental units and agencies and the sheer number of governmental employees in our world today. That is why we need to be an expert in accessing these people as patients and their benefit plans once we are in practice.

"With the Seven Mountains of Marketing a practice focuses on the seven key elements of society that have influence."

> "With the Seven Mountains of Marketing a practice focuses on the seven key elements of society that have influence."

EDUCATION

Education is the mountain where all things are learned and opinions are formed at early ages. The indoctrination of young minds can begin for the professional practice as teacher when team members go into the classroom and present as outside experts what is beneficial to the young patients. This can continue with participation in health fairs, radio talk show appearances and on to hosting our own shows. Being proactive with blogs and social media output from the practice is critical today as the public looks for education on the Internet prior to choosing a professional. You need to be seen as an educator to be considered. Education is about gaining access to those who are to receive care and developing the attitudes of health and wellness early in life. Be seen as a supporter of educational endeavors locally.

MEDIA

Of course, **the Media** controls the flow of information and by-in-large chooses the winners and losers by how they portray news in the public eye. For years dentistry was highly ranked as the most honorable profession but fell from grace when the AIDS scare from Florida struck and the Reader's Digest undercover articles hit the newsstand. Being proactive and creating one's own media buzz is important to capture the third marketing mountain, Media. Having a strong media presence is critical to owning the Media Mountain. In the creation of your Marketing Action Plan, your MAP, having a footprint in print, TV, radio, website and social media is key.

ECONOMY

The Economic Mountain is the business community, the Chamber of Commerce, your neighbors who line Main Street with their shops and stores. Being a mainstay on Main Street is your goal as you develop the marketing savvy to dominate the Economic Mountain. Joining the business community and being a part of what they are doing to raise the banner for capitalism is going to benefit your practice. Be seen as a business person in the community. Participate at the Chamber, the Rotary, Kiwanis, and the Lions Club. Become a resource to them and elevate your sphere of influence. Marketing is all about having influence.

FAMILY

The Family Mountain has as much to do as any other mountain in shaping the behavior of a person. Children usually do what they see their parents doing and are directed by their parents to acquire good or bad habits, especially dental or medical care habits. Health culture is dictated at the family level and what is ingrained into children at home is hard to change. To succeed with the Family Mountain, one needs to bring the entire family into the equation and involve them as individuals in the process.

CELEBRATION

The Celebration Mountain really means the Arts, Sports, and Entertainment Mountain Peaks. This is a range of mountains that make up what establishes our outward expression of who we are and what we value. The creative energy of people flows down from these mountains and enhances our lives, creates our fun and enjoyment. To shine in this environment we must participate and be seen as a key player, adding to their enhancement. Don't see it? Look no further than cosmetic dentistry, cosmetic surgery, weight loss, sports injury protection, image and wellness. Healthy longevity and peak performance are hallmarks of the most desired lifestyles. People take action to achieve what they desire, so being seen as one who can deliver will ensure a constant stream of new clients.

RELIGION

The Religion Mountain can be called the Worship Mountain. This mountain of influence is larger than most would expect in that it is the basis of trust, honor, truth and good. What people want in their doctor is also what they want from their Maker. Because trustworthiness, compassion, truthfulness and faithfulness are traits people wish from their doctor, those professional who operate within the confines of established religion or spiritual communities usually see these attributes conferred upon them as well.

Being a bottom line person, you can see that the summation of the seven mountains being addressed in your marketing methods will total up to more rather than less. Ignoring a mountain in establishing your MAP means you abdicate that mountain to be captured by your competition. The mountain is there and the reason you climb it is just that... because it's there.

CHAPTER 34

Conclusion
But Not The End

WHO IS THIS BOOK FOR?

*M*ARKETING THE MILLION DOLLAR PRACTICE is about growing your practice to the next level, whatever level you desire to achieve. That means this book was written with you in mind. From wherever you are now, the Solstice WebCentric Marketing Action Plan can elevate your success. It provides a solid framework to show you the overall picture. This makes the process much easier to implement. Your website is the hub of your marketing plan, and the WebCentric Marketing Plan is a clear outline of the step-by-step actions to take to improve your primary weapon for success.

Marketing the Million Dollar Practice gives you a step-by-step implementation strategy to add, piece by piece, the necessary spokes to the WebCentric wheel, beginning with your image and how you take the patients into your practice, which is the very essence of internal marketing. You also learned about visibility strategies to attract new patients to your practice.

The range of external marketing and tactics and the sales psychology for each method was developed for your consideration. As you read through the chapters, you saw places where you could "add to" or "shore up" holes in your current

> As you read through the chapters, you saw places where you could "add to" or "shore up" holes in your current marketing plan.

marketing plan. You saw how to develop a game plan
of your own to develop entirely new niches of influence
that could help send new patients to your web site
and ultimately to your front door. You very likely now
understand new possibilities and potential for growth that
you had never considered in the past.

NEXT STEPS

Here's what to do next.

1. Complete a Gap Analysis of where you are currently
   with your practice marketing and your results in
   getting more new patients. Contrast that to where
   you want to be next year at this time, how many more
   new patients per month you want and what level of
   production you'd like to achieve. Employ guerrilla
   marketing tactics. List the specific WebCentric
   Marketing Action plan items you intend to accomplish
   and when you want your team to tackle each one of
   them. Paint a clear picture of your preferred future.
   Start at the end and work backwards with that goal
   in mind. Create your own WebCentric action plan by
   breaking it down to chronological, orderly, sequential
   steps to make it happen, one bite at a time.

2. Review your website and see that it meets the
   minimal criteria for what you need to have control
   of it's content. You'll need to be able to modify, add
   content and to personalize it on a regular basis. Work
   with your webmaster to get the result you want. Don't
   settle for a cookie cutter, rubber stamp, impersonal
   online brochure that is nearly identical to hundreds of
   other dentists across the country.

3. Select your team players, both those inside your
   practice and those outside, who will support your
   marketing and practice growth plans. Choose your
   lieutenant who will help you climb over every

rock, past every plateau. Next, organize your team to implement these specific internal and external marketing ploys and give your team authority to begin building the business, capture ground, and get more new patients into your practice. Clearly identify the tasks that are to be accomplished. Delegate wisely.

4. Put your own WebCentric action plan into action! The Solstice WebCentric Marketing Action Plan (MAP), the second of 12 modules taught in the Solstice 5M, and the Solstice 2-Day Marketing Intensive Workshop can both accelerate this process exponentially.

THE PERFECT "MARKETING" STORM

Let me share with you our perfect marketing storm. In 38 years in dentistry there has to be that one perfect month where it all comes together, where all the forces of nature are aligned to produce that unbelievable result. I compare it to playing in the Super Bowl or the seventh game of the World Series. It's the World Cup and Stanley Cup of dentistry, all rolled up into one. Its center court Wimbledon or the 18th green at the Masters.

For marketing it's all about results. That's what you measure. If you market well and have good management, excellent systems and talented dentists and staff—you win.

Well, January 2008 was our big win—our perfect storm. We had just hired a new dentist in October; our fourth to join our expanding practice. Prior to his coming onboard from his practice in the D.C. suburbs of Virginia, we began our specific WebCentric marketing campaign to introduce him to the public as well as to our current patients. We held events, put out email blasts, wrote newsletters, went on radio and TV, held contests and asked our current patients, point blank, to help us get the new dentist some new patients to treat.

Due to a redoubling of effort we created a groundswell of activity, of interest and of results. By January we were swamped with the most new patients in the history of either Stone Mountain Dental Group, my former practice of 23 years or Suwanee Dental Care, my current practice of, by then, 11 years. We got 170 new patients that month. And, mind you, this was not just the result of doing a massive discount coupon to get hundreds of people in for a "freebie" exam and cleaning like so many do. No, this was a combination of solid WebCentric marketing where we were hitting on all cylinders, attracting high quality patients who just wanted to go to the best dentist in town.

BUT THERE IS MORE

That's not the end of the Perfect Marketing Storm, however. Not only did we attract a record number of new clients, but each dentist and the entire dental hygiene department also had individually it's best month of production— ever! Can you imagine practicing for 33 years, 29 years, 13 years and 13 years as all four of our team of dentists had and each and every one of us having our best month ever in that same month! That was the perfect "production" storm caused by the perfect "marketing" storm.

Are you ready for the punch line—the results? Remember, if it's been done, it's probably possible! If we can do it, you can too!

Dentist #4 produced	$ 88,000
Dentist #3 produced	$112,000
Dentist #2 produced	$150,000
Dentist #1 produced	$250,000
Hygiene Team produced	$150,000
A grand total best month ever of	$750,000

Yes, 2008 was starting out to be a very good year! What we did then was unbelievable. The perfect storm is a perfect analogy of what happened during that time. Since then, we've repeated our strategies and had many, many good months in the $400,000's, $500,000's and a few over $600,000 months. When the forces of nature (WebCentric Guerrilla Marketing, God's promises to those who follow Him, and the psychology of sales in really understanding your patients) are combined and unleashed in your practice, the results are inevitable and strong—very strong.

By learning and applying these time-tested, validated, marketing principles along with the efficiency techniques and leadership skills we've developed and teach in our Solstice 5M Gold Coaching Program you, too, can blow past your competition and enjoy the benefits of the perfect storm!

Epilogue

MY PRACTICE HAS CONTINUED TO FLOURISH during the remainder of the recession which began in Atlanta for us in 2009, averaging $5,000,000 a year from 2007 through 2011. In 2012, I elected to sell at the top of the market and become an associate instead of an owner and continue building on my long-term plan for the next phase of my dental career.

Solstice Dental Advisors was birthed in 2011 as a coaching, consulting and teaching firm to show others how we created our dream practice from scratch and grew it by half a million dollars a year for ten straight years… then maintained it for half a decade more. During the year 2011 I wrote the Solstice 5M and presented to my private clients 14 webinars that catalogued the route to our success in Suwanee.

The Solstice 5M stands for the five million dollar practice, our goal which we reached for a four-doctor practice in one location. The elements of the series include:

1. How To Achieve Expert Status
2. Creating the Ideal New Patient Experience
3. Building Your Marketing Action Plan
4. Getting 100 New Patients a Month
5. Why Decathalon Dentistry is Your Path to Success
6. Efficiency Gold for the Dental Team
7. Key Solstice Systems You Need to Achieve Explosive Growth
8. Key Performance Indicators (KPI) Systems We Utilize
9. Loyal Team and Patient Rewards Programs
10. Team Gold: Finding and Keeping the Perfect 10's
11. Strategic Planning to Reach Multi-Million Dollar Practice Heights
12. The Implementation Secret: The Solstice Gold Key List
13. The Million Dollar Associate
14. How to Beat the Recession

Resources

TO ACCESS THE SOLSTICE 5M and the 13 webinars and online membership website that make up the Gold Member Coaching program go to www.SolsticeDentalAdvisors.com/gold

The Solstice Top Gun Conference in September of 2012 brought together some of my best friends and brightest minds in dentistry to our home town at Lake Lanier Islands, Georgia. We held this three-day event with the presidents of the American Academy of Implant Dentistry, American Academy of Craniofacial Pain, the American Academy of Oral and Systemic Health, the Dental Freedom Academy as well as our top seven Solstice Dental Advisors practice consultants.

This conference alone resulted in the explosive growth of many of the attendees present. A DVD copy of the proceedings is recommended for any dentist wanting to advance his or her practice beyond the common or ordinary. Get your copy here: www.TopGunConference.com

In February 2013 the Solstice Marketing Intensive workshop was presented with all new material, updated to what we were doing at Suwanee Dental Care since this book was written. Our clients attended that two-day intensive and experienced one of the most detailed marketing weekends ever produced in dentistry.

DETAILS HERE:
www.SolsticeDentalAdvisors.com/miworkshop

> Our Solstice coaches are out in dental practices each and every month, teaching the Solstice Way, making the Solstice 5M a reality to those who want to grow their practices.

At this time, I still work in my practice three days a week. We still produce between $425,000 and $475,000 each month and average right at 100 new patients per month.

Our Solstice coaches are out in dental practices each and every month, teaching the Solstice Way, making the Solstice 5M a reality to those who want to grow their practices.

My next strategy to help my Solstice 5M clients gather even more steam in order to climb the mountain of success is to gather a select group of focused dentists to begin our Solstice 5M Platinum Mastermind Sessions. If you have read this book and think that you are capable of learning and implementing what we teach, then this special session may be for you.

Click on the link here to find out more
about the Solstice 5M Platinum Mastermind…
www.SolsticeDentalAdvisors.com/mastermind

Bonuses

BECAUSE YOU HAVE NAVIGATED throughout 34 chapters of marketing material , read my story and seen that there is hope for every size practice to grow and prosper, I want to leave you with a gift for your faithful journey. Choose one or all… these are all free and granted to you in hopes that your life will be fuller, richer and more balanced as a result.

FOR THE MIND
www.SolsticeDentalAdvisors.com/mind

FOR THE BODY
www.SolsticeDentalAdvisors.com/body

FOR THE SPIRIT
www.SolsticeDentalAdvisors.com/spirit

About The Author

DR. WILLIAM B. WILLIAMS, DMD, MAGD, MICCMO, is a highly acclaimed practicing dentist and an expert in marketing and management. During his 25+ years of practice, he has built several multi-million dollar practices, most recently taking a startup practice from zero to five million in just ten years.

His consultancy, Solstice Dental Advisors, equips dentists by implementing strategies to grow and improve their bottom line. Over his career, he has been featured at Dr. Omer Reed's Napili VIII: The Million Dollar Roundtable, lectured for Quest Seminars, Myotronics, Bioresearch, the annual meeting of the Academy of General Dentistry, three international conferences of the International College of Craniomandibular Orthopedics in Japan, Canada and Italy, was Senior TMJ Instructor for the United States Dental Institute and was the founder of TMJ Framework, a mini-residency for head, neck and facial pain.

He was named the Small Business Person of Year in Gwinnett, was the recipient of the Ron Lamb Award from the Christian Dental Society and is the cofounder and director of Kenya Medical Outreach, Inc. Dr. Williams is an author, clinician, teacher and mentor in addition to owning and operating his Suwanee Dental Care private practice. For more information go to: Solstice Dental Advisors and Suwanee Dental Care.

Made in the USA
Lexington, KY
02 May 2014